THOSE YEARS

RECOLLECTIONS OF A BALTIMORE NEWSPAPERMAN

Those Years

Recollections of A
Baltimore Newspaperman

By R.H. Gardner
Former Theatre and Film Critic for the Sun

Sunspot Books

THE GALILEO PRESS LTD., BALTIMORE   1990

Copyright © 1990 by Rufus Hallette Gardner

Published by The Galileo Press Ltd.
7215 York Rd., Baltimore, Maryland 21212

Sunspot Books is the non-fiction imprint of The Galileo Press

Editor: Susan Walsh
Cover Photo: M.E. Warren Photography
Text Design: Terri Anne Ciofalo

LIBRARY OF CONGRESS CATALOGING-IN-PUBLICATION DATA

Gardner, R.H., 1918 -
Those years: recollections of a baltimore newspaperman/ by R.H. Gardner; — 1st. ed.

p. cm.
"Sunspot Books"
ISBN 0-913123-29-3 : $14.95 (est.)I.
Title
PN4874.G32583   1990
070'.92—dc20   90-9717
CIP

ACKNOWLEDGEMENTS

The overall support of The Maryland State Council on the Arts and our annual donors underwrites the operations of The Galileo Press, Ltd., a tax-exempt non-profit corporation organized under the laws of the State of Maryland.

BY THE SAME AUTHOR

Books
The Splintered Stage: The Decline of the American Theater

Plays
Christabel and the Rubicon
IOU Jeremiah

Quotation from Thomas Wolfe's *The Hills Beyond* by permission of Harper and Row, reprinted from the Sun Dial Press © copyright 1941.

Quotation from Tennessee Williams' *Cat on a Hot Tin Roof* by permission of New Directions Publishing Company © copyright 1954, 1955, 1971 and 1975.

Quotation from Tennessee Williams' *The Night of the Iguana* by permission of Two River Enterprises © copyright 1961. Reprinted by permission of New Directions Publishing Company.

Quotation from Tennessee Williams' *The Glass Menagerie* by permission of Random House, Inc. © copyright 1945 by Tennessee Williams and Edwina D. Williams and renewed 1973 by Tennessee Williams.

To Rosie — my heart's bouquet

CONTENTS

Looking Out The Window
1
The Sun Rises
17
The Perception of Form
87
True Love
99
The Quakenbush Letters
125
Baltimore Busts Out
157
Drowning In The Rubicon
169
And Time Passing . . .
181
Never Forget
195
The Sun Sets
209
Digging In My Garden
217
Addenda
231

(preceding pages) The Block, 1934.
(Photo courtesy of Jacques Kelly.)

Looking Out The Window

ONE

As I look back, certain days stand out. The Monday my mother died. The Sunday I arrived in Baltimore. The Saturday I began my first summer vacation.

Winter tended to be cold in Mayfield, the small West-Kentucky town where I grew up. Clothes for grammar-school boys were necessarily complex. Ankle-length underwear, corduroy pants tucked into tightly laced boots, wool sweaters beneath fleeced-lined jackets and leather caps with flaps that pulled down over the ears.

Spring came not so much as a rebirth in nature as a release from weight. The boots gave way to canvas Keds, the caps to straw sombreros with little felt balls dancing around the brim. And, by the time summer burst forth in all its warmth and greenery, it was a simple matter of overalls and BVD's.

The body that during winter had huddled inside its layers of insulation emerged to embrace the world.

So it was on that sparkling June morning I arose, awakened by sunshine and the chirping of birds. I did not dawdle over my buttons but ran, suspender straps dangling, to the kitchen where, under the disapproving eyes of our venerable black cook, I gulped down my breakfast.

Then through the screen door and across the porch to the back yard. Beyond a low hedge, a grove of trees swayed seductively in the breeze. Sunlight, filtering through the branches, made delicate patterns on the ground.

I sprang forward, took the hedge in one leap, flung myself, panting, down and beheld — above the gently swaying canopy — the sky.

The breeze crept under my overalls. I felt light, liberated, deliciously languid.

And, as my near-naked body settled into the grass, I thought with a feeling of infinite contentment "Ain't nothin' I got to do till school starts in September."

I FELT MUCH THE SAME WAY the day after my retirement from the newspaper job I'd held for 33 years. There was no sun in the sky, and the only trees I could see from my second-floor rear window were the few lining the street just beyond a dreary parking lot immediately below. But the sense of freedom — or was it purposelessness? — remained.

"Ain't nothin' I got to do but die."

I had anticipated the moment for some time. A close friend had anticipated it even longer. "What are you going to do?" she had asked anxiously. "You have no hobbies. Your whole life is your work. So what are you going to do?"

I had, if she'd only known, a secret resource. Laziness. I had suppressed it all my life, and it now made me rather look forward to having nothing to do.

The idea, to say the least, didn't bother me. I'd been working, day and night, for 33 years on a metropolitan newspaper and for ten years before that in other jobs. It seemed to me that 43 years of unbroken toil merited one or two of unbroken leisure.

But that was before I discovered how hard doing nothing can be. The difficulty lies in controlling the mind. No matter how hard you try, the damn thing keeps thinking. And to a veteran writer, thinking is a prelude to working. For writing is no more than the recording, in one way or another, of organized thought.

"Stop writing!" Thurber's wife used to yell at cocktail parties when she saw him sitting in a corner with a silly look on his face. "She usually," he confided to his readers, "catches me in mid-paragraph."

Still, I couldn't — however much I might be inclined — sit indefinitely in a room staring at three walls and a parking lot.

How had I managed in the days when I was simply an ordinary happy-go-lucky college jerk? I'd enjoyed myself — mainly, I now suspected, *because* I wasn't working. But what had I *done*?

Apart from girls, most of my interests, I seemed to recall, were athletic. I swam, played tennis and, for five incredible hours three times a week, lifted weights at the YMCA.

But, after a lifetime of sitting at a desk pounding a typewriter, I could not see weight-lifting as the answer.

Something I was sure I wasn't going to do was dig in the garden. Time and again over the years, I'd telephoned retired friends only to be told by their wives that they were outside digging in the garden.

There appeared to be a direct correlation between retiring and digging. The former invariably led to the latter. Except for me and one erstwhile colleague who had found his answer in delivering meals-on-wheels, which I didn't want to do either.

Even had I experienced the digging urge, I could not have brought it off. I live in a house surrounded by inorganic matter — bricks, asphalt, trash. Nothing could grow in it.

Yet, as I sat at my window, looking not at the parking lot but at the pile of accumulated years, I came to realize that there is more than one way to dig in one's garden.

TODAY, AS I SIT AT THE same window, the Baltimore *Sun* — a publication that has always prided itself on being owned and controlled by people residing in the same community that gave it birth — has just been sold to an out-of-state company. The development, coming only a few months before the 150th anniversary of the *Sun*'s founding in 1837, culminates a process of change that has gradually reduced it from a newspaper of outstanding quality to simply another element of the "print" medium competing with television for the advertising dollar.

When I joined its staff in March of 1951, H. L. Mencken was still alive. Laid low by a stroke but still kicking in his Hollins Street home. Richard Q. Yardley was still drawing his political cartoons. A. Aubrey Bodine was snapping his shutter in the photographic department. And Hamilton Owens, Philip M. Wagner, C. P. Ives and that most gentle of all gentlemen, A. D. Emmart, were turning out literate columns for the editorial pages.

For there *were* gentlemen on the *Sun* in those days, and their very presence went a long way toward compensating for the starvation wages. The managing editor, Charles H. Dorsey, Jr., always addressed me as *Mister* Gardner. And that "mister" — combined with the respect he and his successor, Paul A. Banker, accorded my work — gave me a sense of worth far exceeding that represented by my weekly pay check.

In short, though we probably would not have admitted it even to ourselves, we young reporters felt proud to be part of a newspaper whose standards equaled those of the *New York Times*. And this pride created an esprit de corps that, more than anything else, made my early years on the *Sun* continually rewarding. Thus a book recalling those years should be worth not only writing but, possibly, even reading.

My main problem in writing it has been trying to decide what it's about. I started with the intention of doing a straightforward account of my life as a reporter and critic. Then, little by little, other things began to creep in. People and ideas that helped to shape my critical philosophy. The fall and rise of the Baltimore theater. Childhood memories....

What it's probably most about is a little Southern boy who comes to a big Eastern city with which, through the columns of a newspaper, he has a love affair. And the logical place to begin is with my arrival on a sweltering hot Sunday in September of 1941 at Baltimore's Camden Station. I'd heard the city abounded with distinguished and historic associations: Edgar Allan Poe, Francis Scott Key, Johns Hopkins, the Peabody Conservatory, Ford's Theater, museums, monuments, concert halls.

Undoubtedly, it offered great opportunities for acquiring culture and, as one who doted on such things, I was itching to get started. So the first thing I did, after stowing my bags in a Cathedral Street rooming house, was go to a burlesque show.

TWO

What news analysts and other cliche experts of the Thirties liked to refer to as "the gathering war clouds over Europe" filled me with nothing so much as — terror. As a college student majoring in history, I had become convinced that war accomplished little beyond reduction of the world's excess population. I had no desire to die for such a cause. At 21, I had no desire to die at all. To brand me a coward would have made sense only to those placing importance on the value of physical combat — which I did not.

My abhorrence of physical combat and, indeed, all kinds of violence dated from the age of 6 when, as a sickly over-protected child, I had reported for my first day at school. The sun shone blithely from a cloudless sky. The schoolyard rang with the cries of happy children. Suddenly one stepped forward and punched me in the stomach.

The incident implanted in me a distrust of small boys that, along with the suspicion that nine out of ten were bullies, endured. It was the tenth that gave me pause — especially after seeing at recess a few days later the same boy stand up to the school's biggest bully who beat him to a pulp before his classmates' eyes. Again and again he was knocked to the ground. Again and again, nose bleeding, small fists clenched, he returned to the fray. Though the world was brutal, there were, I decided, heroes in it.

But, if being a hero entailed getting one's teeth knocked out for no good reason, I knew I could never qualify. Nor, as it happened, could John Goodspeed — a fellow student at Fort Worth's Texas Christian University, at which many years and punches in the stomach later I arrived.

The thing that drew my attention to Goodspeed's tall, rawboned figure when I first saw it prowling the corridors of TCU was the dramatic contrast between his jet-black hair and a complexion as sallow as wax paper. There was, furthermore, something always wrong with his nose. It ran constantly, necessitating frequent blowing, wiping and a lot of other fancy work with the handkerchief. I never knew whether it was chronic sinus trouble, hay fever or what, but my earliest memories of him are associated with his incessant jabbing at his nostrils trying to make them breathe.

Between jabs, he would utter short, colorful remarks, always vitriolic and usually directed at a fellow student. For in those days he regarded the human race as falling into two groups — himself and others. The two were irrevocably (perhaps mortally) opposed, like capital and labor. Not that he was a follower of Marx. Nietzsche would have been more to his liking. In the mirror of his mind, he shone as a Renaissance figure who, through a historical miscalculation, had been born into a society of imbeciles.

To support the image of himself as artist-intellectual he learned to play the piano, mandolin and musical comb. To the annoyance of his classmates, he read all the English assignments they found unreadable — "Tom Jones," "Tristram Shandy," "Pamela" — and discussed them with authority. Goodspeed loved to discuss things with authority, especially when he didn't know what he was talking about. He developed a flair for cartooning and wrote the gossip (or "dirt") column for the school newspaper in which he managed to alienate everybody who didn't hate him already.

Do I sound vindictive? I'm not. I have unbounded admiration, as well as affection, for John. He has an original mind, is one of the most talented writers I've ever known and possesses a sense of humor as irresistible as it is strange. The following example should suffice.

During our Junior year, elections were held to determine who would occupy certain positions in the student body. John had a hankering to be editor of the newspaper but, as one never overburdened with popularity, he had no idea how to get people to vote for him. Somebody suggested he cultivate a girl then very influential in Jarvis Hall, the women's dormitory. He took her to dinner at a cost of $15.93, an extravagant sum to spend on a date in those days. And his annoyance at having done so was increased by her refusal to kiss him goodnight.

He felt humiliated in his own eyes — especially when it occurred to him that the woman might conclude he had been motivated in his expenditure by her overwhelming physical charms. So the next week in his anonymously written column, he got even with himself. "It is learned," he wrote, "that Goodspeed took Maxine Shaw out dining and dancing last Saturday at a cost of $15.93. Can it be he is after the Jarvis Hall vote?"

In one succinct paragraph he destroyed whatever political advantage his $15.93 might have bought him. But he felt better.

John and I had difficulty agreeing about anything except that men of the sort likely to end up in Arlington Cemetery we had no desire to be. The problem was how to avoid becoming one.

As graduation approached, I learned that a government-sponsored school dedicated to turning out aeronautical draftsmen had set up shop in Fort Worth. I wasn't sure what aeronautical draftsmen did, but because of the emphasis being placed on defense, I suspected that enrollment might defer our induction into the army.

So we took the course. For three sweaty months during the blistering Texas summer of 1941, we wrestled with smudgy pencils, wispy tracing paper, plastic triangles and T-squares. Then we were handed a document certifying us as honest-to-god aeronautical draftsmen. Letters announcing this sensational fact were dispatched to every aircraft factory in the country.

Replies poured in. *Nobody* wanted us. Nobody but the Glenn L. Martin Company of Middle River, Maryland just outside Baltimore. Gathering together his wits, mandolin and musical comb, John departed on September 5. I, for reasons that had to do with Dorothy Ruth Collins, an 18-year-old Fort Worth girl I had become much smitten with, waited until the following week.

ACCORDING TO GOODSPEED, the thing that made the dancer's nipples glow with such electrifying effect was fingernail polish. It was all he could talk about as I alighted from the train. It seemed that the Sunday matinee started at 2 P.M. and if we didn't hurry and get rid of my bags at the room he had rented for us we might miss the opening number.

We really moved after that.

Having majored in journalism, John knew no more about the design and building of airplanes than I did. But in those months of frantic pre-war mobilization, the factories, like the armed services, took anybody. And the existence of a number of surrounding military installations, along with such civilian operations as Martin and Bethlehem Steel, had by the time of our arrival transformed Baltimore from an oversized town rooted in the Nineteenth Century into a metropolis teeming with a floating population of soldiers, sailors and Southern "defense workers" — a good number of which, lacking any better way of spending weekends, attended burlesque theaters.

The city boasted three such establishments at the time, all located within spitting distance of one another in the Block, Baltimore's notorious tenderloin district. The largest and most elaborate was the Gayety. And it was there in an atmosphere combining the odors of a stable and a YMCA locker room that I had my introduction to that fine old American institution, the strip-tease.

Like most urban communities, the Block has since suffered irreparable changes. Then it consisted of four short blocks running east and west along Baltimore Street between War Memorial Plaza on the north and the waterfront on the south. It had been largely destroyed by the Great Fire of 1904. But its numerous gin-mills, cabarets, poolhalls, tattoo parlors, shooting galleries and other assorted clip-joints arose almost immediately from the ashes. Thus the decor of the Gayety, featuring huge bas-reliefs of the undraped female torso, reflected that rococo era of theater design.

Three tiers of gilt-emblazoned boxes flanked the proscenium, the upper two connecting with balconies at the rear. To a spectator seated in the top-most row of the top-most balcony the performers seemed about as close as a batter to the bleachers at Yankee Stadium. But because it cost only 25 cents it was to this section that Goodspeed and I — part of a cosmopolitan throng of servicemen, merchant seamen and West Virginia expatriates (fellow defense-workers every one) — directed our steps that Sunday.

The show had already begun and, as we clambered over the unyielding legs of the soldiers, sailors, West Virginians, etc., a girl far below was writhing in the center of a pink spotlight while a bass drum accented each spasm of her hips with a resounding bang. I sank into the tattered upholstery entranced by this sudden exposure to what Goodspeed had so inadequately described as fingernail polish.

The format of the Gayety's program — for the Sunday matinee became a regular item on our agenda — was simple. As 2 o'clock approached, a pit band ("ten men and a riveting machine" as one visiting comic put it) played an overture in which all the other instruments tried unsuccessfully to compete with the snare drum. The curtain then rose on a big production number performed by a chorus of dancing girls accompanied by an offstage male singer. The singer, usually a barbershop tenor, also doubled as straight man in the comic skits and sometimes even sold candy between the acts. As for the chorus, it was indescribable. Its members' efforts to jiggle on beat seemed to amuse them more than it did the spectators who simply endured their grotesque presence as an unavoidable prelude to the entrance of the top-banana.

The comedians have of course always been the backbone of burlesque. Long before Gypsy Rose Lee popularized the practice of provocative disrobing, these clowns — with their baggy pants and streamer four-in-hands — had established a theater based on stylized vulgarity. For the classic burlesque skit is little more than a dramatized dirty joke.

Because of their dependence upon the performers' ability to improvise, these skits are reminiscent of the Italian commedia dell'arte. And to a person with a sensitive funny bone and a strong stomach, they can be entertaining — especially if he has never seen them before. In the fall of 1941 I had seen none of them. Consequently the Sunday matinee became the highlight of my week.

Fortunately the 25-cents admission did not seriously tax my 75-cents-an-hour salary. Otherwise I might have been forced to pass up such colorful fare for a visit to some dreary movie or even a monument or two.

During the blackout that followed each skit the disembodied voice of the tenor would announce a stripper — usually a girl who had already appeared as a sexy fillip in one of the comic routines. I soon discovered that the law of diminishing returns sets in rather early where stripping is concerned. The sight of undulating flesh seemed to pall on even the servicemen who did not really come alive until the fanfare introducing the headliner at the end of the act.

The big stars in those days, all of whom appeared at the Gayety, were Georgia Southern, Hinda Wassau, Valerie Parks and Margie Hart. Their calculated wiggling had little in common with the disorganized bouncing about of the second-raters. They had only to snake an arm or leg through the central slit in the curtain — one of the standard ways of entering — to provoke an uproar of howls from the audience.

At the conclusion of the headliner's number, the lights would go up, members of the chorus would clump on, the tenor would cut loose and the star, wearing only a G-string and some net over the fingernail polish, would take a final bow. When the curtain descended on this scene that first Sunday I, thinking we'd got our 25-cents' worth, started to get to my feet but was stopped by John's hand on my arm. Though I did not know it, the real show was about to begin.

THREE

No sooner had the curtain descended and the house lights risen than a young man with a microphone stepped from the wings and began to address the audience in the stentorian tones of a drill sergeant.

"Good evening, ladies and gentlemen." He pronounced it "ladeez," his voice rising considerably on the second syllable. "While the girls are backstage undressing for the next act, I'd like to welcome you to the Gayety, Baltimore's only theater featuring first-class traveling burlesque.

"I'd like to remind you that this is only intermission. A completely full and different act will follow. In the meantime those of you who'd like to step out for a drink or a little recreation might be interested to know that we operate a well-equipped bar in the basement and a beautiful poolroom upstairs. For those who prefer to remain we have a nice line of chocolate [pronounced "chawclate"], cold drinks and ice cream, which our sales representatives will be glad to deliver to you right in your seats."

A small army of gorilla-faced, gravel-voiced candy butchers began to roam the aisles rasping "Gitcher chawclate, ice cream 'n' cold drinks here!" The bedlam continued a few minutes; then the young man on the stage cleared his throat, took a firmer grip on his microphone and resumed the stentorian monologue.

"And now, ladeez and gentlemen, if I may have your attention, I'd like to describe a little service we carry on here at the Gayety for our patrons. We know you come here to relax, let your hair down and have a good time. And we know some of you like to have a little souvenir to take home to remind you of the fun you've had here. You know, something a little spicy, a little off-color, a little risque, you might say, in the burlesque tradition. Something you can show your friends when they come over for a game of pool or a bottle of beer.

"Well, we happen to have a wide variety of these souvenirs on hand for your pleasure — plus a large collection of really valuable and beautiful gifts that are sure to interest you. We are fortunate to have been chosen as an outlet by one of the nationally known manufacturers of fine articles who has a lot of new products he's putting on the market. Articles he wants to advertise and is willing to let us give away to you today as a means of distributing them and getting them into your homes.

"For example, we have a large quantity of ladeez' and gentlemen's wrist watches. Now [he held up a watch], I'm going to be honest with you. These are not $100 watches. They're not $75 watches. They're not even $50 watches. They sell for $27.50 at any department store. But they're good time-keepers, as well as a handsome piece of jewelry as you can see.

"Another gift we're offering today is this handy camera [holding up box camera] which allows you to take your own pictures at home. This camera sells for $8.50 at any store handling the best in quality photographic equipment.

"Then there's our stylish pen and pencil set. These pens and pencils are what the manufacturer calls 'seconds' — which means that there's some little flaw in the workmanship but nothing serious enough to interfere with the instrument's operation. This one [holding up set] has a chip in the case so small I doubt you can even see it from where you're sitting.

"We also have cosmetic sets for the ladeez and secretary wallets for the gentlemen, many of which contain genuine lucky-bucks dollar bills [holding up a dollar bill]. Bottles of perfume for the ladeez, electric razors for the gentlemen and so on. The gifts in this group we call Group Number One.

"Now we turn to Group Number Two. *Eye Cue*, the well-known burlesque magazine [holding up magazine] which contains pictures of all the popular strip-tease dancers just the way you like to see them. Here [leafing through pages] is a picture of Margie Hart in a pose that's sure to hold your attention, and here's another one of that famous of all strippers, Gypsy Rose Lee. These pictures, incidentally, can be removed from the magazine and pasted on the wall. Just cut along the margin, and you have a nice piece of art suitable for framing. Or just stick 'em up with thumb tacks in your bedroom and you'll be happy to wake up in the mornings.

"These pictures are spread about the magazine between stories too frank and lurid for other magazines to print. Now, there are ladeez present, so I can't describe the subject matter in detail. But on Page 10 there's an article about a man who was hitchhiking across the country when he was picked up by three Hollywood starlets. He tells how these three gorgeous girls took him to a motel and forced him at gunpoint to fulfill their erotic dreams again and again. And again, ladeez and gentlemen. They told him if he couldn't they'd kill him on the spot. Well, he lived and it's all here in black and white how he managed to do it. The magazine will be offered to you as Group Number Two.

"Group Number Three consists of a series of cartoon books. You know the kind. [Reading] 'What the Chambermaid Saw Through the Keyhole,' 'The Traveling Salesman and the Farmer's Daughter,' 'The Big Squeeze.' Sure they're bawdy and maybe a little bit vulgar, but they make a good burlesque souvenir to take home to your mother-in-law. Maybe she'll get a kick out of it. We call the cartoon books Group Number Three.

"For Group Number Four we have a pair of burlesque dice. At first glance they look like ordinary dice but on close examination you'll notice that the dots are not dots at all but tiny holes, and when you put them together [illustrating] so that the ones on each dice are opposite and hold them up to any light and look through the holes you'll see a man and woman involved in one of the oldest activities in human history.

"Put the twos together and you'll see two men and women, and so on until you put the sixes together, and I promise that you'll see something so unusual, so exciting and so — well, fantastic — it'll take your breath away.

"Now the question arises as to how we're going to distribute these gifts. We could, of course, just toss them up in the air and let you scramble for them. But the chances are the big fellows would get most of them, the little fellows would get only a few and the ladeez wouldn't get any. Obviously that isn't the best way to do it. Also it might get us arrested for causing a riot.

"We've found the best way to distribute these gifts so everyone will get an even chance to share them. We sell a box of very tasty chawclates here at the Gayety [holding up box]. It's good candy, something you'll enjoy nibbling during the second act, due to start any minute now. Anywhere else you'd have to spend 50 cents to a dollar for a fine box of chawclates like this. But we're not going to ask you a dollar for it. We know that you come here to relax and have a good time and don't want to spend a lot of money doing it. No, our price is not a dollar. It's not 75 cents; it's not even 50 cents. Our price is 25 cents, a quarter of a dollar, and we throw in absolutely free one of the gifts mentioned in Group Number One, the magazine, the famous burlesque magazine *Eye Cue*, which is Group Number Two, the cartoon books — 'What the Marine Gave Nellie to Remember Him By' — all in Group Number Three, and the burlesque novelty dice, Group Number Four. "Now [authoritatively, holding up hand], we make you this promise. We're honest people here, not robbers. So if your purchase from our representative doesn't live up to our claims — if it doesn't include one of the gifts mentioned in Group Number One, the magazine in Group Number Two, the cartoon books and the dice — if it doesn't include all these things, keep the stuff, eat the candy and we'll give you back your 25 cents. You can have it all absolutely free!"

Though the faces of the servicemen and defense-workers in my vicinity had exhibited nothing but mild curiosity at the beginning of the pitchman's monologue, I observed a quickening of interest during his description of the magazine's contents and, by the time he reached the dice, they were literally bouncing up and down in their seats. I was not surprised therefore when, with the exception of John and myself, the row went unanimously for the chance to put the sixes together.

While the sailor on my right was squinting hopefully through the "holes," I took a look at his other treasures and found them to consist of a plastic compact, a thin edition of one of the cheaper "girlie" magazines (devoid, as far as I could see, of any article about hitchhikers), a cartoon booklet innocuous enough to have been purchased in any five-and-dime store and (finally) the dice which, as it developed, had only the usual opaque spots on their six sides.

Astounded that any man in his right mind would dare offer such spurious merchandise to a crowd capable of taking the building apart, I was on the point of questioning John on the subject when the speaker returned to the stage, raised both arms and in a voice sharp enough to rattle balls in the pool pockets upstairs, exclaimed:

"Stop the sale!

"Take care of that man," he ordered a perspiring "representative," pointing to an invisible customer in the fifth row, "and come back down here." As the gorillas, their trays overflowing with Groups One to Four, returned to the foot of the stage, he resumed his chatty (would-I-lie-to-you?) approach.

"Now, I can see that some of you are skeptical about our way of distributing these gifts. I know you're saying to yourself 'They can't fool me. Nobody's going to give away such valuable prizes for 25 cents.' All right, I'll tell you what. If I can find ten men in this aisle sporting enough to risk a quarter, ten in the side aisles and ten more in the balconies, I'll make them the most incredible proposition they've ever heard of in their lives.

"I realize that some of these gifts are not as valuable as others. So we'll eliminate them. [To the gorillas] Put down your trays, boys. [As they do] Now, I want you to pick out three of the boxes containing the watches, three containing the cosmetic sets, three of those guaranteed-for-a-year electric shavers and three of the secretary wallets — and be sure that each of them contains a lucky-bucks dollar bill.

"Now my assistants will pass among you. And if the box you select — and I want to emphasize that. You are not going to be handed a box. You will select it yourself. And, if it doesn't contain one of the gifts mentioned — a watch, a cosmetic set, an electric razor or a secretary wallet — with a lucky buck inside — eat the candy, return the box and we'll give you a crisp one dollar bill. If that isn't fair, I don't know what is.

"Have your money ready." With a gesture of dismissal, the pitchman picked up his microphone and strode off the stage, announcing over his shoulder "The curtain rises in one minute."

I had assumed, considering the disappointment they had encountered with their first purchase, the soldiers and sailors would give this second proposition the horse laugh. To my astonishment, they repeated their mistakes with the same eagerness as before. All received in return for their money sleazy oilcloth wallets containing imitation dollar bills. The band re-entered the pit. The drummer attacked his instruments with the same frenzy, and the curtain rose on another miserable chorus routine.

I left the theater that afternoon convinced that, although Baltimore did have more to offer than Fort Worth, I needed time in order to figure out what to do with it.

FOUR

Despite their great significance for the world at large, the Forties for Goodspeed and me added up to so many years of unbroken monotony. It wasn't that nothing happened. As a matter of fact, quite a lot did. We both got married — he to a fashionable Baltimore woman and I to Dorothy Ruth. We also got divorced.

But at the end of the decade we had progressed no farther — in either our professional or personal lives — than where we were when we had graduated from TCU.

The Japanese attack on Pearl Harbor had resulted in the institution of ten-hour shifts at Martin with one day off out of every seven. We lived not so much in a city called Baltimore as in a limbo called the war. We rose before the sun and returned home from the boarded-up heavily camouflaged plant after it came down. Our day off was spent recuperating from the emotional strains of the week that had just passed and gathering strength for the one we knew was to follow.

The work itself, considering our ignorance of aircraft engineering, wasn't too hard. We were both fast learners. At one point I even found myself supervising the activities of more than a dozen draftsmen turning out drawings for the Flying Wing. Goodspeed got along equally well.

But our hearts weren't in it. So neither of us really cared when, during the mass layoffs of January, 1949, we were included among the casualties.

John, harking back to his college major, applied for and got a job on the Baltimore *Evening Sun*. I, hoping for greater glory, spent two years trying to write plays, while supporting myself selling insurance. "Supporting" is a slight exaggeration — since I now can recall not a single policy I ever sold.

Finally, moved by desperation, I wrote a letter to the managing editor of the Baltimore *MorningSun*. And my world — so dim for so long — was suddenly transformed by a shaft of light.

FIVE

It takes time for a meaningful relationship to develop. Thus, though my introduction to the city occurred by way of the Gayety Theater and the Block, it was not until I began writing for the *Sun* that I came to know Baltimore and Baltimore came to know me.

When I got off the train that hot September Sunday in 1941, I was just 23. When I reported to assistant city-editor Clarence Caulfield on a somewhat cooler Sunday in March of 1951 for my first assignment as a *Sun* district reporter, I was nearing 33. The years between were in their own way interesting. If I live long enough I might write a book about them. For the moment, I'd just as soon forget them.

"District reporter" was the first rung of a ladder that, I learned to my surprise, might lead anywhere. Of the various reporters covering police districts when I came on the *Sun*, one went on to become chief of several foreign bureaus, one became a syndicated political columnist and one became chairman of the board.

How did I obtain the right to badger the Baltimore police department under First Amendment protection at the stupendous salary of $37.50 a week? It all started in the Park Plaza Hotel bar over lunch one day with an *Evening Sun* assistant city editor named Richard Tucker. A man whose years in various byways of journalism had soured him on the whole profession, Tucker seemed astounded at the idea that I wanted to be a reporter. Of course he'd never tried to sell insurance.

"If you really want to get on a newspaper, and," he added with a shudder, "I can't imagine why anyone would, you'll have to do some free-lance stuff first. There are rarely any openings on the daily papers, but the Sunday "Brown Section" offers the kind of challenge first-year journalism students have always regarded as a good reason to commit suicide. But you'll have to choose your subjects with care. Nothing vaguely intelligent will serve. What you want is some old man who collects cigar bands."

Tucker, who not long after this encounter was sent to cover the Korean war and disappeared forever from the local scene, was right about the sort of thing the "Brown Section" specialized in. Old-line Maryland. Nothing controversial. Everything strictly from Dullsville. After studying it for several Sundays, I came up with the perfect topic. It was in fact so perfect that "Fritz" Whitman, the section's leather-elbowed, pipe-smoking editor, couldn't believe it had not already been done and wouldn't buy it until he'd checked all the clips in the library.

Baltimore has always been noted for a style of residential architecture known as the "row house." Street after street of these houses, whose sharing of common side walls gives their fronts the effect of one continuous facade, constitute perhaps the city's most noticeable characteristic. It is traditional for the female inhabitants of these houses to come out in the mornings and wash the steps leading up to the doors.

Next to its row houses the most distinctive and indeed historic piece of Baltimore architecture is the Washington Monument that stands in the center of Mount Vernon Place. My article, which appeared in the December 18, 1949 edition of the *Sunday Sun*, began as follows:

> *Baltimore housewives, long accustomed to scrubbing the white steps in front of their homes, should be glad to learn that one of the city's men has a job perhaps 100 times as difficult. As custodian of the Washington Monument, Walter M. Turner's duties include cleaning the 228 stone steps leading from the ground floor to the observation room at the top. This task he has performed . . . at least once a week for the last four years. And without a trace of housemaid's knee.*

THE STORY, REPRESENTING MY debut as a journalist, was followed by others of equally stimulating subject matter: a Baltimore firm that manufactured lacrosse balls, a custom pipe-maker, a wig-maker and a school for expectant fathers. Also included was perhaps the only legitimate scoop in my entire 33-year newspaper career — the first piece ever written about Howard Head, a former Martin colleague whose innovations in ski and tennis-racquet design have since made him internationally famous, not to mention rich.

And all the time I kept writing plays which were not produced (actually one did have a brief off-Broadway run in 1950) and not selling insurance. John, on the other hand, thrived. As writer of the *Evening Sun*'s "Mr. Peep's Diary," he had come into his own.

So we carried on for a couple of years, he in the newspaper business making his mark and I in the insurance business missing mine — until one day when, gathering up my sheaf of boring clippings, I headed for the recently erected *Sunpapers* building at Calvert and Centre Streets. Edwin P. Young, Jr., the *Morning Sun*'s dynamic city editor, was waiting for me with, if not open arms, at least an open mind.

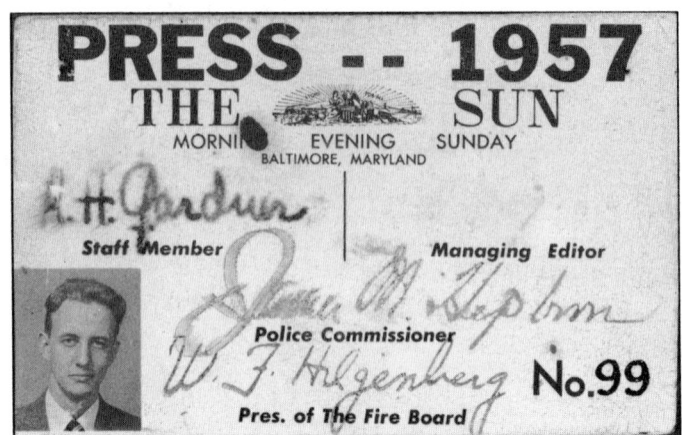

The Sun Rises

SIX

The more common term for district reporter, I learned from Ted Hendricks, the very nice guy assigned by Caulfield that first Sunday to show me the ropes, was "leg man." The description bore no reference to a person's erotic tastes but to the distinction between the reporter who ran about the city collecting news and the "rewrite man" to whom he telephoned his findings for incorporation into the next edition.

The leg man rarely wrote anything and therefore was looked down upon by practically everybody including himself. On the other hand, the rewrite man, who had to bat out reasonably comprehensible copy under the most strenuous circumstances, was looked up to as a sort of king of the city room. The two leading "kings" in those days were the *Evening Sun*'s Odell Smith, who later became administrative assistant to a governor, and the *Morning Sun*'s Russell Baker, who was to win two Pulitzer Prizes, one for his work as a *New York Times* columnist and another as author of a delightful autobiography, *Growing Up*.

Baker slouched in his chair to the right of the city editor as if the whole thing bored him. He was a trained typist, and he made a point of rattling off paragraphs without even glancing at the keys. He was the only man in my experience who could look down his typewriter as others look down their noses.

As a recently hired member of the staff, I was acutely sensitive to these looks and concluded that Baker was an arrogant ass. Possibly he was. He was also the best all-round newspaper man — capable of excelling whatever the assignment — I've ever known. Once, in answer to a question, he told me why he liked rewrite. It gave him the opportunity to bandy words with the district men, who, he said, had a tendency to phone in stories before getting all the necessary information.

I had only one brush with him in this connection. I had been sent by Caulfield to investigate why an empty car had been parked for several days on a deserted street in Hamden. On my way to the spot I passed through an area filled with row houses. In the yard of one, firemen were running around in gas masks, and the odor of decomposition was overpowering. Looking up, I beheld through the open front door two naked bodies caught in the unmistakable act of coition.

I later learned that the victims had died several days before from carbon monoxide issuing from a faulty heater. But my first concern was not with facts. My first concern was that nauseating odor, from which I fled like a coward from the field of battle. My second was notifying the city desk. The news hit Cauly at his worst possible moment — when he was trying to get things shipshape for Ed Young's arrival at 5:30.

"Hold on. I'll give you a rewrite man."

There was a pause, then Baker's dry, always cynical voice came on the line: "Describe," it said, "the nakedness of these bodies."

BALTIMORE, I LEARNED FROM HENDRICKS THAT SUNDAY, was for the purpose of police reporting divided into two areas, the east side and the west. The east consisted of the Eastern Police District, the Northeastern and the

Northern. The west consisted of the Northwestern, the Western, the Southwestern and the Southern. Covering these districts involved going to the stationhouses, attending the magistrates' courts held there in the mornings and afternoons, reading the police reports and listening to the police radio that kept the beat men in touch with crimes then in progress.

At each station-house there was a table in a corner with telephones connecting directly with the city desks of the three daily papers, *Morning Sun*, *Evening Sun* and *News-American* (then called the *News-Post*). We reporters could use these phones at any time except during roll-call at 8 A.M., 4 P.M. and midnight when the shifts changed and all the patrolmen trooped into the stations to receive their orders of the day. While this went on, no outsiders were admitted.

Though I didn't spend much time in the districts, I enjoyed the few weeks I did — especially a magic moment that first afternoon when a kindly faced man, who looked more like a priest than a police lieutenant, came across the dusty floor of Southern Police Station to take my hand in both of his, stare searchingly into my eyes and say "Force against force is not the answer. I keep telling 'em that force against force will never work. The only solution is love and understanding."

Intrigued by a policeman who felt there was a better way of dealing with crime than by force, I asked Hendricks who he was. "Holthause," he said with a slightly disparaging wave of the hand. "Generally considered a character. Don't let the buttons fool you. He's a 'desk' lieutenant, comparable to a sergeant." I didn't at that time understand this distinction, but Holthause, whatever his buttons, impressed me as the most interesting person I'd met that afternoon.

THE TRAINING PROGRAM FOR A *Sun* reporter on his first day was carefully worked out. Hendricks escorted me around various police stations until the 4 P.M. roll call, at which time I was turned over to David Maulsby, the *Sun*'s headquarters man who looked out upon the world and the city's impounding lot from an upstairs window in Central Police Station. If Holthause could be considered a "character," what, oh lord, was Maulsby? He was listed in the Social Register, wore gray flannel trousers up to his ankles over dirty white saddle shoes, spoke with an aggressive lisp and in World War II had been a Marine.

When I entered his second-floor disaster area of an office, with its broken chairs and desks overflowing with piles of debris, he was yelling into a telephone: "Look, Ace! I don't care what size dress your mother takes. I'm trying to find out why you were wearing one!" He slammed the phone down. "These perverts! So what do *you* want?" The question seemed to include me with all the other perverts.

"Oh, you're the new man," he said, after I'd identified myself. He lifted a half-empty fifth of gin from the lower drawer of the desk. "You have a pencil? You may want to take notes."

I had a pencil but, though I kept it poised, I didn't use it. Maulsby was an indefatigable talker who rarely said anything worth recording. Throughout the long monologue that followed, he kept pulling out bottles. All the drawers of the desk seemed to be filled with them. At one point, I drifted over to sit on the leather couch in the corner only to discover that under its lumpy cushions it was filled with them, too.

The principal job of a headquarters man seemed to be keeping in touch with district men by telephone to advise them of things going on in their areas of which they, without advantage of the police radio, might be unaware. Especially fires.

At the time, I knew only two things about fires — represented by the cliche headlines "Forced to flee" and "Taken down a ladder." People were always being "Forced to flee" or "Taken down a ladder" when fire invaded the block or house where they lived. There had been a three-alarm fire earlier that afternoon and, hoping to impress Maulsby with my journalistic savvy, I asked what had happened to the people who had been taken down a ladder.

The question had an electric effect. He almost dropped his bottle of gin. "What people?" There was a definite note of panic in his voice. "Nobody told me anything about people taken down a ladder!" Which was quite understandable, since I had made up the whole thing. "Look, Ace," he said an hour later, as we stood at the stag bar in the House of Welsh having a couple of boilermakers before dinner. "Don't ever do that to me again. I have a hard enough time distinguishing fantasy from reality as it is."

And so he did. But with him it was a lovable trait. After I had become a rewrite man, we Titans of the city desk used to wait with pleasurable anticipation for the stories he called in following a dinner consisting mostly of boilermakers. Maulsby was quite simply a joy who, before his death in the Seventies, made the *Sun* shine brighter every time one encountered him.

After dinner, which lasted until 9 o'clock ("I can't pay you much," Ed Young had said, "but you can take a long dinner-hour"), Maulsby and I looked over the first edition, he to see if any of the tidbits of news he'd delivered had gotten in and I to see if a story I'd written on my own before reporting for my first day at work had been used. The story concerned the closing of an annual flower show and began:

Heads fell over the weekend at the 5th Regiment Armory as, trailing clouds of glory, the National Flower Show pulled up roots for another year. The heads belonged to several hundred tulips, daffodils, hyacinths and other blossoming plants which, according to the show manager, were good for nothing but the dump heap.

TO MY SURPRISE AND EVERLASTING PRIDE, Caulfield had not only used the piece but had put it unchanged in the middle of the back page (then the front page for local news). Maulsby was so impressed ("stunned" would be closer to the truth) that somebody on his first day would have a story so prominently displayed ("You mean that's *your* lead?" he asked incredulously, uncapping a new bottle of gin) that he never again suggested I take notes.

At 11:30 he gathered up the remains of the new bottle and turned me over to Pete Kumpa, the headquarters "lobster" man. I've never really learned the derivation of the term "lobster" as applied to the solitary vigil a reporter has to serve after all his colleagues have departed for the night in the direction of the nearest bar. But what mainly occupied my mind then was something Frank Porter, an *Evening Sun* reporter who shared an apartment with Goodspeed, had told me the night before.

"There's only one person you have to look out for," Frank had cautioned, "and that's a guy named Kumpa. He's a queer."

Police headquarters, like the Oasis and other landmarks in the same area, has since shifted to a new building in a new location. But in those days it was a decaying honeycomb of corridors and back stairs. And, as Kumpa — a bright-eyed pumpkin face of a guy with hair so blond it was almost white and horn-rimmed spectacles — conducted me over the terrain, I was careful to stand at least five feet back of him. He would go running down a flight of steps, pause at the foot and I would stop half way up. The whole thing was based on a ridiculous misunderstanding between Pete and Frank during an encounter where neither had been at his best.

There are two aspects of reporting — gathering the news and writing it. Though sufficiently adept at the latter, Pete's specialty was the former. Give him a telephone and, with a few well-placed calls, he could find out what was going on anywhere in the world. This talent stood him well. He quickly moved up to become, successively, chief of the *Sun*'s Moscow, Hong Kong, London and Washington bureaus. Then he returned to Baltimore to write a column for the *Evening Sun*.

In the face of seemingly unavoidable disaster, he remained weirdly calm — which may have been the secret of the trust he inspired in even the most nervous news sources. He gave the impression of being able to handle any emergency — as he did on the night of the 1952 presidential election when he took on the task of getting me relieved from an unbearable assignment.

Most staff reporters had well-defined "beats," which they covered in both news-gathering and writing capacities. But on election night all became leg men for the political specialists responsible for putting it all together. My job on this occasion was to sit downtown in the AP office and telephone in reports of how voting was going throughout the State.

And so I did, without rancor, until around 2 A.M. when the AP closed up shop and went home. Having nothing to do, I returned to the *Sun* building, hoping to join with my fellows in devouring the free food and drink provided by the management on such occasions. Hardly had I entered the fifth-floor sanctum reserved for this revelry than Banker, then assistant city editor, approached and asked what I was doing there.

"I'm trying to get something to eat."

"Don't you know Dorsey has said he will fire any *Morning Sun* reporter who leaves his post before being relieved by an *Evening Sun* reporter tomorrow?"

"But I no longer have a post!" I protested. "The AP has suspended operations for the night."

Banker shook his head. "You better go back," he said with impressive seriousness, "or you may no longer have a job."

I looked around where everyone — including Banker — was stuffing himself. "You mean I've got to sit in solitary suffering while you guys —"

Here Kumpa appeared and, in his quiet, no-reason-to-get-excited manner, took charge of the situation. "Look, Ace," he said, drawing me aside. "Do what Banker says. I'll talk to Dorsey and get you back within the hour."

It turned out to be a long hour, made even worse by my depressed reaction to the way the election was going. I had been a Stevenson man. Finally, I called Kumpa who told me, shouting above the din of celebration going on in the background, "I'm sorry, Ace. Dorsey is adamant. I don't really think he means it, but if you come back now you're fired."

Before coming on the paper, two months before I did, in January of 1951, Pete had lived for a while in Manhattan, where he had rented rooms from a Japanese chauffeur who lived on the same floor. As he prepared to move in, the chauffeur had told him, "I think you should know that I live the gay life."

In those days the significance of the term "gay" was not as widely known as it is now. Kumpa's response to the landlord's statement was "Fine. I live a pretty gay life myself." But, after weeks of observing crowds of people going in and out of the chauffeur's apartment wearing rouge and other suspicious paraphernalia, he began to get the message.

He'd told this story as a joke on himself, at a party of roistering *Sun* employees, and Frank, who, like everybody there, had probably had a couple too many, had jumped to the wrong conclusion. Exactly how wrong it was I am in a good position to know. Kumpa and I once shared the same Charles Street apartment, and I am godfather to one of his many children.

In time, both Pete and Frank moved to the District of Columbia, Pete to work in the *Sun*'s Washington bureau and Frank to take over a desk job on the *Washington Post*. One evening Frank went to a downtown restaurant, got a steak bone stuck in his throat and died. The man who telephoned me in Baltimore in the middle of the night to inform me in a voice choked with grief of this tragic occurrence was Peter Kumpa.

SEVEN

The *Sun* has always been a morning newspaper, which means that most of the events described in it took place the day before. Evening newspapers describe events taking place the same day and often still in progress. As opposed to the open-ended quality of evening news, morning news has an air of finality. This happened yesterday, and that's it. What happens today is another story.

The better morning papers during the years I worked on the *Sun* did not strive for the sensational impact of their evening counterparts, whose street editions sold according to the size of their headlines. It was assumed that the typical *Sun* subscriber read his copy over the breakfast table with a civilized man's distaste for having his digestion disturbed. The aim was not to release adrenalin but to supply a record comparable in its accuracy to an account in a history book.

In view of this general down-playing of sensational material, the fact that the *Morning Sun* was more interesting to read than the other Baltimore dailies can only be attributed to the personalities of those who, through their occupancy of the city desk, controlled what went into it. This was particularly true of their handling of news-features.

There are two kinds of features. One describes a long-established practice or phenomenon. My story about the cleaning of the Washington Monument steps fitted perfectly into this category. The other always has a topical angle.

The *Morning Sun* had a separate section with a separate editor for the first kind. The second was handled by the city desk, which used the stories (when good enough) to add variety to the back page. How these stories were assigned and played depended on the professional skill and native wisdom of three people. We shall start with Caulfield, than whom there is no better place, whatever the circumstances, to start.

"Shall I," wrote Shakespeare, "compare thee to a summer's day?" And shall I, dear Cauly, compare thee to a gin and tonic with a shot of gin on the side? You called it a "one and one" and, when waiting on you at the Calvert, the barmaid would always know what you meant when you ordered it. Other barmaids throughout the city were not always sure.

Recalling his own early attempts at writing, Max Beerbohm mentions his unflagging quest for the "mot juste" — the exact word — for the person he wanted to describe. The mot juste for Cauly was "merry."

Not that he was the oh-ho-ho-Santa-Claus type. Physically he did not suit the role, having a slight body, reddish hair and freckles. But there was an irrepressible smile always hovering about his mouth and an impish glint in his eye. He was a jolly middle-aged elf who, after a couple of one-and-ones, might lapse into hilarious reminiscences about his early life as a traveling feed salesman or jump to his feet and execute an impromptu jig around the city desk.

Dear Cauly, how we loved you then! How those of us still alive love you now!

Few things contrived to subvert Cauly's natural ebullience. One was Ed Young's coming in so smashed after a ship's launching he was incapable of doing his job.

Under ordinary conditions Ed was the ideal city editor. He had what in Hollywood movies of the Thirties was called a "nose for news." He also had an uncanny ability to inspire devotion in his men — even those who were scandalously underpaid. Much as I tried to repress my own resentment on this subject, the tension between us, as time passed and I continued to receive no merit raises, increased until the middle Fifties when, to everyone's surprise, he suddenly left to take a top executive post on the *Providence Journal*. Unlike others, I did not make a point of mourning his departure, but deep in my heart the devotion remained. I even felt it for his outrageous behavior relative to launchings.

It was the habit of the Bethlehem Steel Company in those days to throw a big bash to publicize completion of a new ship. A fleet of limousines picked up VIP's from all over the area, depositing them finally at the Belvedere Hotel where two banquet rooms on the top floor had been reserved for a Roman-orgy-type celebration. In one room there were drinks and dancing to an orchestra. In the other there was a sit-down luncheon featuring filet mignon with all the trimmings.

As a general rule, newspaper men cannot be bought. They are, however, susceptible to free-loading, which they do not regard as a bribe, because with rare exceptions it has no influence on what they write. Ed Young was to this manner born.

The schedule at the *Sun* ran roughly as follows:

Caulfield came in at 10 A.M. and got out the file for the day. It was composed of bits and pieces — press releases sent in earlier, clippings from newspapers concerning events to take place on that date — all of which he scrutinized over his spectacles with much squinting of eye and screwing up of face. Around 2, reporters began to drift in. He made assignments and listed the stories in the order of what he considered to be their importance. Around 5, the night editor — usually Ed — came in, inspected the list and made decisions as to how the stories should be played, at which point Cauly got to his feet and headed for the Calvert Bar. Except on afternoons when there was a launching.

At such times, the door to the corridor would bang open and Ed, looking like the sole survivor of an Indian massacre, would stagger in. His complexion, normally two shades redder than an over-ripe tomato, would be deep purple. He had a strange way of fingering his clothes, checking to see if his coat was buttoned, his creases unwrinkled. William Manchester, who knew him when Ed was city editor of the *Evening Sun*, claims that this preoccupation with dress derived from the fact that Ed had recently inherited a wardrobe from a relative two sizes smaller than he. But I don't think it was that. His main concern seemed to be with the twin vents in the tail of his coat. He kept running his fingers over them. My theory was that he'd once sat on them improperly and had never gotten over it. As he smoothed them out, he tended to jump up and down nervously. On launching afternoons he literally bounced like a toy animal on a string, as he groped his way across the floor to the city desk and collapsed into the chair opposite Caulfield.

"Mgotanythinfittinprint?" he'd mumble.

Translated, this meant "Have we got anything fit to print?" Cauly was familiar with the question, which never failed to throw him into a fit of depression because it meant he was going to have to stay on at least another hour until the "B" edition had been nailed down.

On one side of the city room was a door opening into a shallow closet. "Shallow" in this instance meant 18 inches. Coats, hung in there, had to be twisted on the hangers in order that the door might be closed. Ed, who always moved like a man standing upright on a speeding motorcycle, would charge through the door of this closet as if there were a corridor of infinite length in the opposite wall. Squeezing inside, he would remain for a moment and then emerge as if nothing unusual had happened.

And it hadn't. He went into the closet to take a couple of snorts from the half-pint of gin he'd just bought at the Calvert. Every night shortly after 12 when make-up for the first city edition (not to be confused with the 8:30 "bulldog") had been completed, he dashed out to get a bottle to sustain him through the rest of the evening.

It was not a morbid dependence on drink that motivated Ed on these occasions but a desire to celebrate the fact that work was almost done. Ed loved to celebrate. We had a lot of after-hours parties in those days and Ed, who had to arrive at them late because of the need to check the back page proof, lost no time, once there, in organizing things.

"Let's hit it!" he'd yell, lifting his purple face to the ceiling. And the assembled group would immediately swing into the alma mater of Ed's school, Cornell.

I remember one evening when, after a night of working rewrite, I arrived with Ed at a party in Kumpa's basement apartment in Bolton Hill. There had already been complaints from irate neighbors, but when we got there somewhere around 2 A.M. everything fell into place.

"I don't want to interfere with your fun," said Kumpa in his quiet undisturbed voice to Ed, who was leading the choir. "I just want to let you know that the cops are on the way." And so they were, but nobody seemed to care, least of all Ed who, as they rapped on the door, raised his arms and shouted "All right, gang! *Hail to thee, Cornell!*"

Among the guests attending these parties was sometimes a statuesque journalism student from the University of Maryland then serving an internship on the *Sun*. During the afternoon she sat at the city desk answering telephone calls in a scoop-necked blouse that, combined with her brilliant red hair and the endowments the blouse did little to conceal, caused many a reporter to look up from his typewriter with an agonized expression. As one who shared their agony, I finally got up nerve enough to invite her to dinner at the Calvert, and on the way back across the vast, intervening parking lot, took a chance on kissing her. She responded with, if not passion, certainly fervor. She almost bit my tongue off.

News travels even faster in city rooms than it does in other places, so it wasn't long after we returned from our poignant tete-a-tete in the parking lot that Ed paused by my desk where I was nursing my mangled tongue. "I understand," he said, "that you took our new employee to dinner?"

"Thass 'ight."

"She — *bit* you?" There was incredulity in his voice.

I nodded.

"Jesus!" He spun around and flung himself into the closet at twice his usual speed.

Paul Banker, the third permanent occupant of the city desk, differed from the other two not so much in spirit as in appearance. A graduate of Yale, he looked Ivy League from the top of his crewcut head to the tips of his Weejun loafers. As a Cornell alumnus, Ed was also Ivy League but, possibly because of his dead relative's wardrobe, he looked more like a well-dressed insurance salesman. As for Cauly, in tam, long scarf and bandy-legged stride, he looked like — well, a leprechaun with a couple of one-and-ones under his belt.

Banker had a perverse sense of humor. Take his insistence that everybody build boats. One could then buy a plastic boat-building kit for a reasonable sum and Banker envisioned all of us spending our weekends on the Chesapeake.

Several actually bought the kits, but all they got for their trouble was a sketch on the city room bulletin board by Jim Hartzell, the *Sun*'s waggish cartoonist, showing a big floppy-lipped cannibal on a tropical island staring at three tiny specks on the horizon and yelling "Get out the kettle, men! Here come the boys from the *Mawnin' Sun*."

There's a lot of boring work to be done on a newspaper. "Shorts," those little paragraphs that fill what otherwise would be empty spots, have to be written. And, whenever there was not enough manpower on the inside to deal with such matters, district men were pressed into service. From the first day, I had jumped at every opportunity to take advantage of this practice, because the districts gave one so little opportunity to write.

It was while sitting at my typewriter one spring afternoon, looking forward to dinner, that I saw Banker approaching from the city desk, his crewcut head bristling, his Weejun loafers gleaming. "Cover this," he said, handing me a clipping.

The clipping announced that members of the Charcoal Club were holding their annual dinner in honor of the distinguished Baltimore painter, the late Ignatius Loyola Glutz. The meeting would be held that night at the group's studio on Eutaw Place, where, with bright eyes and sharpened pencil, I arrived a few minutes before the appointed hour.

The room was large with a long banquet table running down the center and walls hung with specimens of the master's art. Harry Pouder — with whom I later became close friends owing to the fact that, as drama critic of the magazine put out by the Baltimore Association of Commerce, he sat right behind me at the theater — showed me around. "This is one of Glutz's early experiments," he said, pointing to a realistic portrait of a hotdog with pickle and mustard. "And this, of course, is indicative of his blue period." He waved a hand in the direction of an enormous blue weenie.

I looked down the row of paintings. "He seems to have been obsessed with a certain subject matter."

"Oh, yes." I got another careless wave. "Like all true geniuses, Glutz occupied himself with recurring themes." That, as other members of the group arrived and the ceremonies got under way, I decided no one could deny.

First there were speeches. Though dead many years, Glutz had apparently left behind a veritable trove of art treasures, remnants of which were being unearthed regularly from the ruins of demolished rowhouses. The past year had yielded a particularly juicy cache in an abandoned sewer.

Banker, his tongue invisible in his cheek, had quite clearly presented me with a challenge. My only concern in meeting it was with time. I had never written a story requiring any kind of style on deadline.

I got back to the *Sun* building after 11. Ed Young was on the desk, routing with characteristic decisiveness the copy that flowed over to him from the other reporters around the room. "Did you cover Glutz?"

I nodded.

"Good." He glanced at the clock. "You've got twenty minutes."

Stories were then typed triple-space and sent over to the desk in one-page takes. The editor read them and sent them, also page at a time, across to the copy desk. There they were copy-read, the heads returned to the editor for approval and the whole mess shot down the tube to the composing room — where they were set into type and transferred by techniques I've never really understood to large rotating cylinders, eventually ending up in print.

The story I wrote that night, which appeared in the second city edition of the April 1, 1951 *Sun*, read:

Full of the spirit of April Fool, plus perhaps that of the Roman god Bacchus, members of the Charcoal Club met last night to celebrate in an atmosphere of mild hysteria their fifteenth annual dinner in honor of Ignatius Loyola Glutz.

Glutz will be remembered by Baltimore art-lovers — to use the term as loosely as the language allows — as the man "responsible for the course of American art for the last 75 years."

To judge by the frenetic canvases adorning the Eutaw Place studio where the banquet was held, everyone who ever wielded a brush copied Glutz. Picasso, Rouault, Rembrandt, the early cliff dwellers — they're all pure Glutz.

The degree of this achievement reaches its true staggering heights when one considers that Glutz was born in Baltimore only 86 years ago.

This man who "spent two weeks at the Maryland Institute," "painted signs for which he was paid in baloney," "camouflaged guns during the first war," had a humble beginning in a garret on South Poppleton Street. He had an even humbler end in a garret in France, according to the legend of the Charcoal Club.

If the atom bomb ever falls on Baltimore a veritable cloudburst of Glutz masterpieces is sure to result. For somewhere in the foundation of each building, planted no doubt concurrently with the cornerstone, is a Glutz original.

How did they get there? Who knows? That's Glutz every time.

Last night's banquet began with a reading of the "works" by G. Harry Pouder, club president.

These included a thumbnail biography written by the late John McGrath, founder of the cult, and several poems. An idea of the latter can be derived from the following deathless lines:

I am Glutz.

I am not nuts.

After the poetry session came a long series of toasts. Richard Brady toasted "Glutz the man." This was followed in turn by Col. James P. Wharton's toast to "Glutz the artist."

It was at this point that the entire assembly turned as one man to admire the paintings, many of which showed sausages done in various styles and periods.

The highlight of the evening involved a presentation of Glutz's diary, entitled "Glutz Confidential," unearthed and translated from the original Greek by Joseph G. Shaner. Its contents must, unfortunately, remain a secret. Most of the Glutz material seems to deal primarily with his exploits with the ladies. He was apparently a blend of Casanova, Lothario and Harpo Marx.

Whether or not Glutz is real is probably something the world will never know. One thing, however, is certain. He is real to the members of the Charcoal Club, and the more they toasted him last night the "realer" he became.

ED YOUNG READ MY PIECE WITH AN INDIFFERENT AIR. On the last take, however, he chuckled. "Good tag line," he said, spiking the carbon before sending the original over to the copy desk. I had been in the business too short a time to know that a "tag" was the last line in a story. Still, I felt I had succeeded, and my euphoria was increased the next afternoon when Banker, with a sheepish grin, congratulated me on my performance.

Actually, there was a fourth permanent occupant of the city desk. Though classified as a rewrite man, Jay Spry possessed a quality that made him ideally suited to the job — an uncanny ability to absorb and categorize trivia.

The *Sunpapers* in those days published an average of ten daily editions — plus a number of feature sections on Sunday. Most reporters tended to read only those stories concerning their own fields. Not Spry. He read them all. When he departed for home at the end of a working day, he carried such a pile of newspapers under his arm that he was sometimes accused of peddling them on the side.

He didn't. What he did was to subject them to intense scrutiny, clipping items and placing them in the file to remind Cauly of things to come. The *Evening Sun* clip about Glutz that Banker had passed on to me had doubtless come from him.

This daily pouring over of newsprint gave Spry an expert knowledge of what was happening not only in the columns of the *Sun* but also in Baltimore. His job was to come in early and hold down the desk until Cauly appeared. He spent much of this time arguing with people who, annoyed by something they had read in the *Sun*, called in threatening to cancel their subscriptions.

The standard way of dealing with such irritants is to get rid of them as soon as possible. Spry took the opposite route. He would sit there, puffing on a long cigar, and go on and on, pointing out the flaws in their arguments. Years later Burks was to say "Every paper needs a guy like Spry, who not only knows everything that has been printed but what to do about it."

When in the middle Fifties, after 15 years of dedicated service, Spry decided to leave the *Sun* for a better-paying job with Standard Oil, we put out a dummy front page announcing the fact under a banner headline written by copy-desk slot man Pierce Fenhagen: "Spry Leaves Cul-de-sac To Become An Oil Tycoon." There was also a mock obituary by Catling, which began "Spry was the kind of man who sharpened his pencil to a needle point and expected the same uncompromising perfection from others."

And it could be said that he did that. It could also be said that he was an extremely nice guy. I heard he had once declared that I was the most promising new reporter to come on the *Sun* during the entire 15 years he had worked there. I don't know if it's true. In view of Baker and Catling I doubt it. But I like the idea anyway.

BANKER'S ASSIGNING ME TO COVER THE GLUTZ BANQUET was in the *Sun* tradition of testing the mettle of new reporters by seeing how they reacted to jokes played on them. There was, for example, an elderly lady who called the city desk two or three times a month complaining of people peeking through her windows. Though obviously a lunatic, she had once been married to a *Sunpapers* reporter, which prevented the gentlemanly trio of Banker, Young and Caulfield from hanging up on her.

Instead, they transferred her to one of the new men who, because the call had been passed to him by the city desk, was dumb enough to think it was legitimate. And, since the woman's first words were usually "Have you got a pencil? Take this down!" the poor cluck recorded reams of unusable notes, including prolonged denunciations of her ex-husband.

Along with others, I suffered these jokes. But it was not until the afternoon Ed Young introduced me to two strangers standing at his elbow that I grasped the full scope of the city desk's insidiousness. "This is Mr. Bright and Mr. Hall," said Ed, rising and running his fingers through his vents. "They have a story to give you."

During the hour or so that followed, the tall, thin Mr. Hall did most of the talking, and it was evident that the dozen or so drinks I had seen him consume at the Calvert earlier that afternoon had not been in vain. For his part, Mr. Bright just sat there with a stupid grin on his face.

They, it seemed, represented the vanguard of a movement to capture the 1952 Republican presidential nomination for Maryland's Governor Theodore R. McKeldin. In pursuit of this end they had telegraphed invitations to all the country's outstanding Republican politicians to attend a meeting in Baltimore later that year. I had in fact overheard them doing it while eavesdropping outside a Calvert phone booth and thus was inclined to accept the validity of their statements.

But when, after giving them the benefit of all my doubts I bade them goodbye and walked over to the city desk to report, I received a shock. Without even looking at my pile of notes, Ed flung them into the wastebasket. Tim Bright, I was told, was a wealthy used-car dealer who, with the help of Douglass Hall, a public-relations hack, was trying to worm his way into local politics. The whole interview had been a fraud perpetrated by my superiors on — me.

Of course nobody, including McKeldin himself, accepted the invitations to what had been described by Hall as an "unofficial presidential nominating convention." Like so many of Doug's schemes, this one came to naught. Yet I could not help but think of him when, from the podium of the real convention a few months later, McKeldin put Eisenhower's name into nomination.

I call him "Doug" because this was the first of many meetings, during which I came to feel something like affection for him. He was always popping up with some idea or other — such as the time he claimed to be representing a tribe of Indians he said were arriving the next day to pitch their wigwams in City Hall Plaza preliminary to powwowing with the mayor. Banker actually sent me out on this one, but all I was able to turn up was a chorus girl that Doug had dressed in a department-store Indian costume.

Yes, I got to know Doug pretty well, and it was impossible to know him without liking him. He had the charm of a man who knows he was born to lose but keeps trying anyway. I have always felt that the highest sense of humor is possessed by those capable of applying it to their own shortcomings. In addition to having this kind of humor (even while trying to con you, he couldn't help laughing at himself) Doug showed moments of true brilliance. Take his monument to McCarthy.

Because of the Wisconsin senator's determination to capitalize on the average voter's fear of Communism, Joe McCarthy became the most controversial American politician of his day. Liberal Democrats hated him, Right Wingers of both parties loved him. He was particularly admired by Richard Nixon, the 1952 Republican vice-presidential nominee, who had used tactics similar to his in defeating Helen Gahagan Douglas in the 1950 race for the U.S. Senate in California. He was particularly disliked by the Baltimore intelligentsia for his unfounded charges that Johns Hopkins professor Owen Lattimore was a Soviet agent. Douglass Hall persuaded Baltimore used-car dealer Tim Bright to get publicity for himself by erecting a monument to this man.

There was no question that the idea provoked coverage. As time went on and rumors continued to fly, more and more references to it appeared in the press. Then the day of the unveiling arrived. The "monument" turned out to be an unadorned concrete shaft of the sort sometimes seen in old cemeteries. Even so, it got good play on the back page of the *Sun*.

Doug's last shot for Tim Bright occurred a couple of months later when he sent in an elaborate press release announcing that he was suing his former employer for monies not received. The release cited examples of his getting Bright's name in the papers through such devices as the McKeldin caper and the McCarthy monument — for which services he had, according to the release, not been paid. The typical kicker (one could almost see the grin on Doug's face) came in the last paragraph.

The amount being sued for was $8.37.

EIGHT

When I first met him at Goodspeed's house a year or so before I started on the *Sun*, Patrick Skene Catling was in his middle twenties and well on the way to becoming the star he'd made up his mind to be. He had a lot going for him — talent, drive and, above all, charm. He looked like a combination of Cary Grant and Prince Philip. He was willing to settle for the former — particularly where women were concerned — but in his heart of hearts he preferred the latter.

He was the man who would be king, prince, duke, marquis, earl, viscount, baron — anything so long as it carried the tag of aristocracy. He had been born in Britain, son of a Reuters correspondent, and it was his private tragedy that he had all the attributes of the nobility without belonging to it. He spoke with an upper-class English accent. The cut of his clothes was impeccable. The quality of his writing was probably the best, Baker's included, of anyone then on the *Sun*.

But in place of a seat in the House of Lords, his expectations consisted only of those available to a $75-a-week reporter on an American newspaper. He endured this indignity with style. Style was what Patrick (he didn't like to be called Pat) had the most of — along with proper appreciation of the fringe-benefits offered by his job. These included introductions to important people, travel expenses to faraway places and the ability to avoid such annoyances as paying the check at Pimlico.

One afternoon, turning in an expense account containing the cost of two Scotches and sodas imbibed with a news source at the Baltimore race track, Catling was told by Charles H. (Buck) Dorsey, Jr., the *Sun*'s acid-tongued managing editor, that he would not sign any authorization for such use of company funds. "But I spent it!" shouted Catling, furious at the thought of not getting his money back. "What am I supposed to put down?"

"I don't care what you put down," snapped Dorsey, "just so long as it doesn't involve booze!"

Catling rewrote the expense sheet, listing the objectionable items as "two double-rich malted milks." Dorsey signed it without hesitation, and the business of the world went on.

As you can see, Catling had, in addition to those qualities already mentioned, gall — examples of which became legion. I shall cite only a few.

There was a character at police headquarters who fixed parking tickets. You'd go down and give him a couple of bucks and he'd see that your case never came to the magistrate's attention. Catling breezed down one afternoon and, finding no parking places on the street, put his little Morris Minor in the police lot. He was immediately descended upon by an obnoxious individual who told him he'd have to get out or suffer horrible consequences.

Catling said, "Keep an eye on the car. I'll be back in a minute."

He passed into the building, finished his business and on the way out paused thoughtfully.

He took the elevator to the top floor, went into the police commissioner's private quarters and informed the commissioner's secretary that he was there.

"For what purpose, Mr. Catling?"

"To interview the commissioner, as arranged by my editor yesterday."

"What is the subject of the interview?"

"Crime," said Catling.

The secretary inspected her calendar. "I don't see any notation —"

"Look" — Catling began to get peevish. "I only know my editor —"

"Wait a minute." She punched buttons. "Mr. Commissioner, there's a reporter here from the Baltimore *Sun*. He says he has an appointment to interview you."

Catling was ushered into the inner sanctum, where he was proffered stammered apologies for the evident foul-up that had occurred between the commissioner's office and his. As he was leaving, he said "Oh, by the way, I seem to have a problem with your parking attendant. He thinks —"

"Oh, don't worry about him!" The commissioner picked up a phone and Catling returned to the *Sun* smelling of roses.

By the time I came on the paper, Catling had established himself as a force to be reckoned with. He had courted and married, if not the boss's daughter, the next best thing. Susan Watson was not only a canny and beautiful woman (she later won renown, first as a London free-lance journalist, then as wife of the Labor Party's Anthony Crosland), she was also daughter of Mark S. Watson— who, as the *Sun's* military analyst, could, it was said, telephone the prime minister of any country in the Western alliance and be immediately put through.

Such advantages combined with Catling's natural assets to make him in the area of feature writing what Baker was in all the other areas. And it was as a feature writer that I hoped to make it myself. Facts, as facts, did not particularly interest me. I was interested mainly in what a good writer could do with them. Straight news reporting was bound by its own strict rules. Feature-writing, on the other hand, offered maximum freedom for invention. Because of the triumvirate of Young, Banker and Caulfield, no reporter ever had more of this freedom or encouragement to use it than existed on the *Sun's* local staff in the 1950's.

Patrick, as I've mentioned, had a lot going for him. He also had a lot going against him. When a copy-editor changed one of his sentences, he did what all writers dream of doing but don't. He punched the man in the nose. When the chairman of the *Sun's* Board of Directors sent him a note praising a piece he'd written (all in lower case about the poet e. e. cummings), Catling replied with a request for a raise — which, to everyone's astonishment, he got. At this point, Dorsey summoned Catling to his office and, recalling the nose-punching incident, told him, "You've got two strikes against you. One more and you're out."

But gall, wedded to talent, is hard to beat.

Undaunted, Catling parlayed an assignment to interview actress Jane Russell into a six-month leave of absence to go to Hollywood at the expense of RKO's Howard Hughes to write (while living it up at the famous Garden of Allah and driving around in white Cadillac convertibles) a biography of the big-bosomed star. The book never materialized but, in the way it demonstrated Catling's ability to make the most of every opportunity, the episode won him the envy, if not necessarily affection, of his less-resourceful colleagues.

Before leaving the *Sun* to accept positions — first on the *Manchester Guardian Weekly* and later on *Punch* — Catling attained just about every goal he had set for himself. He wanted to be chief of the *Sun's* London Bureau. In February, 1956 he became that. He wanted to move in exalted social circles. Among those he met and interviewed as a *Sun* reporter were Gloria Vanderbilt, Evelyn Waugh (whose work he much admired), Vivien Leigh and the ex-Queen of Egypt. His romance with singer Peggy Lee, met during another *Sun* assignment, made news on both sides of the Atlantic.

He wanted to write novels of the sophisticated sort associated with Waugh and Graham Greene. In time, he wrote several, one of which Greene, during an accidental encounter with him in a London pub, expressed a liking for. He wanted to travel widely, first-class and, preferably, at someone else's expense. He did.

He went to Korea for the *Sun* and created a furor with his account of a bloody battle seemingly staged for the benefit of visiting brass. He went to Central America and created a similar furor with an intentionally phony story sent through the censors to demonstrate that Guatemala's government was in control of the Communists. Wherever he went he made waves. And the waves — at least in this early period of his career — contrived to lift him to the top.

THIS WAS ONE OF TWO PEOPLE I had to compete with in fighting for recognition as a *Sun* feature writer. The other was a woman of formidable background. Janetta Somerset was a graduate of Oxford, the daughter of an English peer and a direct descendant of the Lord Raglan who had ordered the charge of the Light Brigade. Even Catling didn't quite know how to handle that!

Janetta had spent a short time working as a clerk in the *Sun*'s London Bureau. In the early Fifties, she moved her sphere of operations to this country and all of us on the local staff braced for the shock. And well we might.

Writing is a difficult job. "Do you find it hard getting through a piece?" Baker asked me on one of his periodic visits to Baltimore after leaving the *Sun* to become a *New York Times* columnist.

"Oh God, yes."

"I'm finding it harder and harder," he said.

Writing is like navigating a boat through unfamiliar waters. You feel your way, trying to avoid the reefs and shoals — and the tributaries that lead nowhere, thus compelling you to turn around and work your way back through streams already traveled.

But there is a current which, if only you can find it, will carry you home. The basic problem in writing lies in locating this current. Some writers never do. Janetta lived in it.

She wrote with an ease that was almost obscene. The rest of us would be sitting at our typewriters biting our nails and staring about uneasily, while she sat at hers banging away. It may be that her pieces did not always have the cleverness of Catling's. But who cared? They were articulate, literate and nicely composed. She talked the same way.

Her first story, after her arrival in Baltimore, was an account of the annual blessing of the hounds on Thanksgiving morning at My Lady's Manor in Monkton. Having come from a country where fox-hunting was an age-old tradition, Janetta let her specialized knowledge hang out. Indeed, so crammed with esoteric references was her article that Catling suggested to Ed Young that adding a glossary might help. Ed's positive reaction to the unconventional idea of a newspaper having to explain a writer's vocabulary was typical of the flexibility that made the *Morning Sun* more interesting to read than other newspapers of comparable stature at the time.

In the months that followed, Janetta, Catling and I filled its columns with some of the liveliest features ever knocked out daily on deadline for a metropolitan newspaper. There was always one, often two, sometimes three and even as many as four appearing in the same edition. And inasmuch as space and the number of choice assignments were both limited, the struggle for them unavoidably took the form of a contest in which I always felt out-classed.

Janetta spoke fluent French, belonged to the English aristocracy and in England lived in a castle. Catling, quite apart from his ability to promote himself in the world of "beautiful people," was probably the most talented writer I had ever known personally. Both were paid at least twice as much as I. It was only logical that, in their eyes, I would seem a rather bumbling immigrant from the most uncivilized part of the United States, plodding a course to nowhere. Yet they never gave me that impression but always treated me as a respected colleague and friend.

This was especially true of Janetta who, following the newspaper strike of 1965, left the *Sun*. For the next 20 years she served the Baltimore community in a number of capacities — always with distinction. Her prolonged battle with cancer during the last part of this period was carried on with the courage and grace that, more than her aristocratic heritage, bespoke her real nobility. She remained until the last moment of life every inch a great lady.

As for Catling, only once did his and my relationship reach a crisis. On those afternoons when we found ourselves stuck in the city room writing shorts, we often slipped off for a bite or sip in the *Sun*'s cafeteria. Sometimes he took the order and carried the tray from the counter, sometimes I did. This afternoon he'd asked me to bring him a cup of tea. As I approached the corner where he sat, sunlight sparkling on his multi-colored weskit (fancy vests were in then) and immaculate beige trousers, something got caught in my machinery and I ended up dumping the whole tray into his lap.

He staggered to his feet, his face contorted by an expression in which violent indignation vied with incredulity. It was evident that, while tea might be spilled on some people, it should *never* be spilled on him.

It just wasn't done.

ONE FINAL CATLING STORY.

At some point during my first year Ed Young, pretending that an out-of-town assignment would be good for my morale, sent me to Williamsburg, Virginia to cover a flag-raising ceremony at the historic old State House. The ceremony consisted of — well, raising a flag at the historic old State House.

I watched it go up, then sat down to ponder what I was supposed to do about it.

I now realize that the only reason I was dispatched on such a fool's errand was because Ed owed a favor to the woman who handled Williamsburg public relations. Thus a couple of paragraphs with a Williamsburg dateline would have been sufficient. But this was my first out-of-town assignment, and, by heaven, I wasn't going to let it go at that!

I thus proceeded to compose what is probably the most overwritten story in the history of journalism and, certainly, the *Sun*. In describing how that little flag went up the pole I mentioned every famous Virginian from Patrick Henry to Thomas Jefferson. Then, just to be sure, I threw in Light-Horse Harry Lee and Randolph of Roanoke.

"He must be drunk," said Banker when I telephoned the atrocity in to the city desk.

Catling had been standing at his side, reading the takes as they came out of Baker's typewriter. "No," he said with a sorrowful shake of the head. "When he wrote that he was stone cold sober."

NINE

I think it was my first day on the paper that Hendricks — or maybe it was Maulsby — told me a story about Dorsey I include here not so much because I believe it as because it accords with the image Dorsey himself liked to project as a crusty, Front-Page-type managing editor who brooked no nonsense from anybody. Actually, he brooked nonsense from everybody. At least, from everybody he liked.

The story concerned an effort by a *Sun* reporter to get a look at a document the police did not want released at the time. The reporter was nothing if not persistent and, having talked his way from one ascending rank to another, he finally found himself before the district's captain.

Captains, I might explain, occupy the same position of authority in their districts that their sea-going counterparts do on ships. They may not be authorized to impose inhumane punishment like Captain Bligh or marry people, but they can do just about everything else.

After much bickering, the reporter called Dorsey — who'd just returned from the Maryland Club, where he'd had a couple of rye whiskeys. "Mr. Dorsey," said the reporter, "I've been trying to get the captain to let me see the document we need. He refuses. I wondered if you'd speak to him?"

At this point (according to the story) the reporter handed the telephone to the captain, who'd been standing there uncomfortably all the while.

"Speak to him!" bellowed Dorsey, unaware that he was no longer talking to the reporter, "I wouldn't wipe my ass on a police captain!"

Hearing this, the captain (again according to the story) handed the telephone back to the reporter and gave him the document.

Shortly after his retirement, I confronted Dorsey with this story, which he denied. His argument was that he would never have been so rude or vulgar, and I believe him. But I still like to think it happened because, as I have said, it fitted with the gloriously arrogant (and somewhat romantic) role of a fearless newspaper editor that came natural to him.

Take the way he entered the office every morning. A tall, elegant-looking man with a cigarette-holder jammed between his teeth and a hat cocked jauntily on his head, he pushed through the corridor door with an aggressive step and jaundiced eye that dared anybody, as he swung across the floor to his desk, to interrupt the rhythm of his stride.

Actually, he had two desks — one in a cubicle at the rear of the city room where he carried on business of an administrative nature, and one in the city room proper where he made up the front page and sometimes summoned us incompetents to task for our sins. But it was all show. Underneath his terrifying exterior, Charles H. (Buck) Dorsey, Jr. was a pussycat.

DRINK, ACCORDING TO PURITAN ETHIC, is the curse of the working class. It is not, despite all popular notions to the contrary, the curse of the working press. During my 33 years in the profession I've known many hard drinkers — indeed, I can think of only a few who weren't — but there were even fewer who qualified for AA's definition of an alcoholic as a person for whom drinking has become a problem in his or her daily life.

The difference, I suspect, is that whereas the alcoholic drinks to escape reality, the old-time newspaper man drank to celebrate it. Rather than an impediment to work, drinking became a complement — something to be looked forward to throughout the day with the idea that, after the last take went down the tube, he could devote himself to it with enthusiasm.

Ed Young in his nightly dash to the Calvert *after* getting out the paper (launchings constituted an understandable exception) is a good example. But there are others — such as Ned Burks, who because of economics drank a cheap brand of bourbon called Colonel Lee.

One night, having a drink with him in his home, I noticed a bottle of bonded Old Fitzgerald sitting on top of a cabinet. I asked what we were doing drinking Colonel Lee when he had that available. He replied with some embarrassment that the bottle had been a gift from a local politician to whom he planned to return it. I challenge anybody to prove that a man who lets professional ethics stand in the way of imbibing choice whiskey is a problem drinker.

The next time I saw the bottle was in my office a few months later on the day Burks, who had been chief of the *Sun*'s Bonn Bureau, was departing for a job with the *New York Times*. It sat in the middle of my desk with a note, which read "I'm leaving this with you. Hope you don't mind that I took a drink." A drink from a bottle belonging to me was all right. But not from one sent by a politician. So much for alcoholic reporters.

IN THE FIGHT AGAINST LIQUOR as a corrupting force in journalism, Dorsey was a leader. He issued a proclamation that none could be consumed on *Sun* premises and that any employee doing so (except on election nights) would be "summarily" — a word he loved — dismissed. As an employee himself, he took pains to live up to the letter of his law.

As his car glided out of the *Sun*'s parking lot at 5:30 every afternoon, he unlocked the glove compartment and produced a bottle of Maryland rye from which those riding with him took a couple of snorts. In view of the problem of communicating with him later, it was evident he continued the practice on his own after letting the rest of us out.

The difficulty in talking to Dorsey on the telephone after he reached home was his marked tendency to dispose of all matters concerning members of the staff with orders to fire the person involved. Somewhere in the Fifties, district reporter Tom Ward got into an argument with the personnel of Eastern Police Station and was put into a cell on a charge of disturbing the peace.

Tom, who was studying law (he became a judge), was furious. He called Banker, who called Dorsey. "Fire him," snapped the latter and hung up. Instead Banker took up a collection from those in the office, which I was delegated to carry to the station to spring Tom. And the next afternoon the case against him was dismissed by the presiding magistrate.

Not long afterward Dorsey, passing through the *Evening Sun* city room, saw Janetta sitting at a typewriter banging away at her usual express-train speed. "What's Janetta doing in the *Evening Sun*?" he asked, on arriving at the *Morning Sun*'s city desk. "Don't you remember?" said Cauly innocently. "You fired her over the weekend, and now she's working for the *Evening Sun*."

"Tell her to get her tail over here and stop acting stupid," growled Dorsey, indignant that she had taken his firing seriously.

He also liked the idea of men settling scores with their fists. Kumpa was supposed to have had such a confrontation with him during a party at the National Press Club just before Dorsey appointed him chief of the *Sun*'s Moscow Bureau. I say "supposed," because neither Kumpa nor Dorsey was very clear afterwards about what had happened.

Probably the most memorable incident in this connection occurred during an informal staff party in the basement apartment of Helen Delich Bentley, who before entering politics was the *Sun*'s maritime editor. At the time, I was seeing a Swedish nurse, who had to be back at her dormitory by 11 P.M. in order to gain admittance.

When I left to take her home, the room had been filled with people yelling at each other over the noise of a record-player. I returned to an embarrassed silence. Dorsey sat in a corner looking pleased with himself. He beckoned to me.

"Hear about Ridgely?"

Joe Ridgely was a night copy editor working during the day for his Ph.D in English at the Johns Hopkins University. For reasons nobody understood, Dorsey had developed a violent antipathy to him. Ridgely, who, after his marriage to Janetta, became a Columbia University professor, understood the situation least of all.

"What about Ridgely?"

"He invited me outside."

"You mean —" My jaw dropped at this well-known euphemism for a challenged fist-fight. The twinkle in Dorsey's eye reinforced my worst fears.

"Oh, yes," he said, looking more and more pleased with himself. "He wanted me to step outside."

I glanced around the room, filled with the anxious expressions of my fellow reporters hovering around the walls. Ridgely stood on a patio just outside a pair of open French doors. "What," I demanded, going up to him, "happened?"

"I haven't the slightest idea." He had a nervous habit of flicking the ash off his cigarette between puffs, even when there was no ash to flick.

"We were in the room talking," he continued, pausing only to flick. "I could hardly hear him because of the noise. I said 'Mr. Dorsey, wouldn't you like to step outside?' Next thing I knew he was taking off his coat."

It was traditional on the night before a correspondent left for assignment overseas for Dorsey to take him to dinner at the Maryland Club. These were, from what I've heard, chummy affairs with booze and bonhomie flowing like mad. But they sometimes took bizarre turns.

The night before Burks was to leave for Bonn, Dorsey gave him the standard treatment. They had a good dinner with drinks before and after. In the process, Dorsey discussed the situation in Germany and expressed confidence in Burks's ability to do it justice. Then he offered him a lift back to the *Sun*.

Just as Burks was getting out of the car Dorsey leaned into the open door. "Oh, by the way, Burks," he said, "you're fired."

Of course Burks was not fired. He went to Bonn and distinguished himself by doing, among other things, a first-rate job covering the Hungarian revolution. Tom Ward was not fired, nor was Janetta. It was not so much that Dorsey's bark was worse than his bite; he seemed to feel a strange compulsion to substitute bark *for* bite. He was basically kind-hearted and the best friend I ever worked for. He stood up for his men and, if he liked you, you could do no wrong.

One of the reasons I was able to go as far as I did on the *Sun* was that he liked me. He always gave me the feeling that, whatever attacks I might suffer from other directions, at the top I was in solid. And for this feeling — so necessary to any writer if he is to do his best work — I shall be forever grateful.

For example, not long after being appointed theater critic I learned that the man who operated most of the movie theaters in town had launched a campaign to get me fired. People were calling up *Sun* subscribers urging them to register protest in regard to my review of *The Ten Commandments*. Philip M. Wagner, then editor of the editorial page, mentioned the matter one day when I happened to encounter him in the hall. As one only recently elevated to a new position, I expressed concern. An hour later I was summoned to Dorsey's office.

"What's all this horseshit you've been talking to Wagner about?"

"Well, Mr. Dorsey, I've been told that subscribers are being encouraged to write letters denouncing my review of *The Ten Commandments*. There are apparently a lot of them."

Dorsey rose to his feet. Standing, he looked tall. "Mr. Gardner," he boomed, "it doesn't matter how many letters come in denouncing you. Don't you know that when the Indians are attacking the fort Bill Schmick (the publisher) is the person to have protecting your rear?"

He was a very good man. I wonder what he would have said had he lived until the day when the Indians, having breached the fort's defenses, started attacking from within.

TEN

In his preface to *Newspaper Days*, H. L. Mencken described his life as a young Baltimore reporter as the "maddest, gladdest, damndest existence ever enjoyed by mortal youth." I hadn't been on the *Sun* long before I began to understand what he meant. Most jobs amount to little more than an endless repetition of the same thing. Certainly this had been true of the two jobs I had held previously. Now every day seemed to bring forth a new adventure.

I happened to be at the Town Theater one evening in September, 1953, watching a bad movie version of Mickey Spillane's bad novel *I, the Jury* when FBI agents, tipped off by a Los Angeles newspaper editor, swarmed into the place and shot a West Coast fugitive to death in the mezzanine phone booth. From his position at headquarters Pete Kumpa managed to get wind of the shooting — which resulted in the death of an FBI agent as well — in time to have the story covered by the district staff. But, as the only reporter in the audience, I was able to get some good quotes.

I was not on assignment then, but I was the night of March 6, 1952 when, a few minutes before opening of the Sonja Henie Ice Revue at the Fifth Regiment Armory, disaster struck. Just as the petite Norwegian skater was preparing to make her grand entrance a large segment of the bleachers collapsed, dumping scores of screaming spectators into a pile of debris and injured bodies 20 feet below.

Having fought my way to a telephone and received assurances from Jay Spry that reinforcements were coming, I emerged from the booth to run into — of all people — Banker! Spry, I concluded, was nothing less than a magician. It wasn't until much later that I realized that, though I might have been the only member of the working press present, innumerable members of the free-loading press were on hand to back me up.

Aided by this off-hours staff, Banker achieved such complete coverage of the story, which ran (with pictures) on both front and back pages, that Dorsey congratulated everybody with a posted memo the following day. During the same period I was arrested for drinking beyond the 2 A.M. curfew at the Baltimore Press Club.

Of the more than 70 people on the premises, I was the only employee of a newspaper and thus the only one with any right to be there. Others consisted of advertising-agency executives, public-relations men, friends of friends of friends. There was also a fair sprinkling of off-duty policemen from the same Central District that carried out the raid. The next afternoon Dorsey, pursuing his usual course from corridor door to cubicle, paused at my desk to observe "I understand you and thousands of other so-called press people were hauled off to jail in paddy wagons last night?"

"That's right."

"I want you to write an eye-witness account, omitting no embarrassing detail." He thrust the cigarette holder back into his jaw and strode off. It was typical of him that the account, together with all its embarrassing details, led the back page the following morning.

IN THE LAST DECADE OR SO, much of the fun has passed out of newspaper work owing to the elevation of unimaginative martinets who insist that reporters observe the same rules as people in ordinary jobs. For it is characteristic of the mediocre mind to try to trample talent beneath the heel of regimentation. After all, what other defense does it have?

In my day, it was different. Reporters worked not to the tick of a clock or the beat of the slave-driver's hammer but for the sheer joy of the job. They had to fill out time slips, but that was just a formality to satisfy the business office. If you had something to cover, you covered it, regardless of the hour, day of the week or whether you were supposed to be on or off.

Seeing your story published as you had written it — and you could usually count on that — was sufficient reward. If you were scheduled to come in at a certain hour, you did, and you worked your prescribed shift. But, if at the end, you still wanted to work (knowing you'd be given extra time off later), you did that too. It was all very informal and, compared with what was eventually to follow, carefree.

I was sitting at my desk around midnight on Friday, May 18, 1951, putting together a color story on the Diamond Jubilee running of the Preakness I had been assigned to cover the next afternoon, when the first alarm on the Cross Street Market fire sounded. When the twelfth came in Banker — who by then had sent out everybody but the copyboy and cleaning lady — looked across the rows of deserted typewriters at me and said "I know you're off, Gardner, but you've got to go."

I minded going not because I was off but because I hated fires. I had not yet figured out any intelligent way of covering them. Today television crews sail through police lines in their fancy-painted vans and are given every co-operation by the municipal authorities. But when I staggered out the back door of the *Sun* building that night toward one of the biggest fires since the great one of 1904, I possessed no such means of identification. I did not even have a press card. Press cards had to be countersigned by the police and fire commissioners — which took time — and I had been on the paper hardly two months. "I don't know," said the cop to whom I showed my American Newspaper Guild membership card. "It doesn't look right to me."

Still, he let me through into the usual bedlam of firemen running around in slickers, brandishing axes and spraying water on everybody. The rule in such situations is to seek out the man in the white hat, the theory being that, as fire chief, he should know what's going on. And well he may. But, between yelling at one man to get that hose connected and another to get that ladder up, he rarely cares to tell you about it. At any rate, I got few answers to my questions that night. All I really got — apart from annoyance over the interruption to my brilliant description of how the horses thundered down the track at Pimlico the next day — was wet.

It was not long afterward that my status changed from district man to general-assignment reporter at a big $2.50 a week increase. Instead of sitting around station houses, hoping something would happen, I sat around the city room, writing shorts and competing with Catling, Janetta and others for the few decent feature stories that turned up every week. I soon discovered a basic law of general-assignment reporting.

Don't wait for the city desk to tell you what to do. Become so busy on your own that, when you come in at 2:30 in the afternoon and are handed something like the Flower Mart or the Johns Hopkins Turtle Derby you can say "I'm sorry, Cauly. I have a 3 o'clock appointment with the director of the Baltimore Museum of Art."

In line with this rationale, I covered subjects over the next year that might never have been covered otherwise (with no, I suspect, loss to anyone). I wrote a story about a 90-year-old man who drove his sister crazy by going up a ladder every day to inspect the roof. I wrote another about a man who built an entire house, brick foundation and all, inside another entire house. Among the characters I interviewed were Boxcar Betty, "Queen of the Hoboes," and three birds belonging to a nightclub act called "Polly and Her Parrots."

And this is perhaps as good a place as any for me to pay tribute to those members of the *Sunpapers'* photographic department — men such as Walter McCardell, Clarence Garrett, Joe DiPaola and Ralph Dohme — who went out with me daily to snap pictures of some of the outstanding crazies of the time. Dohme was a particularly interesting case.

One night, after several months of working with him, I stood at the Calvert bar, elbow to elbow with a man I had never seen before. He seemed to resent the fact that I was a reporter, and the more he drank the more hostile he became. Suddenly, as he was on the point of becoming physical, I sensed a new presence at my side.

"If you need help," said Dohme, "I'm here."

He made no effort to keep the man from hearing him. Dohme never dillied or dallied about a fight. A few months later a guy who had been courting Dohme's estranged wife swaggered in a few drinks the worse for wear. Dohme wasted no words. "Look," he told the drunk, "if you want to tangle assholes, I'm ready."

Catching sight of Janetta standing at the bar on the other side of the newcomer, Dohme changed his tone. "Oh, gosh, I'm sorry, Janetta. I didn't mean to use that kind of talk in front of you." Then, whirling back to the other, "Anytime you want to tangle assholes," he shouted, "just let me know!"

I've had some close friends in my life — Goodspeed, Charley Flowers, Edgar Jones. But I doubt that any would be willing to "tangle assholes" on my behalf. On the other hand, Dohme — who moved out west shortly after this episode — would.

WHEN BANKER YELLED ACROSS AT ME ONE NIGHT during my second week on the paper to go to the Belvedere Hotel and interview Oscar Levant, then in town for a concert the following evening at the Lyric Theater, I became excited. Levant had always interested me because of his reputation for devastating witticisms. He was credited with having replied to a stuffy woman who, resenting his insults, demanded "Who do you think you are?" with "Who do you have to be?" It was, I felt, a hell of an assignment, and if nothing else it was that.

To begin with, I arrived at the hotel before Levant himself. "Christ!" he groaned when I cornered him in the lobby. "I just got off the train. Give me a minute to collapse."

He was further annoyed by the piano the management had put in his suite. "What do they expect me to do, play in my sleep? All right." He turned testily to me. "Don't ask me any standard questions."

Considering I had not been a reporter long enough to know what standard questions were, the remark confused us both. Eventually, however, the interview was obtained, duly telephoned in to the city desk, and I found myself — I can't remember exactly how — in the back bar of the Chanticleer nightclub having a drink with him.

As time passed and my career progressed, I met and interviewed many celebrities — from Marlene Dietrich to Arnold Toynbee, from Clifford Odets to Joan Crawford. But none packed quite the punch for me of this early encounter with Levant who, at the approach of a woman with something for him to autograph, took off as if he had a rocket attached to the seat of his pants.

Later, wending my lonely way homeward, I was attracted by a hissing sound from the recesses of a street-corner phone booth. "Hssst, Gardner. Has that woman gone?" It was obvious from the way he hovered in the darkened corner of the booth that the man known the world over for his fearless behavior in social situations was scared to death.

NONE OF US YOUNG REPORTERS in those days made a decent living. In order to get from payday to payday we had to pool our resources. Kumpa and I found ourselves sharing an apartment with two other members of the local staff — Charley Reiter and Carleton Jones. The apartment was located over the Mount Vernon Restaurant in the 900 block of North Charles Street, and it was a doozy. There were no windows in the high-ceilinged living room, which gave one the sense of sitting at the bottom of a well. The kitchen was a whole floor below the living room, the bathroom a whole floor above. It had only two beds to accommodate four tenants.

Actually, this was not as bad as it sounds. Charley — a tomcat at heart — spent most of his nights in other beds. I had interests along similar lines — which left the premises more or less free for Kumpa and Jones. Carleton was a large, lumbering man with a Southern accent you could cut with a baseball bat. He was called the "Colonel" by most of his friends on the *Sun*.

The nickname was mildly patronizing, but Carleton was not a man to be patronized. The son of a professional army officer and a South Carolina socialite, he had accompanied his parents all over the world in his childhood, acquiring a lot of knowledge in the process. He had a habit of dropping this knowledge, bit at a time, into his barroom conversation. During those late nights at the press club, while we were in one room playing pool he'd be in another playing the piano and singing selections from Mozart's *Cosi fan tutte*. His voice made up in volume for what it lacked in training.

Many years later he became the Sun's restaurant critic.

Another reporter with whom I fraternized in those early, semi-hysterical days was Nathan Miller. Nathan joined the staff in 1954, three years after receiving a master's degree in history from the University of Maryland. Like the rest of us, he served his time in the districts, but there was a difference. He was the only police reporter I ever knew who had *two* cashmere overcoats.

He also had other distinctions. Catling had hit a copy editor for changing one of his stories. Nathan hit an assistant city editor for calling him a kike. I witnessed the incident, which took place in a downtown bar we were temporarily using as a substitute for the defunct press club. Nathan gave me a ride home afterwards. He seemed unusually depressed.

"I guess I have no choice but to resign," he mused, as we sat in his Alfa Romeo outside my house on Saint Paul Street. I tried to convince him otherwise. I don't know what I said, but the next day he didn't resign, and it wasn't long before he was appointed chief of the *Sun*'s Latin American Bureau with headquarters in Rio de Janeiro.

A few years later he returned to this country and began writing books on the American navy, F.D.R., the Roosevelt family and other historical subjects—all of which added to his reputation and bank account. I've often wondered what would have happened had he gone in the day after punching the assistant city editor in the nose and quit.

I AM AS FAR AS I'VE BEEN ABLE TO ASCERTAIN the first reporter anywhere to do a story on Blaze Starr, who started out as a teen-age barmaid at Baltimore's 2 O'clock Club and ended up owning it, together with other real estate in the same area. A spectacular redhead with a bosom that didn't know where to stop, Blaze rose to national fame through her much-publicized friendship with Louisiana Governor Earl Long. When I met her early in 1952 she had just decided to become a stripper. She figured she possessed all the necessary equipment but an animal.

Zorita had popularized the notion that there was nothing more erotic than the contact between naked female flesh and the scales of a disgusting beast. Zorita used snakes. Blaze opted for a baby alligator.

But there were problems.

"First," she told me as we sat in the shadows at the rear of the 2 O'clock Club one night, "I've got to have its teeth pulled. Then I have to have its toenails clipped. It's going to cost a fortune before I even get started."

Meanwhile, across town in a nightclub on South Broadway, a young woman was attracting a lot of attention with another snake act. But whereas Zorita had used harmless reptiles, Princess Naja was using cobras with their poison sacs intact.

One night we on the city desk received a call to the effect that one of these vipers was missing from her apartment in the 1200 block of North Charles Street. The police, after evacuating the block, conducted a nothing-if-not cautious search, looking — as Maulsby, who wrote the story, put it — "upstairs, downstairs and in my lady's chamber" without locating the slimy creature. The question of its whereabouts continued to haunt the mind of the Baltimore public for almost a week via repeated speculations in the three daily papers.

Coming in the following Sunday, I was called over to the managing editor's desk. "Hal," said Dan Meara, Dorsey's likable low-key assistant, "I want you to go up there and break that woman down. I don't believe there ever was a missing snake. The whole thing's a publicity stunt."

So, donning my best woman-breaking-down air, I went up to the Princess's block, still vacant of its usual tenants. I had decided on an angle. Following her discovery of the allegedly missing reptile she had sought the advice of Arthur Watson, director of the Baltimore Zoo, himself no novice where publicity was concerned.

He had, for example, promoted a young female baboon, whose talents ran to finger-painting, into a city-wide celebrity, with frequent TV appearances and several one-ape shows. Why, I asked the princess, when she discovered her loss, had she called him instead of the police? Her answer surprised me. She was afraid the police would hurt the snake.

The quickest way to get your name in the paper is always to call the police, whose reports are open to the press. And this, it seemed to me, was especially true of a case where stripping and poisonous snakes were involved.

"Dan," I said, on arriving back at the *Sun,* "I don't know. She's no great brain. Yet the answer she gave me, assuming she's lying, would require one."

"The next time that woman gets into the paper," declared an exasperated *Evening Sun* editor during the week that followed, "she's going to have to die." And she did. A couple of days later. Of snake bite in the middle of her act.

Under the head "Each man his own world," editorialist Price Day remarked "To most of us her world seemed strange. Our own private worlds might have seemed as strange to her."

SOMETIME IN THE EARLY FIFTIES, the *Sunpapers* management realized it could no longer ignore television as a maker of news. Accordingly, it assigned Donald Kirkley, for more than 30 years the *Sun*'s theater critic, to do a daily TV column. This raised the question of who was to take over his job. Janetta, Patrick and I came in one afternoon to learn that we were to divide it among us.

It was typical of the what-the-hell attitude all three of us had at the time that we accepted this peculiar arrangement as an opportunity to kick up our heels. Janetta paraded her manifold talents as drama (and movie) critic one week, Patrick the next and I the next. In between, I worked as a general-assignment reporter for three days and on late rewrite the other two.

Also, I covered meetings of the Liquor Board and, with the *Evening Sun*'s William Manchester, Housing Court — as a result of which I wrote the first series on the dangers of lead-paint poisoning to children ever printed in the *Sun* and, for all I know, anywhere. Suddenly, everybody knew me! Politicians, encountering me in public, smiled familiarly. Producers, theater operators and press agents greeted me with warm handshakes, slaps on the back and offers of food and drink. I was probably the only $40-a-week man in Baltimore to whom both mayor and governor made a point of speaking.

My name began to pop up in the *Sun*'s Letters-to-the-Editor column in connection with articles I had written. Hundreds of people I had never heard of were beginning to hear of me. And respect me. And because of their respect I began to respect myself.

I was no longer a kid trying to find a place to light. I was a professional writer with a growing readership. Walking home at night after checking the proofs of my copy for the next day, I looked at the Baltimore skyline with a new sense of identity.

The city, which had so long defied me, had suddenly become mine.

ELEVEN

Having made it locally, so to speak, I began to think of branching out. I recalled an evening shortly after Goodspeed's and my arrival from Texas when we had gone to the Block and seen Diane Berton, a big, Slavic-looking brunette with hips like a threshing machine, dance naked in the middle of a nightclub floor. The nightclub, it seemed to me, should make a good subject for a national magazine story that might even be expanded into an in-depth treatment of the Block itself.

The district — whose four short blocks along East Baltimore Street contained nineteen bars, fifteen eating places, five theaters, six sporting arcades, five tattoo parlors and eight strip-tease cabarets — had its origins in the Nineteenth Century when seafaring men surged periodically into port to divest themselves of energies built up during long days at sea. A story about it would require considerable research and, inasmuch as one can't spread piles of old newspaper clippings over one's desk without attracting attention, everybody in the city room soon became aware of my project. Baker particularly showed interest and asked to see the story after I'd whipped it into some kind of shape. I made the mistake of letting him.

I had anticipated criticism but not to the extent that I got it. He attacked the piece as if he had been a teacher grading a Freshman theme. Over and over again he denounced my use of "dangling participles." I had majored not only in history but also in English and knew all about dangling participles. It occurred to me that Baker didn't. He couldn't tell a dangling participle from his Aunt Fanny.

When I started this book the first sentence I wrote was "Looking back, certain days stand out." It had a dreamy, stream-of-consciousness quality I liked. But I knew I couldn't use it because it contained a dangling participle. "Looking back" didn't modify days but an absent speaker. Hence it dangled.

Baker apparently thought any participial phrase coming at the end of a sentence dangled. "I sat down and ordered a hamburger, knowing nothing about French cooking" would to his mind be guilty. Yet the sentence is perfectly sound, though "I sat down and, knowing nothing about French cooking, ordered a hamburger" would be stronger.

I sent the manuscript to *The New Yorker*, which after a few weeks returned it with "We all read your story on the Block and liked it. Unfortunately, we do not publish articles about out-of-town subjects except for our own peculiar reasons."

To this day the article has not been published. I submit the following excerpts from the segment on the nightclub partly because they illustrate the literary style (dangling participles, etc.) I employed at the time and partly because they represent an authentic part of Baltimore's past.

Please bear in mind though that they were written in the early 1950's and that almost everything they describe has since passed into history:

—0—

The story of the Oasis, said to be the only nightclub on the Block with an international reputation, is closely interwoven with that of its founder and guiding genius. Leaving school at the age of 14, Max Cohen drove a taxicab until the first World War landed him in Camp Meade, where he made a small fortune buying the cast-off civilian clothing of new recruits and selling it at a nice profit in Baltimore.

After the war he became successively a waterfront restaurateur, operator of a small loan business and proprietor of a North Howard Street nightclub called the Jungle. In 1927, he bought the Music Box at the corner of Baltimore and Frederick Streets, renamed it the Oasis and launched himself on a career that created a new pattern for nightclub entertainment. Under his management, the place expanded into a thriving business employing scores of waitresses, bartenders, musicians, showgirls, bouncers and other attendants —the only "dine and dance" establishment in America according to Max with a favored rating in Dun and Bradstreet.

Harry's Cabaret at street level carried on the Music Box tradition of catering to stevedores, merchant marines and servicemen, while the Oasis in the basement went all out for the carriage trade. It became a favorite of government officials seeking escape from the long Washington weekend, and there was rarely a celebrity who, while visiting the city, didn't include it on his agenda. Willie Gray, veteran Oasis master of ceremonies, once compiled a list of such people. Among the names were John Steinbeck, John Barrymore, Bob Hope, William Gaxton, Sophie Tucker, Al Capp, Legs Diamond, Ralph Capone, Dutch Schultz, Joe DiMaggio, Jerry Lester, Joe E. Lewis, Bugs Baer, Alice White, George Abbott, Russell Crouse and Fredric March.

One reason for the Oasis's popularity with visiting VIP's is the publicity it has consistently received. Over the years it has been described in glowing terms, from *Variety*'s "one of the real wonders of cafe society" to *Time*'s "perhaps the worst nightclub in America but without doubt the best time in the world." A good example is an item appearing in the *American Mercury* of April, 1946:

"A cabaret in Baltimore called the Oasis," wrote George Jean Nathan, "last year advertised its master of ceremonies and star entertainer as follows: 'Willie Gray has just completed another year in this menagerie. It's his sixteenth and that's some sort of record as so-called nightclub entertainers go. His worn-out gags are so terrible they make you laugh in spite of yourself and the awful show he paces is enough to drive you nuts. That's really what we're after, so everybody's happy. Slum on down tonight.'"

The subject of these remarks is a bland, wispy gent of around 50 who, according to Oasis legend, passed out under a table one night and hasn't been out of the place since. Actually Willie has been emceeing shows at the Oasis ever since they replaced those of the Music Box in 1927. During most of this time he has worked a straight seven-day, two-performances-a-night schedule with no breaks. Every now and then he is fired, but the management always takes him back, which is fortunate — for them.

Because if there is any real style left on the Block it resides in the person of this slight, usually bleary-eyed Irishman. Certainly, he is most responsible for the peculiar mixture of wit and vulgarity that has made the Oasis such a success. The quintessence of this mixture may be said to be insult — directed partly at the establishment, partly at the clientele. And though other clubs have tried to duplicate it, none has ever succeeded. A reason may be that there is only one Willie Gray.

During the progress of an evening Willie roams the ringside circle exchanging quips with the table occupants and transmitting the best to the audience by means of a tall standard-borne microphone, his only prop. These explorations continue until he encounters someone drunk enough or dumb enough to fancy himself a celebrity. "Ladies and gentlemen," he will then announce, "we are fortunate to have with us tonight none other than Mr. Joseph P. Doakes of Wistful Falls, Idaho. Let's give him a big hand." As the yokel rises grandly to his feet, he is met with an electrically amplified bellow: "Sit down, ya bum! Wha'cha trying to do? Steal the show?"

Only a few out of a long succession of "bums" — including Jack Dempsey, Bob Hope and Bing Crosby — have taken offense. "One time I yelled 'Sit down, ya old bag, at Liz Whitney!" declares Willie, "and she didn't like it at all." Rudy Vallee was another who seemed to think the joke not very funny.

Rather than alienating his audience, Willie's behavior has won him friends from all over the world. Harry James thought it was a great gag one night when Willie invited his wife Betty Grable to do a strip act in the show. He still receives letters from soldiers that were stationed at Fort Meade during World War II. One was recently discovered in a bottle floating off the Atlantic coast. Another, sent in a more conventional manner from California, informed Willie that his song "Who Hit Nellie in the Belly with a Douche Bag?" was becoming a nation-wide hit.

Such indications of his popularity both please and amuse Willie, but the supreme tribute came when Ezra Stone, the Henry Aldrich of radio fame, named a race horse after him. To Willie that is as close as one can get to immortality.

Offstage, Willie — who before the microphone manages to make more noise than a presidential nominating convention — becomes a quiet mild-mannered fellow with a limp handshake and a wistful air. In appearance he is slightly cadaverous, possessing hollow cheeks and thin hair over a long bony head. Standing five feet seven inches in his round-heeled shoes, he weighs a bare 130 pounds.

It might seem paradoxical to Willie's many admirers that the man, who for them represents the sum and substance of the Block, away from its lurid environment appears to be nothing more than an average middle-class Baltimorean living in a well-kept suburban row-house and driving to work every day in the family car. The location of his present home (stocked with every domestic gadget advertised in Good Housekeeping) was chosen because it lay near a school which his three little girls might attend with minimum inconvenience and danger.

In his club cellar — surrounded by daughters, wife, television set, deep-freeze, electric stove, dish-washer, tropical fish, turtles, dogs and countless photographs taken with celebrities that have visited the Oasis through the years — Willie likes to relax with a glass of rye (he doesn't like beer) and recall some of the colorful characters he has known on the Block since he became its principal colorful character in 1924.

Such men as Diamond-Tooth Sharkey, Charley Gaither ("the only guy in Baltimore ever taken for a ride"), Xavier Gehring (a V.D. specialist who used to stalk the streets in shorts and a pith helmet), Nookie Thompson and Sweetcakes Dorsey Calk, a bookie who owned so many clothes he felt compelled to change them every hour. Sweetcakes, according to Willie, "was a real good-looking guy with a lot of women chasing after him. Eight or nine girls kept him at one of the Block hotels, and every hour on the hour he'd go up to his room and change clothes. They were high-class clothes too."

Sweetcakes ultimately was found dead on a park bench. There were no girls around, and his clothes looked as if they hadn't been changed in a long time. He was 57 years old.

Willie also told me about the Folly — a combined hotel, theater and cabaret memorable for, among other things, a legend about how the Block got its name.

"In the old days hookers used to sit around tables at the Folly waiting for a sucker to drop in. Outside a guy named Shipley kept a couple of limousines, and for two bucks you could rent one for a five-minute drive. The driver went slow so you could get your money's worth, and they always went the same way. South on Front to Lombard, east on Lombard to Fallsway, north on Fallsway to Baltimore and back to the Folly again. They called it taking a ride around the block."

Around ten each night Willie downs the dregs of his last at-home drink, kisses his wife goodbye and gets out the car for the drive to the Oasis — where customers, lured by signs suggesting they "walk down one flight and save nothing," may see him an hour or so later presiding over what he affectionately describes as the "lousiest show in the world." Entering the door at the bottom of the stairs, the would-be merry-maker is stopped in his tracks by a mountain of unyielding flesh.

Since 1937, the job of bouncer at the Oasis has become something of an institution. It was early that year that Max announced that he was hiring Mickey Steele, a six-foot female acrobat who had received her training working bars in the Pennsylvania coalfields. Every ton a lady, Mickey it was claimed always ascertained what city a rowdy customer hailed from and then hurled him in that direction. Another Oasis bouncer, Philip Giardina, bore the nickname of Machine Gun Butch, and patrons, calling in for reservations, were instructed to ask for Mr. Butch.

Having gained admission, the Oasis patron finds himself in a dimly lighted room of about 25 yards square with a medium-sized bar at one end and an orchestra hidden in shadows at the other. Occupying every bit of floor space, with the exception of a few spidery aisles and a small dance floor near the center, tiny tables, like cloth-covered postage stamps, provide the only seating facilities for the almost 300 people the Fire Department allows in. The women sitting at these tables will doubtless arouse the curiosity of a man visiting the Oasis for the first time — since they all affect the same sexually flamboyant attitudes and attire. An item on the back of the reservation card on his own table should help to set him straight.

The item, an extract from Ed Sullivan's column in the *New York Daily News* of May 6, 1936, reads as follows:

"The feature is a line of chorus girls, whose ages range from 23 to 47. They sit around at tables in evening gowns, but when the Master of Ceremonies starts the show, they stand up at the tables, peel off their evening gowns and are revealed in their chorus costumes. When they finish a number they wriggle back into their evening gowns and sit at the tables again. John Barrymore on one of his Baltimore visits spent hours at the Oasis and wound up on the floor reciting Hamlet's soliloquy. The patrons were pretty mad at him for introducing a melancholy note and Barrymore had to square himself with the irate customers by buying drinks for the house."

What Sullivan failed to make clear was that sometimes the costumes under the evening gowns weren't there. The girls, in exchange for a juicy tip from their table companions ("They think nothing of asking a guy for 50 bucks," says Willie) deliberately leave the costumes off and make a public ceremony of donning them in front of the orchestra just before showtime.

As the magic moment approaches, Willie appears, wraith-like with his long-necked microphone. The girls arise from the tables where they've been fleecing the customers and converge upon the dance floor. The band swings into "The Stars and Stripes Forever," to which Willie provides an ear-splitting accompaniment of "Hoo-rays" and assorted bird calls. Following an interval when the girls are all shaking it up in unison the floor is cleared and Willie takes over.

"Good evening, good evening, ladies and gentlemen," he says, squinting at them warily through the clouds of tobacco smoke. "Welcome to the worst show in town. Fifteen beat-up old bags will sing and dance for your entertainment." He crouches over the microphone, which he never allows to sit squarely upon its base but swings in pendulum-like motions both exuberant and threatening. His speech is erratic, broken intermittently by whistles and yells. His enunciation is slurred. His watery eyes, as he surveys the sea of faces, seem to hold the malice of a madman. Pointing first at this one, then at that one, he begins the attack. He insinuates, he upbraids, he accuses. No doubt about it, he scares hell out of the audience.

At length he gets down to business.

"And now, ladies and gentlemen, I'd like you to meet a little girl who has performed before all the crowned heads of Europe and in some of the better houses in Harrisburg, Pennsylvania — Jackie Lamont! And remember," he adds sagely. "The more you applaud the more she takes off."

Jackie then slinks on and does her stuff. Most of the girls at the Oasis belong to the walk-around-and-wiggle school. They strut about for a while, then pause in the middle of the floor and squirm. Somewhere in the process the drapery comes off. Few are talented enough to be called dancers in the technical sense. But what they lack in skill they make up for in enthusiasm.

The extent to which their enthusiasm may at times take them was demonstrated in 1943 when Patrolman Andrew Berger and his wife, a policewoman, visited the Oasis under orders of Captain Joseph Itzel, then commander of the Vice Squad. Patrolman Berger later testified that he and his wife arrived about the time the master of ceremonies was introducing a 28-year-old dancer named Corine Harper with the words "The more you applaud the more she takes off." For eight minutes, Patrolman Berger said, Miss Harper danced, and for eight minutes the applause was deafening. Finally, she stood in one corner of the floor clad only in a wisp of lace around the middle. "She opened the lace and went off the floor." On the way she gathered up her garments from where she had dropped them in the laps of the customers.

This little vignette, related with such admirable attention to detail by Patrolman Berger, cost Max and five of his employees a total of $80 in fines for producing an indecent show. One reason for the small fine may have been that among those testifying for the defense were the head of the investigating department of the Maryland War Production Board, a former dean of the University of Baltimore, two prominent attorneys and a retired broker. All had been present on the night in question and all maintained that they thought Max's shows stayed within the bounds of good clean fun.

An outstanding feature of this fun consists of an actual tactile relationship between the performers and customers — a sort of audience-participation gimmick as it were. After strutting and squirming, the girls will often make a tour of the ringside, plumping their nude posteriors down in a patron's lap or hugging his head to their bared bosoms. This clubby little practice has been known to take some rather bizarre forms, depending upon the imagination of the dancer and intoxication of the patron. Needless to say, there is usually a scramble for ringside seats.

The interminable line of strippers and head-huggers is broken from time to time by banshee-voiced vocalists, chief of whom is Battleship Maggie, an overblown doxie who sings "Kiss Me Sweet, Kiss Me Simple, Kiss Me on My Little Dimple," and a somewhat thinner version who sings a song about a peanut vender specializing in the sale of (God help us) "Hot Nuts." But no matter how dirty the lyrics, this part of the program is regarded as something merely to be endured. "If you think that was lousy," observes Willie after the "Dimple" song, "Wait'll you hear the next one." Another time he will dismiss the whole business with a brisk "No applause is necessary. Our girls know they're rotten."

—0—

YEARS LATER, AFTER I BECAME A THEATER CRITIC, I began to debate with myself the question of where my primary obligation lay. Whether to art or to humanity? Should I worry about the personal feelings of the writers, directors and actors involved in the productions I criticized? Or should I be true to the demands of my profession?

Whenever this question gnawed the most painfully at my vitals it always helped to remember Willie Gray and an incident that occurred one night as I sat with him at the Oasis bar a few minutes before showtime. A roving waitress stopped to whisper to him that a couple of newlyweds were in the house. "What the hell they doing here?" snapped Willie churlishly. He had a rattling laugh which he used as a follow-up to many of his lines. "What the hell they doing here? Heh, heh, heh." The effect could be pretty unsettling.

"They're so cute," said the waitress. "I thought you might like to introduce them during the show."

A few minutes later Willie stood before the table pointed out by the waitress. "Ladies and gentlemen," he announced into his microphone, "we're going to dedicate a song to a couple here that's been man and wife for only a few hours. What's your name, son?" He bent solicitously over a boy of about 18, who was obviously embarrassed to the point of agony by this public proclamation of his altered marital status. The girl at his side turned her face away, as Willie's leering countenance was shoved forward. "Come on." he said. "Tell me what you'd like to have us play for you."

They murmured something — probably "Stardust" — while the girl giggled and again turned her face away. I stiffened to attention. She was about the same age as Willie's eldest, whom I had reason to believe he would not have subjected to embarrassment for anything in the world.

But he was Willie Gray —a comedian whose reputation rested on an ability to create crass jokes at others' expense. So what would he do? To which loyalty would he prove faithful?

"Can you beat that?" he bellowed into the microphone. "These kids have been married only seven hours and, after seven continuous hours of marital bliss, he wants to be 'On Top of Old Smoky' and she wants 'Hot Nuts.' Heh, heh, heh."

TWELVE

Though I was to rise to greater glory in the city — and, to some small degree, the world at large — I now know my happiest moments as a newspaperman were spent during the period I covered the theater with Janetta and Patrick on alternate weeks and divided the rest of my time between general assignment and weekend stints on the rewrite desk. Because it involved a combined effort by the two desk men (usually Albert Sehlstedt and myself), Banker (who on weekends functioned as city editor) the copy-desk slot man (usually Pierce Fenhagen) and the district reporters (with whom we were in touch by telephone), working rewrite generated a camaraderie I never experienced afterward and always missed in my rather lonely job as theater critic.

We sweated under the pressure of deadlines, conflicting information and faulty air-conditioning to produce reasonably accurate reports of fires, storms, strikes, assaults, riots, murders, robberies, accidents and other calamities until 1 A.M. Then, hanging up our telephones and rolling down our sleeves, we sallied forth into the night to let off steam.

As a general rule, our steam-letting consisted of going down to the Press Club — which, since the raid, had relinquished its liquor license, thereby giving the police no excuse to interfere with our carousing — and shooting pool until dawn. But first we stopped by the Calvert for a quick one to speed us on our way.

During my years of dedicated patronage, the Calvert — located in the block south of the *Sun* building on Calvert Street — passed through successive metamorphoses until it finally became an establishment one might take a sweetheart or mother to without fear of her coming away scarred for life. But in the early Fifties, its bar was not a tight circle jammed into the forward half with padded stools for the shapely rears of secretaries dropping by to flirt before going home. It stretched in one gloriously unbroken line from front to back. It was a friendly, if somewhat gamey, place where printers, reporters and other disreputable types came after work to celebrate. And the only females likely to venture in were those whose recreational habits placed them on a par with the male customers or an occasional wife in search of an errant husband.

NEWSPAPER WIVES HAVE ALWAYS HAD IT ROUGH. In addition to the boozing, late hours and all-round undependability of their spouses, they are sometimes subjected to unexpected humiliations, such as the following example (passed on to me by Maulsby) involving Ned Burks's lovely wife Trudy. When Ned had nothing better to do he accompanied authorities on raids of Block bars and pornographic bookstores. After one of these, Trudy, while driving the family car, was stopped for some minor infraction of the traffic laws. Rummaging through the glove compartment in search of the registration certificate, she was appalled to find her lap suddenly filled with dirty photographs. "I-I'm sorry," she stammered, trying to meet the cop's shocked stare. "You see, my husband is a newspaperman."

THE BARTENDER AT THE CALVERT was a cherubic, mild-mannered, 225-pound Irishman from Pottsville, Pennsylvania, whom we all knew as Roy but whose full name was Leroy Aloysius Landers. Ordinarily disposed to padding quietly up and down behind the bar, catering to the demands of his loud-mouthed customers, he created something of a sensation one night with the remark that on the day before he had drunk 70 bottles of beer.

Seventy bottles add up to around six-and-a-half gallons, an amount that even the pickled regulars at the Calvert found prodigious. Roy, however, did not share their reaction. He and his wife, he said, were accustomed to bar-hopping on his days off, in the course of which he might consume up to 50 bottles interspersed with a dozen or so shots of whiskey. His wife also liked beer and could "knock off 25 bottles any night."

Such an accomplishment, I thought, deserved recognition. So on the back page of the *Sun* the following Monday appeared a story about Roy, together with a six-column picture of him sitting at one end of the bar with 70 bottles of beer lined up along its great length like soldiers at attention. It was an impressive shot and, added to the photographs and stories that followed, sparked a city-wide controversy that raged off and on throughout most of the summer of '53.

Beer-drinking contests were something of a tradition in Baltimore. Mencken describes one occurring shortly after the 1904 fire between a printer on the Baltimore *Herald* and a man who, like Landers, also came from Pennsylvania. But even as late as 1935 a 30-year-old man named Emil Cella had set a world's record before members of the Eastern Democratic Club, their wives and children by gulping down a half-gallon of beer in 17.2 seconds.

It was in the hope of flushing Emil, or "Feets" as he was always known, out of the woodwork that I included a reference to him in my story, along with an unintentionally inflammatory remark by Roy.

"Down here they call me the beer-drinking champion of Baltimore," Pottsville's leading expatriate had declared. "Up home I was always considered the same."

I had hoped for a reaction. It came at 9 that evening when a city desk phone rang and a gravelly voice almost shattered my eardrum, bellowing "Bottle for bottle, glass for glass, gulp for gulp, I'll drink that goddamn Irishman under the table!" It was Feets.

Grabbing a photographer, I raced over to the bar in the 800 block of Eastern Avenue that Feets had given me as an address. And there I got the most explosive interview of my life. Using a gavel to pound home his points, he yelled "I'm challenging him! And if I don't drink that son-of-a-bitch dry before the day's over I'll pay him $1,000. But I want three weeks to train."

I asked what training for a beer-drinking contest entailed, whereupon Feets became mysterious. "That's my secret," he said with an enigmatic smile. "I don't let anybody in on that!" A couple of minutes later he was confiding to his "manager," William Brichetto, that it meant putting away 50 or more glasses a day without eating.

"I've retired from eating," said Feets, who was once credited with eating six chickens at one sitting. "I can't eat while I'm drinking. And I drink all the time." He added that he would be willing to take Landers on at any date after the three-week training period and tentatively set it for June 29.

"I'll do it with either bottles or draft," he said, "and the first one to go to sleep loses."

"What if one of you drops dead?"

"Then —" Feets brought the gavel down with a resounding bang — "the other guy wins!"

Sun photographer Joseph DiPaola got some truly horrendous shots of Feets, ranting, raving and flinging his arms about. The photograph of the gentle-faced Roy, despite the array of beer bottles, had aroused no immediate protest. But when DiPaola's studies of what looked like a mad man appeared on the next morning's back page, the dam burst and the letters poured in.

One from a prominent minister compared people that drank beer by the gallon and ate six chickens at one sitting to "pole-sitters, marathon-dancers and other such maniac-fringe" types who should not be glamorized by the press. But most of the protesters were concerned over the disastrous effects the story might have on the young. In its sentiments, the following excerpt from a letter signed by the chief of the alcoholics studies section of the Maryland Department of Health, is typical:

Articles such as Mr. R. H. Gardner's, which appeared in the Sun *on Monday, June 8, are unquestionably harmful to the effort toward proper education of the public about the effects of ethyl alcohol upon the human body. Mr. Gardner's unworthy pastiche has nothing to do with temperance or moderation .... What do you, the writer and the editors who permitted the story to appear, men who hold a public trust, honestly think would be the reaction of young people and beginning drinkers who may read the article? What have you gained if even one young person tries to emulate or duplicate the 'feat'... I hope the writer will answer the questions I've posed above and if he would care to familiarize himself with reasons why alcoholism is today our fourth largest public health problem, I will be happy to be of any assistance to him.*

IN THE HECTIC YEARS SINCE MY STORY APPEARED, the mindless young have repeatedly demonstrated their eagerness to be influenced by the bad examples of their heroes — rock musicians, actors and TV stars. But no one by the fartherest stretch of the imagination could have described either Roy or Feets as a youth idol. Moreover, it takes considerably less stamina to pop a pill or smoke a joint than it does to swallow six-and-a-half gallons of beer.

Casual research has uncovered no evidence that beer-drinking increased to any measurable degree in Baltimore during the summer of '53, so I shall respond to the questions posed in the above letter with a reference to "Mencken's Law":

"Whenever A annoys or injures B on the pretense of saving or improving X, A is a scoundrel."

Of course, Mencken, who distrusted all professional reformers, dealt in hyperbole. Personally, I never considered the alcoholics-studies man a scoundrel. As a writer, I admired his vocabulary — particularly "unworthy pastiche," an expression you don't run into much. I was thus surprised when, at our next meeting, Roy used it. My report of the encounter, printed on the back page of the *Sun* of June 10, read in part:

Leroy Aloysius Landers, capacity beer-drinking champion of greater Baltimore and Pottsville, Pa., yesterday accepted the challenge of Emil Cella, fastest suds-gulper in the world, to a no-holds-barred contest to be held on the evening of Monday, June 29."Dismissing his opponent's claim that he would 'drink that son-of-a-gun dry before the day's over' as an unworthy pastiche, the ebullient Mr. Landers set his jaw and, with modesty becoming an Irishman and a champion, asked 'Who does that guy think he's kidding?'

THE DAY AFTER THE ABOVE ITEM APPEARED, Dorsey summoned me to his desk and, removing the holder from his clenched teeth, said "Who thought up this beer thing?"

"I'm afraid I did."

"Don't apologize. It's a good story. But it has inflamed the blue noses. So I don't want any more references to it until the contest, which we'll cover with our usual thoroughness." By all indications, that would be no time soon. Without issuing an official statement, the Baltimore Liquor Board let it be known that it would not countenance any such contest held on premises licensed for the sale of alcoholic beverages. Its adamant position on the subject caused a series of postponements until my old pal, Douglass Hall, called one day to say he'd arranged with the proprietor of a Middle River restaurant for it to take place on Sunday, August 16.

Dorsey had said we would cover it with our usual thoroughness, and we did —a six-column picture layout on the back page and 34 inches of type. Burks, then on the road with the Orioles, told me that when he saw my story in the Monday-morning paper he couldn't believe the amount of space the *Sun* had given it. Neither, for that matter, could I.

The essence of the story was that Cella, who had been a legend for 18 years in Baltimore beer-drinking circles, couldn't deliver. After hardly more than an hour and seven 14-ounce mugs, the man who had been screaming all over East Baltimore about what he was going to do to Landers, laid his head down on the table and mumbled "Roy, you gonna be new champion."

Ostensibly, it seemed to be a matter of over-training. During the hours immediately preceding the contest, Feets had drunk 18 glasses as a warm up, as opposed to the simple breakfast of bacon and eggs his opponent had consumed — along, of course, with 10 bottles of beer.

All the way to Middle River from the East Baltimore bar where I picked him up around noon, Feets lay in the back seat and begged for beer. His trainers, fearing his thirst might abate, fed him fillets of anchovy — the "secret" he had referred to on our first meeting. But it was a weapon that fizzled, much to the disappointment of all who had made the dreary trek into Baltimore County that Sunday and the disgust of the various newspaper men, including, in addition to representatives of the local press, correspondents from Washington and *Life* magazine.

Still, it was a good story, and I was proud of the *Sun* for giving it, in the face of all the criticism, the play that it did. Banker felt differently. He and I had carefully planned the picture layout so that the two contestants would be photographed at progressive stages of intoxication. The obvious "kicker" was Feets, the loser, passed out with Roy, the winner, still swigging away.

But Dorsey wouldn't go for it. He flatly refused to include the shot of Cella with his head on the table, and Banker became so incensed at what he considered destruction of the layout's impact that he flung all the pictures down on Dorsey's desk and strode away. In all the years I worked with him it was the only time I ever saw him lose his temper in the office.

I understood his attitude and respected him for it, because journalistically speaking he was right. But I understood Dorsey's, too, and I suspect that Banker, who succeeded Dorsey as managing editor in the Sixties, came to also.

The same edition that carried the results of the contest carried a story about one Valeriano Cardona Jimenez who that very day had become beer-drinking champion of Saragossa, Spain, by downing twelve-and-a-half pints in an hour. Civic-minded Baltimoreans immediately began to agitate for an international match that would pit Roy against him. It was a good idea, but nothing came of it.

And so ended the Great Baltimore Beer-Drinking Contest of the Summer of '53. Feets, according to an *Evening Sun* story in the early Sixties, became a broken man so ravaged by dissipation he could not swallow even one glass of beer without dire effects. And, although I have been unable to confirm it, I suspect both he and Roy have long since passed on.

It's too bad, for I'm sure either could have taken the Spaniard with one tonsil tied behind.

THIRTEEN

There are two periods in the day when people habitually drink — immediately before dinner and, if obliged to put in late hours as we did on the *Sun*, after work. For our late-night drinking, we went to either the Calvert or the Press Club. The cocktail hour was spent at Martick's in the 200 block of West Mulberry Street.

Martick's was run by an elderly Jewish lady who had come to this country from Poland in 1915. By the time I began going there in the late Forties, her husband had died. Sanford, the oldest of her five children, had withdrawn from active participation in the business so that he might establish a separate one of his own. And Jeanette and Alex, the two youngest, were working for their degrees at the University of Maryland. Only Rose, the older daughter, and Morris, the middle son, were able to give the bar their full attention.

Also by this time, the mother had suffered a series of physical setbacks including cancer, diabetes and glaucoma, the last of which robbed her of the sight in one eye and seriously weakened the other. But that eye, handicapped as it was, didn't miss much. My earliest recollections of her were as a little gray-haired lady hunched on a stool behind the bar reading a newspaper with a magnifying glass. Every now and then she'd raise her head to yap at a customer or one of her children for, despite her ancient and frail appearance, she had the kind of toughness of which pioneers are made.

It had been through her determined efforts that the small-time bootlegging operation she and her husband had masked behind the facade of a neighborhood grocery store made the transition at the end of Prohibition to a legitimate and stable business. Success, however, did not come immediately.

At first a typical old Baltimore bar, with an unshaded overhead light bulb that gave it an indescribably dreary appearance, Martick's changed on the assumption of its management by Rose and Morris around 1950 into a place suggestive in atmosphere of Greenwich Village. And, with the change, came a new problem.

Where previously it had been patronized almost exclusively by lower-class alcoholics, it now drew a clientele of middle-class homosexuals, who seemed intent upon turning it into their own private club. The Marticks had no prejudice against homosexuals. They were glad to get the business. What worried them was the effect upon heterosexual customers who were made to feel uncomfortable. Overnight and through no intention on their part, the place had become a gay bar and, as such, was under constant surveillance by the police. After a number of visits by various officials (including on one occasion the FBI), they decided something must be done.

The Fifties saw a rebirth of hot jazz not only in Baltimore but throughout the country. Such stars as Muggsy Spanier and Dizzy Gillespie filled week-long engagements at the Spa, a nightclub in the 1300 block of North Charles, while just across the street at the Bandbox a local group headed by former Dixieland Jazz Band pianist Wilder Chase drew capacity crowds with their Sunday-afternoon jam sessions.

Among Martick's regular customers was a recent St. John's College graduate, John Alexander, who had developed a piano style so similar to the great Jelly-Roll Morton's it was eerie. On the theory that if he could attract heterosexual customers in sufficient quantities to outnumber the homosexuals the situation at his bar would be reversed, Morris hired John — together with Tylden Streett, a sculptor who was also an accomplished drummer, and cornetist Howard Simpson — to play at the bar Thursday through Saturday nights.

The plan worked. Considering its limitations, the Southland Trio was excellent and on opening night — attended by well-known artists, teachers and professional men from all over the city — sounded so imposing as described by me in a six-column spread on the back page of the *Sunday Sun* of March 24, 1954 that for several years running people had a hard time getting in.

I had met Rose Martick in the early Forties when we were married to other people. She had sat in a third-floor room of a moderately elegant house on Mount Royal Terrace among mutual friends listening to jazz records with a dour expression on her face. It was an expression I later grew accustomed to as, night after night, she stood before the cash register in her mother's bar staring out at the customers. As one forced to put up with drunks all her life, she had developed an almost physical aversion to them. She was also painfully shy. After establishing sufficient rapport with a person to feel safe, she might creep out from behind her defenses and reveal the many facets of her delightful self. Until then, one had to deal with the expression. Encountering it for the first time, Danny Kaye was plainly perturbed.

THE ENCOUNTER TOOK PLACE in Baltimore's famous Miller Brothers' restaurant a few years before it was demolished to make way for the Charles Center. Accommodations had been arranged by David Polland, press agent for Washington's Carter Barron Amphitheater, where we all were to attend the opening of Mr. Kaye's one-man show at 8 o'clock that evening. There are two kinds of press agents — those who endeavor to fulfill the duties of their job with the least expenditure and those who seem to derive satisfaction from going all-out in the opposite direction. Like his lifelong friend and fellow PR man Sid Zins, Dave's charm lay in his determination to be a perfect host. He seemed forever to be thinking up new ways to spend his employers' money for the pleasure of his guests.

Naturally he expected his efforts to be appreciated. Thus, having thrust a corsage of orchids into Rose's hand at one of his dinners, he was stunned when she asked in all innocence "What am I supposed to do with this?"

"Oh, that's the girl that always gives me a hard time," he said when I told him I was bringing her to the Danny Kaye press conference. Little did he know.

When we arrived a few minutes late, everyone was seated. On one side of the long table were members of the press including a *Life* magazine reporter. In the center on the other side was Mr. Kaye, his personal press agent, representatives of his movie studio and a couple of empty chairs which I soon realized had been reserved for Rose and me.

With her usual shyness she tried to edge into hers without attracting attention. She might as well have blown a trumpet. At the first glimpse, Kaye straightened like a birddog sighting quail.

"Why do you look so miserable?" he cried, leaping to his feet. "Who are you? What's your name?" Rose shrank back, almost falling over the legs of the chair.

She muttered something, her face crimson. "How do you spell it?" he boomed. "Is it —?" He rattled off a number of ways Martick might be spelled.

"Please —"

In the performer's frenzied efforts to get at Rose I, who had been placed next to her, was in the way. "Look!" he said in obvious exasperation. "Why don't you sit here and I'll sit there?"

"But I'm supposed to interview you," I protested as he began literally to pull me from the chair. "I'm supposed to ask you about your future plans?"

"Where on earth did you get that expression?" he demanded of Rose, having successfully effected my transfer. "Why don't you smile? Aren't you happy?"

"Don't do that," whispered Rose, her eyes fixed on her plate. "You're embarrassing me."

"I'm not embarrassing you. I'm trying to find out what makes you look that way."

"It's just that" — she took a deep breath — "I don't have a very outgoing personality. Especially when I've just got off from work."

"Tell me." Mr. Kaye leaned closer. Everyone took a grip on his fork and strained his ears. "Are you more outgoing the more you drink?"

That did it for me. "Don't worry about her drinking!" I bellowed. "Just tell me about your future plans!"

"I never drink," said Rose.

"Is he always like this?" I asked the female press agent who had been traveling with him about the country.

"Always."

"How do you stand it?"

"You get used to it."

"Why," said the subject of discussion, resuming his onslaught on Rose, "are you so sullen? Don't you like me?"

"For God's sake!" I groaned.

It was here that the *Life* magazine reporter tried to get in a word about the tour the actor was making. What cities did he like best.

"It's not the cities I respond to but the people in them. And speaking of—" The pointed nose swung back to Rose.

"Why do you insist upon embarrassing me?" she almost screamed. "Why are you making me look ridiculous to the whole table?"

"I don't mean to make you look ridiculous," the other said in a more subdued tone. "I'm merely trying to find out why you don't like me."

"Who says I don't like you? Just because I don't swoon at the sight of you!"

And so it went until Rose realized what was required of her. Danny Kaye could not suffer any hint that he was anything but a person whose very presence brought joy to the world. Around him, one even had to take care how one looked. So she told him she had always been a devoted fan (which, as it happened, was true) after which he was quite willing to let her alone and be interviewed.

The experience had put me in a bad mood, which I did not attempt to conceal from Dave Polland. "Let me get you a drink," he said after we had arrived at the entrance to the Washington amphitheater.

"No thanks."

"Oh, come on." Dave belonged to the breed of public-relations men taught from birth that, when in doubt, buy a reporter a drink. "Just a little one."

"I don't want a drink," I said, growing madder by the minute. "No amount of liquid could quell —"

"Please!" He suddenly had become desperate. "Please have a drink!"

"Okay!" I shouted, figuring it was the only way to shut him up. "Get me for God's sake a drink!"

"What would you like?"

"I don't know. A Coca Cola. I'm not going to drink it anyway."

"Let's have a Coke here," said Dave, rapping on the counter of the concession stand.

"We're closed up," said the woman on the other side.

I've often thought that Dave's reaction to this simple woman's simple statement might well be the most outstanding example of *over*reacting in history. For at least five seconds he stood there speechless. Then he found his voice. "What do you mean closed up?" he roared.

"We ain't selling no more drinks."

"What do you mean you ain't —" He stopped, seemingly incapable of continuing. "I am the publicity director of this theater, and if you don't — "

Well, I got my Coca Cola, which I didn't drink, not having wanted it in the first place. Later, sitting next to Rose in the forty-first row of the immense amphitheater, I heard Danny, struggling to be heard over the waves of applause, announce:

"And now I want to dedicate a song to some friends who have come over from Baltimore tonight to see me." There was a moment's silence. Then he sang;

Rosie, you are my posie.
You are my heart's bouquet.

Rose has soft, velvety eyes that when she is experiencing confusion (which is most of the time) somehow produce the impression of rotating wildly in their sockets. They were rotating now. "That's me he's talking about," she said with something that was not so much pride as satisfaction. "He's singing that to me."

And, be it ever to the credit of this grossly self-centered but enormously talented man, he was.

A JEWISH GIRL BORN AND RAISED in a section of the city hemmed in by Chinese on one side and blacks on the other, Rosie never believed anybody — particularly a person of importance — could be interested in anything she might have to say. When she began to accompany me on interviews, she tried as best she could to be invisible. Unfortunately, her diffidence sometimes made her seem rude.

Following a screening of his *Guns of Navarone* in Washington, producer Carl Foreman, who had written the screenplay for the award-winning *Bridge on the River Kwai*, was puzzled when, throughout our interview, Rosie sat across the coffee table, head hidden behind a newspaper. "I gather she didn't like it," said Foreman, as he got up to go. "What's that?" The head popped out from behind the newspaper. "I said," repeated Foreman, "that apparently you didn't like the film." "Oh, no," said Rosie quickly. "I just don't have anything to say."

At length, I came to realize that, apart from shyness, her refusal to be carried away by the presence of celebrities stemmed from what she considered her priorities — namely the family business and her health. One night a stranger came into the bar with a regular customer, passed directly from the front room to the back and proceeded to beat hell out of the piano. "Tell that guy to stop pounding the piano," said Rosie to the friend when the latter came up front for a drink. "He'll break it."

"Don't you know who that is," said the customer, visibly awed. "It's Leonard Bernstein."

Rosie knew who Leonard Bernstein was, but her concern for family property outweighed her pleasure at having a genius in the house. "Well, tell him to take it easy," she said. "We just had that piano tuned."

Later that evening, taking drinks back to the table occupied by Bernstein and his group, Rosie was asked if she'd like to attend a party that night in his honor. "Well, actually no," she said. "I've worked all day and by then I'll be tired."

"You mean —" Bernstein seemed shocked that any girl, and a barmaid at that, would turn down the great Lenny — "you won't go?"

"I can't," she said, stacking empty bottles on the tray. "I'll be too tired."

In offering this explanation Rose was being completely honest. Fatigue has always plagued her tentative steps. Her sister Jeanette says she was born tired. While taking a night course at Johns Hopkins University, she decided that the only way she could stand the additional strain was to sleep a couple of hours between leaving the bar and going to class. Rushing to her apartment one afternoon with this in mind, she was hailed by a friend she hadn't seen in years. "Rosie!" he cried from across the street. "Rosie, darling!" "I'm sorry," she yelled, plunging on. "I'd like to stop and talk, but I've got to go home and take a nap."

Rosie and Jeanette engaged in a running competition of bosom measuring. Both bosoms were roughly the same size, but because Jeanette had a larger frame, Rosie's, by contrast, always looked bigger. To reassure herself, whenever they were sitting around the house doing nothing, Jeanette always said "Let's measure."

The Fifties were a time when big bosoms were in, and Rose and Jeanette had a disturbing habit of wearing jersey pullovers as they waited on customers. One man, apparently driven mad by frustration, went into the men's room and wrote on the wall "Has anyone noticed the tits on the girls behind the bar?"

Morris was so infuriated he spent two days scrubbing the offensive reference out. Which brings us, at long last, to the most eccentric Martick of all.

He manifested it in many ways, the most obvious of which was dress. Patrons attending the weekend jazz sessions were met at the door by a man who might be wearing anything from a mid-Nineteenth Century dress suit, complete with stovepipe hat, to a bush jacket and pith helmet. He either purchased the stuff from Goodwill or rented it from a Howard Street costume shop. But his real eccentricity was of the heart.

Stopping by one afternoon on my way to the paper after interviewing a bunch of gypsies, I found him brooding at a table just inside the door. "What do you do," he asked, "with a pigeon that can't fly?"

The question had never occurred to me. And, while I was deliberating upon it, he related a story so doleful in its implications about the nature of man that I got out my pencil and began taking notes.

Earlier that afternoon, while standing in the doorway, he had observed a small boy kicking a pigeon from the alley that ran alongside the bar into the middle of Mulberry Street. The fact that the pigeon didn't fly away aroused Morris's curiosity as well as sympathy for its plight.

Suddenly, seeing an enormous truck bearing down upon it, he rushed out waving his arms and shouting. The truck ground to a stop. "What the —" The driver leaned out the window.

"Don't move!" cried Morris. "You'll kill the pigeon!" The driver seemed unimpressed. "Get that goddamn pigeon out of my way," he snarled, "or I'll mash it flat."

"So," continued Morris, "I went out and began kicking the pigeon back into the alley." But his and the bird's worries had just begun.

A tractor-trailer jounced down the alley and paused momentarily before swinging out into Mulberry Street. As it sat there, snorting, the pigeon waddled underneath it. "Watch out!" shrieked Morris. "There's a pigeon under your truck!" While the driver reflected upon this unwanted bit of information, Morris got a broom and prodded the pigeon to safety. Still, the problem of what to do with it remained.

Hoping for suggestions, he telephoned the Society for the Prevention of Cruelty to Animals only to be told that the organization had no facilities for looking after ailing pigeons. He was advised to call City Hall where the operator gave him another number (Edmondson 6-0200). The following is an account of what then transpired.

Morris (into phone) — "I have a very sick pigeon here. It can't fly, and I'm afraid it's going to get squashed by some car. What should I do?"

Man's Voice (at other end of line) — "Wring its neck."

Morris (shaken) — "You mean — I should kill it?"

Man — "Sure. We don't bother with sick pigeons. If you don't want to wring its neck, get a stick and beat it to death."

One look into the bird's beady eyes convinced Morris he was not the man for the job. He couldn't even find a stick. So he took the pigeon to a Eutaw Street pet shop. There he learned that the reason the bird couldn't fly was because it couldn't eat and was therefore too weak. The reason it couldn't eat was that its bill had grown down in such a way that it couldn't open its mouth. The proprietor of the shop offered to trim the beak for a dollar but said he felt the best solution would be to kill the bird because pigeons, like any other animal, need care and love to keep alive.

As he recounted this, Morris — who has always been the loneliest of loners — gave me a despairing stare.

My report of this episode, which appeared in the March 7, 1956 edition of the *Sun*, created a sensation comparable only to the beer contest. The paper's switchboard was crowded with calls from people wanting to do something for the homeless pigeon — which, by then, had found haven in a sumptuous pigeon coop above an oil refinery.

The thing that seemed to have captured the callers' imagination was not only the helplessness of the bird but, even more to the point, Morris's concern for it. He had a talent for involving himself in matters inherently newsworthy.

Take his enquiries into the question of what makes art? Since his and Rosie's assumption of the primary responsibility for management of the bar, they had combined the dispensation of alcohol with rotating exhibitions of paintings by local artists. These exhibitions attracted not only the artists and their camp followers but also such scavenger newspaper types as Goodspeed, Catling and myself who were always on the lookout for interesting things to write about. Actually Martick's had always been a favorite haunt for *Sun* people. Yardley, the nationally famous political cartoonist, patronized it long before it became fashionable among the younger reporters. According to Rose, he was the fastest drinker she'd ever waited on. Hardly had she set a highball on the bar before he was shaking the ice in the glass to indicate the need for a refill.

Bob Murray, the irascible head of the copy desk, was shot there one night in a hold-up attempt. The thing that made it an "attempt" was that Sanford, then still working behind the bar, chased the miscreant to a nearby street corner and retrieved the loot before the man could get away. Murray, who received only a minor wound, lived happily to make whole generations of copyboys miserable.

Newspaper accounts of more recent happenings at Martick's made people curious about a place they had heard little of in the past but now were beginning to suspect bore investigation. In writing these accounts, Goodspeed, Catling and I drew upon not only the colorful personalities of the Marticks themselves but also of those regulars whom, without any apparent effort, they had always managed to attract.

There was the man who stood at the bar and shot birds. He had the habit of rolling his eyeballs up until only the whites showed. Every now and then, he'd raise his arms to the ceiling, as if aiming a gun. "Bang," he'd say. "Got'cha."

Then there was Wallace, who carried a small mouse with which he created havoc among female patrons unaware that it was a toy. Most of all, there were Tombstone and Snowfoot.

Tombstone and Snowfoot were the black vestiges of a once-flourishing breed — the minstrels who wandered through medieval literature and, at the beginning of this century, the back alleys of the New Orleans French Quarter. Somewhat startling in appearance and even more in aroma, Tombstone and his common-law wife would take up positions on a street corner and, until chased away by police, fill the air with their presence.

Tombstone played guitar, harmonica and the musical spoons. Snowfoot played a garbage pail with a string through the bottom which she thrummed in the manner of a bass fiddle. The effects they achieved with these instruments were nothing less than phenomenal. But then both were natural musicians — especially Tombstone who could play anything.

There was rarely a day that Tombstone and Snowfoot didn't show up at Martick's, partly because they felt at home in the bohemian atmosphere but mainly because the proprietors let them come in and make a few bucks playing for the customers. I included them in my back-page story about the jazz-opening of March 24, and *Sun* rewrite man John Van Camp did a funny piece on their appearance before a magistrate who, after witnessing their performance, dismissed the charges against them of disturbing the peace.

Indeed, Martick's began to occupy so much space in the local columns of all three papers that, after David Culhane — later to become a TV reporter but then working for the *Evening Sun* — wrote an elaborate story about an exhibition of traffic signs Morris had just hung in the bar, the same editor who had said something similar about Princess Naja declared "The next time that place gets into print it'll have to burn down." He did not take into account the force he was dealing with.

One day, going into the men's room of a West Baltimore garage, Morris was struck by the way dust had formed on a section of the wall to create an image of horses rearing in the wind. He asked the proprietor how much he would take for that section. Fortunately, it was of cardboard, easily removable, which Morris purchased for a nominal sum. He fixed it with chemicals, trimmed it, framed it and, under the title "Dust Horses," entered it in that year's Peale Museum Show where it won an honorable mention.

The episode did little to enhance Morris's popularity among Baltimore artists, who regarded it as a slur on their professionalism. But, as reported by me in the *Sun*, it — along with Morris's theory that art could be "found" as well as created — achieved wide distribution in not only this country. I know, because Jeanette — who by then had married Nathan Miller, recently appointed chief of the *Sun*'s new Latin American Bureau — sent me a wire service copy from Rio de Janeiro. Written in Portuguese yet.

Through a combination of inspiration, perspiration and the help of a few Baltimore newspaper men, Martick's surfaced at a time when college, martinis, Dixieland jazz, crewcuts and Brooks Brothers clothes were the fashion. And since it fitted in with this trend, it — at least for a while — thrived.

But times do not remain the same. And somewhere in the Sixties the immaculate, crewcut, liquor-imbibing, Ivy League conformists changed into the unwashed, uneducated, hairy dissidents at first called beatniks and then hippies, whose dependence on drugs and generally slovenly habits proved so aesthetically offensive to Morris that in June of 1967 he closed up and went to Europe.

He reopened the bar, after extensive remodeling, as a French restaurant in July of 1970. He did most of the remodeling himself and achieved some striking effects with a tile floor in the front room and a mixture of snakeskin wallpaper and riveted metal plates in the back. It was quite elegant, and the food, also created by him, received praise from restaurant critics all over the area.

But I missed the nights when tobacco smoke hung in clouds beneath the low ceiling, with the Southland Trio blasting away in a back room packed shoulder-to-shoulder and Rosie, her little heart momentarily liberated from its usual burden of gloom, dancing in the aisles.

FOURTEEN

It didn't take Janetta, Patrick and me long to realize that our biggest problem in covering Baltimore theater was there wasn't any. There were plenty of movies, which we loved because they offered such wonderful opportunities for ridicule ("*Thy Neighbor's Wife*," wrote Catling of a Hugo Haas film, "stinketh"). But of professional theater there was precious little. A shrinking trend had been in progress since the introduction of talking pictures in the late Twenties.

People have always loved dramatic performances and for centuries the only place they could see them was in a theater. For a small segment of the American population, this meant New York. For others, it meant cities visited regularly by touring companies having their origins in New York. The name for this string of cities was "the road." As the only means by which people living in such places as Cleveland, Detroit, St. Louis and Baltimore could see plays, the road during the first two decades of this century thrived.

But suddenly it became possible to see talking-picture versions at a fraction of what it cost to see them on the stage. And since this coincided with the pinch applied to the consumer's pocketbook by the Depression, it progressively reduced the audience upon which the road had always depended. In this slowly dying process, television came as a sort of coup de grace.

Given the chance of watching Milton Berle for nothing, people stayed home in such droves that Ford's — built by the same man at whose Washington theater Lincoln had been shot — was unable to attract enough shows to keep its stage lighted more than a few weeks out of the year. Other factors complicated the problem.

The expense of touring made it financially unfeasible to bring a show into a town without a guarantee. Through its annual subscription series the Theater Guild provided one. Cities with the most subscribers offered the best guarantees and were thus favored by producers. Compared to its two principal competitors — Philadelphia and Washington — Baltimore rated a poor third.

Washington made Baltimore's chances particularly difficult. As the nation's capital, it boasted a highly developed social life. Its theater (the National) consistently sold enough Guild subscriptions to guarantee each show a healthy two-week engagement. Ford's could not guarantee even one.

It was another example of the chicken or the egg. The number of shows Baltimore could attract depended upon the number of subscribers it could muster, and the number of subscribers it could muster depended upon the number of shows it could attract. To make matters worse, producers discovered that it was less of a gamble to rely upon Baltimoreans' driving the 40 miles to Washington to see a show than to risk a precarious week at Ford's. It thus became customary to bypass Baltimore for Washington.

Even those shows booked into Ford's at the beginning of a season did not always materialize. And the cancellations tended to undermine the Baltimore theatergoing public's morale. A great lassitude set in which eventually became so notorious as to provide excuse for the "shooting deer in the balcony" slur in the musical *Kiss Me Kate* by a pair of playwrights who did not even know how to spell the theater's name.

The situation reached a crisis during the fall of 1953 when *The Love of Four Colonels*, a Peter Ustinov comedy starring Rex Harrison and Lilli Palmer, closed literally on the city's doorstep. Because it had been the focus of that year's subscription campaign, the producer's decision to cancel its tour immediately after the Washington run had a devastating effect.

Morris A. Mechanic, owner of Ford's, telephoned me to say he could not afford to keep the theater open under such circumstances and was considering accepting a local department store's long-standing offer to convert the property into a parking garage. I was made the *Sun*'s drama critic soon afterwards and spent the next ten years trying to keep him from doing what I maintained would put an end to professional theater in Baltimore.

Which wasn't entirely true. We still had Don Swann and the Hilltop.

Though cut from different cloths, the Martick and Swann families had much in common. One was immigrant Jewish, the other threadbare Maryland aristocracy. Professionally, the Marticks relied on the support of artists and intellectuals, the Swanns on those belonging or aspiring to the Blue Book and Social Register. The Martick children went to public school and the University of Maryland, the Swanns to Gilman and Princeton.

But underlying both families was an iron will to survive and, through the means selected, both managed to add a distinctive color to the society of their day.

Don Swann, Sr. was a talented artist whose etchings of familiar local scenes continue even today to sell. For 25 years, his wife, Rita, worked as an editor and columnist for the Baltimore *News-Post*. Francis, their younger son, was a successful playwright. His *Out of the Frying Pan* was produced first on Broadway and then as a Hollywood film starring Eddie Bracken and Robert Benchley. Lyn, their daughter, indulged in a number of careers ranging from public-relations consultant to television producer. It is with Don, Jr. however, that we are concerned here. In 1938, together with Dan Cedrone — brother of my friend and erstwhile colleague Lou Cedrone of the *Evening Sun* — Don founded the Hilltop summer theater at Ellicott City, Md. Like all such ventures, it underwent recurring crises and, after much moving about, settled finally in Greenspring Valley on a tract of land named after the man who invented Bromo Seltzer. As it happened to be "my week," I covered its seasonal opening on June 24, 1953. And for a brief period its history and mine — not to mention Janetta's and Patrick's — were uneasily joined.

Talent may take different forms. Don's seemed to lie in a remarkable gift for persuading people to invest time and money in his projects. He sold not simply a season of shows but a chance (through building sets and painting scenery) to become actively involved in their creation. Also a social life — for favored patrons were granted the privilege of attending receptions where they could rub elbows with the actors.

During summers at Emerson's Farm these consisted of a resident company of unknowns. But in the winter when Don presented a more ambitious program — first at the Belvedere and then at a remodeled movie theater on North Avenue — they could meet real stars.

Added to these inducements was the possibility of being seen among diners in the Belvedere's luxurious John Eager Howard Room on a weekly TV show produced by Lyn. This show, sponsored by local merchants catering to the expensive tastes of the Swanns' patrons, was a good example of the family's ability to use one sibling's efforts to advance the cause of another. For the highlight of Lyn's show was an interview with the actor starring that week in Don's.

There was nothing wrong with this. Producers must find ways to push their products and, because of the shoestring nature of his operations, Don had to take advantage of every opportunity. About this he made no bones. But the very brashness of his eagerness to use anybody (not only relatives) to promote himself created in Janetta, Patrick and me a resentment that may have helped to blind us to the good qualities he possessed.

For though playing the part of a con-artist and clown, ("There's no charge for the drink," he used to tell the Hilltop audience before it went out for intermission refreshment, "only for the cup we put it in"), Don, aided by his invaluable assistant, Ray Hamby, managed to provide Baltimore with a weekly program of professional theater it would never have had without him. During a period when the Theater Guild could not persuade the producer of *The Love of Four Colonels* to allow Rex Harrison to appear at Ford's, Don gave the city a steady stream of name performers: Basil Rathbone, John Carradine, Edward Everett Horton, Elaine Stritch, Veronica Lake, Joan Blondell, Ilka Chase, Chester Morris, Constance Bennett, Margaret O'Brien, Billie Burke, Jeffrey Lynn, Charles Coburn, Arthur Treacher and Magda Gabor. It went on for years — and without any help from the "public sector."

It was a fantastic accomplishment, which has never been properly acknowledged — at least by me. I hope that, belated as it is, this will in some measure compensate.

Among the many fading memories of that rapidly changing scene, a few brilliant moments stand out. When, much to Lyn Swann's horror, Veronica Lake went on television with curlers in her hair. When Basil Rathbone, shoveling in the John Eager Howard Room's hors d'oeuvres as if he hadn't eaten for weeks, told Don the night before his opening in *The Winslow Boy*, "I can't go on television with your sister. My obligation is to give you the best performance I can and I haven't yet learned my lines." Then there was Sherry Britton, a former stripper whom I remember with special affection. And — the Gabors.

By the time I began to encounter them — here, there and God knows where— they had become a legend. They were said to have escaped from their native Hungary at the end of World War II in a car loaded with champagne, which they used to bribe the guards at border crossings.

Also in the car (it was alleged) were jewels with which Jolie, matriarch of the clan, opened a posh shop upon reaching New York.

Dazzling as these gems might have been, they were nothing compared to the treasure represented by Jolie's three breathtakingly beautiful daughters — Magda, Zsa Zsa and Eva — whose obvious assets began to be exploited soon after their arrival on these shores. At least, Zsa Zsa's and Eva's. Magda did not immediately follow her sisters into show business but stayed home to help mama mind the store. Then around the end of 1952 Don persuaded her to come to Baltimore and make her stage debut in a revival of Clare Boothe's *The Women*.

I went to the Belvedere, where the company was in rehearsal, to interview the future star. But she wouldn't receive me. Only after the opening, she said.

There's nothing that raises the hackles on a reporter's neck quicker than somebody's refusal to be interviewed. Especially if that somebody is in show business. I went away and did some homework. I discovered that just before leaving New York she had told an interviewer that, if she didn't like her performance in this, her first, appearance on the stage, she'd give acting up.

"I'll do the best I can," the article quoted her as saying, "and if it doesn't satisfy me — never mind what others say — I'll quit."

As presented in the Belvedere's Charles Room, *The Women* — which Kirkley, still drama critic at the time, reviewed — was interesting to me in only one particular. It was in the round, and a bathtub where a supposedly nude girl was bathing was only a few feet from where I sat. In the process of soaping herself the big toe of actress Michaele Meyers accidentally pulled the plug. The water receded and what had originally seemed a rather dull scene gained momentum.

Lights went out, the lovely Michaele emerged from the tub unobserved, and the play ended. While waiting for Magda to appear, I approached Jolie, center of a large table of glittering visitors in the lounge. Unlike her daughter, she showed no reluctance to talk.

"I'm happy that all my daughters are now in the theater," she said. "I'm a prima donna myself, you know. In my business. All the jewels worn in the play tonight came from my shop."

She displayed her neck, swathed in pearls. "These come from my shop."

"Magda," she went on, "was thinking only of me tonight. When Zsa Zsa is on TV she calls up afterwards and asks 'How was I? How was I?' She cares only about what I think.

"The same was true of Magda tonight. She didn't care about what the others thought. She only cared about what I thought."

Here Magda, in tights and a black sweater, came swinging through a door, surrounded by adoring fans. I had a hard time getting near her. When I did she was anything but friendly.

"May I now interview you, Miss Gabor?"

"No!" she cried with unconcealed annoyance. "I just come off stage. My mother and all my friends are here! Why should I be bothered with you?"

She was right. I should not have bothered her then. But she had made such a point of my waiting until after the performance.

"I have only one question," I said. "In New York last week you told a reporter that if you didn't like what you did on the stage tonight, you'd leave the theater forever. Did you like it? And, if not, when are you planning to retire?"

For at least five seconds she stared at me with wide, incredulous eyes. Then — "Wait," she said. "I go get mama."

FIFTEEN

My experience with Magda taught me something about interviewing celebrities. When Oscar Levant said don't ask any standard questions he was referring to the tendency on the part of reporters to always rely on the same dull subjects.

"At what point in your life, Mr. Levant, did you decide to become a concert pianist?" Or "What is your favorite musical composition?" Such questions, aside from their ability to drive a sensitive soul like Levant to drink, become a bore to the reader who has already encountered the answers in a dozen other interviews with the same celebrity. Thus a reporter's only hope of writing a fresh interview lies in finding something that will set his story apart from all others.

It may pertain to an incident.

With Magda, it was something that happened during the opening-night performance. As I've mentioned, in-the-round productions place the audience in close proximity with the actors. *The Women* called for an actress to light a cigarette. As she placed it between her lips, a spectator in the front row leaned forward and snapped his lighter. She drew a blank and, if Magda hadn't given the next speaker the appropriate cue, the show might have stopped right there.

Such at any rate was the tale told me by the director.

True or not, the incident gave my interview with her a lift it would not have possessed if I'd had to depend on the repeated accounts of her and her family escaping with the cases of champagne.

Or it may arise from the physical circumstances under which the interview is conducted.

Learning that Edward G. Robinson wanted to see Ford's Theater where he was to appear the next night in *Darkness at Noon*, I suggested after meeting him at the Belvedere that we go have a look. It was a balmy fall evening and, having decided to walk, we soon found ourselves at the foot of the Washington Monument in Mount Vernon Place. Robinson, known for his patronage of the arts, was momentarily stunned. "Magnificent," he murmured, staring up the 188-foot spotlighted shaft. Then, as if the thought had just occurred to him, he added "But it's awfully phallic."

He was, to put it mildly, right. The monument — designed in 1814 by Robert Mills, a Philadelphia architect — is like nothing so much as an erected penis with a life-size statue of George Washington perched on the head. It lives.

A couple of years later during a press luncheon for Barbara Rush in her Belvedere suite, the actress casually mentioned that after everybody left, she was going to have her hair done. I asked to be present and, as a result, got a little gem of a story. For the hair-dresser brought along his press-agent who was an idiot. Having played no part in setting up the interview, he did his best to disrupt it — thereby frightening the hair-dresser, annoying me and amusing Miss Rush, for whom I wish to express unbounded admiration. Few professional beauties would be willing to appear before a stranger with soaking wet heads. It did not bother her.

"You see," she explained as she was being doused with water, "I've got darling hair."

Not long afterwards, I interviewed Tallulah Bankhead while she was lying in a Philadelphia hotel room watching the movie *Ninotchka* on television. The reason she was lying was that she was nursing a hand broken during the performance of a play then on its way to New York. Though accustomed to adversity, Tallulah did not take to being on her back for no good reason. Throughout the movie she kept making unkind remarks about Greta Garbo's co-star Melvyn Douglas.

Ninotchka was filmed during Mr. Douglas's callow period before he achieved distinction as an aging character actor, and I concluded that Tallulah's comments stemmed from disgust that such a superficially slick performer should have been cast opposite the great Garbo. On the other hand, she may have at some time had dinner with him and gotten stuck with the check.

My own meeting with him took place in a Baltimore restaurant while he was appearing in a Broadway-bound play called *Spofford*. Inasmuch as meetings with members of the press usually result in several thousand dollars' worth of free publicity it is customary for the actor to bear whatever expense (which, of course, he passes on to the producer) is involved. In this instance, I had assumed there would be no question since I'd had only a token drink, whereas Mr. Douglas had consumed a whole meal.

Yet when the check came he sat there like a statue, staring stonily ahead.

Only one other celebrity ever played this game with me — Elaine Stritch who, following my favorable review of her performance in the Hilltop production of *Pajama Tops*, had invited me to dinner. It was the first time any actress had ever invited me to dinner, and I accepted eagerly. Then at the end of the meal I was treated to the staring-stonily-ahead routine.

Later in the run of *Spofford* I was having a happy-hour drink in the lounge of the Baltimore hotel where Douglas was staying. The barmaid, an old friend from the Sunday afternoons she had waited on me at the Bandbox jam sessions, picked up the telephone. "Yes? Yes. Yes, Mr. Douglas," she said into the mouthpiece. "That cheapskate!" she cried, slamming down the instrument. "He hasn't time for a full meal before his performance tonight and wonders if we could send up some of that nice *free* cheese dip we use on the bar as an hors d'oeuvre!"

But Douglas and Stritch were exceptions. Most visiting celebrities were as generous as they were charming. Which brings me to Van Heflin.

Every opening at Ford's in those days was preceded by an interview with the star whose arrival on Sunday night made it possible to get a story in the next morning's paper. It was thus that I met Mr. Heflin, then touring in a road production of *The Shrike*. In the course of our conversation I happened to mention that I spent most of my wee hours at the press club shooting pool. To my astonishment, Mr. Heflin stiffened as if jerked by a string.

"I *love* press clubs!" he shouted. "I also love pool!" The upshot was an agreement that I was to call for him the following evening and show him the town.

But when I appeared at the stage door a few minutes after the curtain fell on the opening-night performance I was informed by his wife Frances that they had a previous engagement. It did not disturb me. As a reporter of no particular importance, I had few illusions. I went away not so much hurt as puzzled as to why he had made such a point of setting the thing up in the first place.

I was awakened the next morning by a woman who was literally sobbing into the telephone. "Mr. Gardner, I didn't know Van had made a special appointment with you for last night. He has given me no peace. Please tell him that you forgive me."

Heflin then came on.

"Hal! I spent all last night after Frances told me what happened trying to reach you. I called your paper. I called the press club. I called the homes of several of your associates. Nobody knew where you were. Can we set it up again for tonight? I'll meet you wherever you say."

There were a number of times afterward that my work brought me into contact with Van Heflin — such as when he was appearing in *A View from the Bridge* on Broadway — and he always treated me as a close friend.

The Shrike was written by Joseph Kramm. Sometime during this same period he wrote another play, *Build with One Hand*, which had its world premiere in Baltimore. I was much impressed with him during our initial meeting at the Belvedere the Sunday before the Monday-night opening. Not so much with Kramm, the artist, as with Kramm, the man, whom I found to be rather sweet. I hoped his play would be a good one. It wasn't.

Build with One Hand starred Elliott Nugent with a supporting cast that included Geraldine Fitzgerald and Sheppard Strudwick who did their best. As to why the show (the only one I ever "killed") closed the day after its opening here I would just as soon not say — though I suspect it had something to do with the personal problems of its playwright, on the one hand, and its star, on the other.

I suppose something similar might be said of any show that doesn't make it. I'm reminded of Clifford Odets's *Flowering Peach*, a play about Noah and the Ark which tried out in Baltimore. I asked Menasha Skulnick, who portrayed Noah, what he thought the play was about. He said he hadn't the slightest idea. "But haven't you asked Odets?" He gave a shrug worthy of a veteran of the Yiddish theater. "He told me just to read the lines and to not worry about it."

Having dinner with the playwright one night at the Lobster in midtown Manhattan while the production (which Odets also directed) was in rehearsal a few blocks away, I asked the same question. I got the same answer. "Don't worry about it."

Elia Kazan, who'd known Odets for years, was seated across the table. "How can you," he asked, "direct a play you have written? How can you maintain any objectivity?"

"Oh, that's no problem," said Odets. "When I direct one of my plays I'm a completely different person from when I wrote it."

The Flowering Peach folded soon after its opening in New York.

Exactly why Gore Vidal's *Weekend* suffered the same fate I've never been sure. When I saw the Washington tryout I thought it had everything to insure success in the America of that day. The year was 1968, and the play concerned a Republican candidate in the coming presidential election. It had a racial theme (then very good), sex (always good) and, above all, its author's caustic wit. I especially liked his comments about Richard Nixon and said so in my review. Then I called him up at the Mayflower Hotel in Washington and requested an interview.

"Of course, Mr. Gardner," he said in his characteristically ironic tone. "Your review was the only 'grown-up' one I've received so far. I shall be delighted to see you."

At the time, Vidal was obsessed with the fear that President Johnson might use nuclear weapons in Vietnam. He could talk of nothing else. I mentioned that, if Johnson did, we were on the brink of Armageddon. As I left shortly after Vidal's half-sister (who is Jackie Kennedy Onassis's step-sister) arrived, the writer pressed a copy of his just-published *Myra Breckinridge* into my hand. It bore the inscription "Best wishes. Pre-Armageddon. Gore Vidal."

Undoubtedly the most unusual interview I ever did was one that never took place. Sometime in the Seventies I was invited to New York to meet Harold Pinter in connection with *Butley*, the Simon Gray play he had directed for the American Film Theater. Gray showed up. Pinter didn't.

I felt robbed and, in anger, I concocted a frankly fictitious interview in which Pinter's replies to my questions were taken from public statements made by him in the past. It was a funny idea but, owing to Pinter's determination to be evasive, the story itself was rather dull.

My anger here was directed not so much at Pinter as at the Madison-Avenue types that had set up the interview. Actually I sympathized with his distaste for such affairs. I didn't like them either.

They were blatant attempts by money-minded promoters to get free publicity for products at the expense of the dignity of the artists involved. And with the approval of my paper — which then had standards — I resisted them. There were occasions, however, when the pressure made resistance next to impossible. Such an occasion arose in October of 1959 when the American premiere of Robert Bolt's *Flowering Cherry* opened a split-week at Ford's.

The term "split-week" refers to opening an engagement not at the beginning of a show's week's run but in the middle. Ordinarily Ford's did not book such engagements, but the Bolt play was having problems in rehearsal, so the opening was postponed from Monday to Thursday. This meant that no reviews would appear until Friday—which in turn meant the show's run would amount to only two days. It was therefore essential to build up an advance ticket sale sufficient to make those two days profitable. And for this they needed publicity. I was asked by the press agent to do an interview with the star, Eric Portman.

Baltimore got few Broadway tryouts in those days, and I did not want to discourage the practice. At the same time, *Build with One Hand* had taught me how difficult it was to maintain objectivity about a production after meeting somebody intimately involved with it. I had great respect for Mr. Portman, but I had no wish to interview him. Still, I agreed to.

The interview was set for 11 o'clock after the Tuesday-night rehearsal. I was then devoting every spare moment to writing a book and had found the late hours to be the most productive. I resented having to break off in the middle of a chapter to go down to the Lord Baltimore Hotel and discuss with Eric Portman matters I was sure neither of us cared a damn about. And the resentment increased when I arrived to find him not there.

I waited 30 minutes then departed, leaving a note saying I would be at my office if he wanted to arrange another interview. His call came in shortly after midnight.

"Eric Portman heah." His clipped British accent was more than usually noticeable. "Sorry to have missed you, but you know how rehearsals are." He paused, then went on briskly. "I plan to be up a while. So if you'd care to stop by—"

I told him I was in the middle of something that might take another half-hour. But if he wanted me to come then—he agreed that would be fine. It turned out to be a mistake for both of us.

From the moment he admitted me to his hotel room I could see he was filled with hostility—not to mention liquor from an assortment of bottles on a corner table. After all, I had kept him waiting 30 minutes! But then he had kept *me* waiting 30 minutes! Who did we think we were?

The statement that I would have been there earlier had I not been trying to finish a chapter in a book I was writing on criticism was pounced upon. I was writing a book on *criticism*!

"You know, you remind me of our young author," he said, going to the table to pour himself another drink. He left the reference dangling. It wasn't clear how I reminded him of Robert Bolt, though the adjective "young" should have provided a clue.

Though it changes the older I get, I have always looked younger than I am. I was then 41, but I looked 30. On the other hand, Mr. Portman was 56 and, in dressing gown and slippers, looked 70.

He had, I learned later, been having difficulties with the play he was rehearsing. In his last Broadway venture (O'Neill's *Touch of the Poet*) he had been roundly criticized for affecting an Irish brogue so broad it made almost everything he said incomprehensible. So he was in anything but a state of unshakable self-confidence, and my appearance seemed only to aggravate the condition.

He chose to interpret my first question — what is *The Flowering Cherry* about? — as proof of my incompetence. Hadn't the play run for a year in London, receiving an award for the best of the season by a new playwright? How could I presume to review it without knowing its history?

For a while after that the conversation took the form of a name-dropping contest in which Mr. Portman and I attempted to out-drop each other. Had I read Hazlitt? Had I read Shaw? Had he read Archer? Never heard of him! Never heard of William Archer, theater critic of the *London World*? Oh, that Archer, but his name wasn't William. Mr. Portman then proceeded to bet me $100 that William Archer's first name wasn't William.

As the evening wore on and his supply of liquor diminished, the conversation became more animated. Not to mention confused. I have, however, retained certain impressions:

1. The trouble with critics is they do not make as much money as actors and therefore resent them. He had me there.

2. The trouble with American critics is they are not as good as English critics, which adds to their resentment.

3. The trouble with American critics is they are American.

Everything good in the American theater comes from England. There are no good American playwrights. The only good playwrights are English.

When I ventured to suggest that Mr. Portman's opinions might derive from a slight bias based on the fact that he, too, hailed from that empire upon which the sun never used to set, he declared "I am an Englishman." The statement became a refrain uttered whenever he could think of nothing else to say. "I am an Englishman."

"And I am a newspaperman," I felt compelled to point out. "What if I print all your anti-American remarks?"

I could print anything I wished, he said with a winning smile. Throughout, he was charming — and the mere fact we were yelling at each other in such deafening tones that the occupant of the next room began banging on the wall does not mean we were ever angry. It was delightful he said to sit down with a critic and discuss matters of real importance instead of the trivialities that usually pass between people at such times. And when at one point I asked him why he went out of his way to be obnoxious, he seemed downright hurt.

"'Obnoxious' is not a word we use in England," he said.

Finally the hotel's house detective came up and begged us to lower our voices. We were disturbing all the other people on the floor.

"I am the house man," he explained when Mr. Portman opened the door.

"I am an Englishman."

"And I am an American. I mean a newspaperman." After all those drinks I wasn't sure what I was.

THE MAIN THING THIS EXPERIENCE DID was to convince me once and for all of the folly of interviewing anybody connected with a production before passing judgment on it. For, after the account of my meeting with Mr. Portman came out in Thursday morning's paper, I feared that any negative remarks I might make about the play or his performance would be interpreted as a continuation of our fight in the hotel room. So I leaned over backwards in an effort to like the damn thing. The honest truth is I didn't like it at all. And I particularly didn't like him.

PERHAPS THE BEST WAY to wind up this discussion of interviewing celebrities is to print the following, which I wrote for the *Sun* of June 5, 1972:

—0—

One of the minor headaches of the working journalist is the press luncheon held in honor of some actor touring the country to plug a film he or she has just made.

True, you get a nice meal, and you get to meet some nice celebrities. But in exchange for these goodies, you're expected to write a story. And that isn't always easy.

You can't, for example, simply say "Mabel Murgatroid was here today and said her latest movie was great." No reporter worth his lunch would do that. You're supposed to find what is known in the trade as "an angle" — something that, when you hand the piece over to the editor, will make him resist his natural impulse to throw it into the wastebasket.

My usual apprehensions in this connection were doubled recently when Sid Zins, prince of public-relations men, invited me to meet Marsha Metrinko. I had just seen *Stand Up and Be Counted,* the film in which Miss Metrinko appears, and loathed it — not because it concerned women's lib. God knows I'm used to that. But because it's so badly done. There's not a believable character in it.

I was, however, encouraged by a fact-sheet Sid gave me as soon as I entered the room where Miss Metrinko — a tall, willowy woman with a charming face and tastefully streaked hair — was being interviewed by several of my colleagues.

"Fluent in Russian, French, Italian and Spanish," the sheet stated, "Miss Metrinko is, in addition to her work in films, a licensed real estate agent in California and a licensed broker on the New York Stock Exchange." That should give us something to talk about, I thought and read on. "Along with her academic honors (a graduate of the New York Institute of Finance and of Georgetown University), she is also Miss Love Bundle of 1972, a title won on the basis of her dark brown eyes, ash-blond hair and the curvaceous manner in which her 135 pounds round out her 5-foot, 10-inch height."

Choosing a language at random, I said "Hello, there" to Miss Love Bundle, who gave me a rather strange look from her dark brown eyes before whirling her ash-blond head back to the others again. As I feared, they were discussing *Stand Up and Be Counted,* and I racked my brain for something positive to say.

I remembered that one of the crises in the film occurs when Jacqueline Bisset, having made a women's-lib-type pact with an airline pilot to live with him in his apartment as long as he did his share of the housework, discovers that he is slacking on the job. The reason: he doesn't like housework.

I asked Miss Metrinko who she thought did the airline pilot's housework before Miss Bisset moved in. She gave me another strange look and said she had never thought about it.

"Don't you imagine he had a maid? And, if so, couldn't the maid have continued doing the housework?"

"I suppose," she said with an abstracted air.

"Do you feel that the picture of men given in this film is an accurate one? Do you personally know any men like that?"

"No," she said, staring stolidly at the window. "I don't know any men like that myself, but I'm sure there are some."

"But don't you think —"

"Look," she said, springing to her feet, "I've got to speak to you in private about something."

I rose and followed her dumbly to a distant corner of the room.

"I can't talk to you," she said, "because your fly is open and it's breaking me up."

She was right. My fly *was* open. Anxious for an angle, I had concentrated too much on my subject and her appearance and not enough on my own.

—0—

AS STATED AT THE BEGINNING OF THIS CHAPTER, the rule when interviewing celebrities is to find something to set your story apart from all others on the same subject. With Miss Love Bundle, I think I did.

SIXTEEN

There was a Stratford-on-Avon in England, a Stratford-on-Avon in Ontario and a Stratford-on-the-Housatonic in Connecticut. Around the time I became the *Sun*'s drama critic the two Stratfords on this side of the Atlantic chose to follow the example of the one on the other and produce an annual festival of Shakespearean plays. American audiences, desperate for any kind of theater, responded with enthusiasm and the contagion spread. In 1962, a festival dedicated to the works of George Bernard Shaw opened at Niagara-on-the-Lake just across the Canadian border from New York. The following year another opened in Minneapolis.

All four festivals were responsible for the construction of playhouses incorporating changes that set them apart from those around Times Square. Of these, the most significant was the one director Tyrone Guthrie and designer Tanya Moisiewitsch created for the original Ontario festival.

The seats, rising in steep tiers, swung in a semicircle around the stage. The stage itself was no more than a platform, devoid of proscenium or any kind of framing. Somewhere between its rear wall and steps leading down to the orchestra level was a structure similar to a gazebo, within whose slender columns action could occur.

Opposite the two front corners, concealed ramps descended diagonally into the basement. By means of these vomitories and doors in the rear, the stage could be filled or emptied within a matter of seconds.

I have described the interior of this theater because I feel that it and the philosophy it represented (to be discussed later) played an important part in sparking the revolution in American stage techniques that followed. The Minneapolis playhouse (named after Guthrie who is credited with getting it started) was both similar and different. And the same was more or less true of its productions.

As for the Connecticut Stratford, its playhouse, though promoted as a modernized version of the Globe, was anything but. Not only did its rectangular auditorium push the bulk of the audience away from the stage, but the hugeness of the stage itself (especially its towering proscenium arch) tended to dwarf the actors. By comparison, the Shaw Festival Theater seemed both intimate and charming.

At least part of its charm derived from its setting. Niagara-on-the-Lake has a restful, remote-in-time atmosphere that combines with its lovely, park-like appearance to make it as pretty as its name. Perched at the tip of a peninsula formed by the Niagara River and Lake Erie, it dates from the American Revolution when loyalists from New York, Pennsylvania and Connecticut settled there. Once the capital of Upper Canada, it was burned during the War of 1812 and had to be rebuilt from scratch.

Little seems to have changed since. Most of its shops and public buildings have been carefully preserved or restored — so that a walk through its shady streets gives one the feeling of stepping into another century.

Indeed, a noticeable freedom from the tensions of modern life prevails at both Ontario festivals. At Niagara-on-the-Lake, it is the illusion of entering the past. At Stratford, it stems from an exhilarating, spring-like quality suggestive of madrigals and maids dancing around a May-pole.

The playhouse sits on a knoll from which a well-tended lawn, broken only by patches of brilliant flower beds, slopes down to the Avon where (so help me) swans glide. Patrons wind their way up from parking lots in leisurely fashion. On matinees some picnic on the grass. Relaxed as the scene appears, there is always an undercurrent of excitement which reaches a peak when trumpeters appear on the balcony to announce the opening curtain.

The word "excitement" needs no definition, but it has a special meaning here. People attending openings at Ford's when I first began reviewing its productions always seemed to be undertaking a chore — as if they were not really interested in what they had come to see. Even in Washington, opening-night audiences had seemed more attuned to the presence of senators and other VIP's in the audience than to the happenings on the stage. The atmosphere at Stratford was different.

Coming as they did from all over the continent and, indeed, the world, the spectators had only one thing in common — the expectation of sharing a joyous experience. And rarely were they disappointed.

In time Rosie and I got around to all the festivals. We attended the grand opening of the Connecticut one on July 14, 1955. The production — *Julius*

Caesar, starring Jack Palance — did not exactly knock us out. Nor for that matter did the theater. We were more impressed the half-dozen or so times we visited Minneapolis, and we loved *everything* we saw at Niagara-on-the-Lake. But it was Ontario's Stratford that contributed the most to our understanding of what theater in the big sense was all about.

From our very first visit we seemed to have sensed that here at last was where it was "at." The theater's banner-hung lobby with its life-size photographs of scenes from current productions excited us enormously, as did the pomp of the trumpeters' fanfares and the playing of "God Save the Queen" before the performances.

Arriving in town one afternoon a couple of hours before the festival's scheduled opening that night, we were surprised to find all the inhabitants drawn up on both sides of the street down which we alone were driving. Many carried little Union Jacks which they waved at us encouragingly.

"They knew we were coming," I told Rose.

A few minutes later, having discovered the cause of the demonstration, I called Dorsey in Baltimore.

"Buck, Princess Margaret is due in here any minute to officiate at the opening of the festival theater tonight. Would you like me to file a separate story on her?"

"No." He sounded testy. "Stick to your last."

"What?"

"Stick to your last." Again the words were snapped out.

"My last? My last what?"

"Mister Gardner! Haven't you ever heard the expression that a cobbler should stick to his last? Yours is the theater. So stick to it!".

"Oh. That last," I said, feeling a little annoyed at the implication that I was capable of reporting on only one aspect of human activity. Especially after the splendid job I had done on the flag-raising at Williamsburg.

STRATFORD IS A LONG DRIVE FROM BALTIMORE, and on a subsequent visit Rose and I didn't arrive for Christopher Plummer's *Hamlet* until just before the curtain rose. We didn't even have time to eat, and this deprivation, combined with the strain of worrying for ten hours over whether I was going to pass the car ahead before the approaching car reached us closed in on Rose. She slept through half the first act and all of the second.

She hated herself in the morning. We'd come all the way to Canada to see a masterpiece performed by one of the outstanding companies in the world. The least she could do was stay awake.

As the afternoon wore on, she became more and more ashamed. Finally, seeing how the wind was blowing, I suggested we turn in our tickets for the play we'd planned to see that night and have another go at *Hamlet*. She responded with such puppy-like gratitude that I was touched.

So we went back, and she slept through it again.

THE ABOVE OCCURRED DURING THE SUMMER OF 1957. In the spring of 1959 I took her to a production of *The Tempest* at the Johns Hopkins Playshop, one of the few non-professional theaters in Baltimore that, owing to my respect for its founder, Hopkins professor N. Bryllion Fagin, I regularly covered. And once more the madness struck.

How we conducted ourselves at Stratford was not significant, because nobody knew us. On the other hand, everybody knew us in Baltimore and, aware of my position on the *Sun*, watched us at theater openings continuously. The sight of Rosie, collapsed on my shoulder dead to the world, was sure to upset not only the actors (to whom she was clearly visible from the stage) but the more sensitive members of the audience as well. I felt compelled to acknowledge and, if possible, provide an explanation for it.

The Tempest contains an oft-quoted passage, which goes:

We are such stuff as dreams are made on,
And our little life is rounded with a sleep.

ON APRIL 8, MY REVIEW, PRECEDED BY THIS QUOTATION and bearing the headline "Perchance to Dream," appeared in the *Sun*:

—0—

I have a friend who can't sit through a Shakespearean play without falling—rather precipitately—into the arms of Morpheus.

Something about the cadence of the verse, especially when pronounced "trippingly on the tongue," acts upon her like an opiate.

Hot milk, caffeine-free coffee, barbiturates—nothing produces quite the instantaneous effect of a passage like

Tomorrow, and tomorrow, and tomorrow
Creeps in this petty pace from day to day
To the last syllable of recorded time...

On the last syllable of the first "tomorrow" her face automatically assumes a helpless, hangdog expression. On the first syllable of the last "tomorrow" her eyelids droop. Her breathing shifts to iambic pentameter and, by the time the actor has hit his "petty pace," she is well on the way to dreamland.

This acute susceptibility to the somniferous power of Elizabethan verse, combined with a comfortable seat and a convenient arm-rest, has resulted in her sleeping through some of the most celebrated theater of our time—the Old Vic productions at the National in Washington, the Stratford festivals in Connecticut and Ontario and, most recently, a performance of *The Tempest* at the Johns Hopkins Playshop.

The noise arising from the intense activity of the sailors in *The Tempest*'s opening scene delayed the reaction for a while but, as soon as Prospero and Miranda entered a moment later, she dropped off, thereby missing probably the most static sequence in Shakespearean drama — the interminable and virtually unbroken bit of exposition in which Prospero tells his uninterested daughter (who already knows it) everything the audience must know to understand the play.

I noticed, however, that, though she awoke only twice during the evening — once when Joseph Bandiera, in the role of Caliban, was vigorously protesting the unnumbered torments of his lot and once during intermission — her rest seemed more troubled than usual.

"It was all right," she said later, "but somehow I couldn't get that real deep sleep I get from Old Vic and Stratford."

I tried to make her understand that she could hardly expect the same effect from an amateur production as from a professional one — especially one created by a company as renowned as those she had mentioned.

I pointed out that the play itself was difficult to stage, being generally episodic and having little conflict in the strictly dramatic sense. I spoke glowingly of Mr. Bandiera's make-up, Walter Koehler's demeanor as Prospero, Noelle Sullivan's beauty as Miranda, Diane Kaplin's enthusiasm in the physically taxing role of Ariel and the valid comic effects achieved by David Howell and Kenneth Campbell as a pair of clowns.

Director Alice Harwood Houstle, I declared, had done a fine job, considering the manifold problems and the limited facilities at her disposal. And I concluded by saying that Baltimoreans with a special interest in the play might welcome the opportunity afforded by the remaining performances scheduled for 8:30 P.M. tomorrow through Sunday in the Playshop's barn theater.

A groggy stare convinced me I wasn't getting through. For her, Shakespeare was the stuff that dreams are made because of. Obviously, her evening at the theater needed rounding with a sleep.

—0—

SOME PEOPLE, AS THE YEARS MOUNT UP, CHANGE. It has always been one of Rosie's more endearing qualities that she doesn't.

SEVENTEEN

The summer festivals, which became permanent items on my annual agenda, helped to crystallize an idea that had been germinating in my head. The gist of it was that the reason so many of the new plays I found myself having to review seemed depressing was the sick way they portrayed man.

Whereas the classical poets had depicted him in heroic terms on a large canvas, modern dramatists presented a knothole view of him in such roles as a traveling salesman unable to face his failure as a father and a spoiled rich boy wrestling with latent homosexuality. One view was inspiring, the other morbid. I later developed this idea at length in my book, published under the title *The Splintered Stage* by Macmillan in 1965.

Though they limited themselves to no particular period, the summer festivals favored the classics and, by demonstrating just how great great drama could be, added to my education. Moreover, by thumbing their noses at Broadway, they pointed to the possibility that the future of the American theater lay not in New York but in localities capable of creating their own productions, such as the two Stratfords, Niagara-on-the-Lake, Minneapolis and, conceivably, Baltimore.

But how was it to be accomplished? For even if Morris Mechanic fulfilled my most extravagant hopes by building a new theater to replace Ford's, there remained the problem of finding a managing director comparable to Guthrie who would know how to use it for the creation of new shows. There was also the always sticky question of financing. Such was the nature of my thoughts when I met the Rev. Gilbert V. Hartke, head of the Catholic University of America's drama department, and Zelda Fichandler, founder of Washington's Arena Stage.

In the early Fifties, Father Hartke had instituted school tours of productions his graduate students had mounted during the year. The tours, which eventually extended all the way to Europe, were surprisingly successful. But it was as administrative director of Olney, a professional summer theater located halfway between Baltimore and Washington in the minuscule Maryland community of the same name, that he became known to me.

Our interview took place one afternoon in the sun-lit lounge of Olney Inn, a picturesque country restaurant nestled in a grove of trees not far from the frame structure lent by a local philanthropist for Father Hartke's use as a non-profit theater. The establishment that sprang from this gift (for the loan was later made permanent) was in the priest's opinion one that might well serve as a model for all future theaters connected with academic institutions (like Catholic U.) and devoted to the production of classical drama.

Whether it was the historic associations of the inn (it was reputed to have been patronized by presidents) or the rainbow-like sports shirt Father Hartke wore beneath his priestly garb I can't say. But I sensed I was on the verge of something, and the following week, attending Olney's opening show of the season, I got my first hint of what that something was.

With the play, T. S. Eliot's *Cocktail Party*, I was already familiar, having both read and seen it. I hadn't particularly liked it, but the Olney production changed my mind. In the June 4, 1954 edition of the *Sun* I wrote:

The opening of the Olney Theater last night was a triumph for everybody — the actors, the director, the set-designer and T. S. Eliot whose poetic probings of the human psyche, "The Cocktail Party," constituted a perfect beginning for the 14-week summer season.

And it was a real inspiration to see, for a change, a near-capacity audience beating its approximately 1,000 hands together and shouting "Bravo!" at a cast which deserved every bit of the applause.

Headed by Bramwell Fletcher and Marjorie Gateson, the eight participants performed Mr. Eliot's fascinating, if at times exasperating, play with an understanding and competence that matched and in some ways exceeded that of the road company that visited Ford's two years ago.

LOOKING AT THIS REVIEW TODAY, I realize I went a bit overboard. But having assumed that light-weight plays hastily produced for one-week runs (as done at Hilltop) were typical of summer theaters, I was bowled over to find one offering a program of Shakespeare, Shaw, Wilde, Fry, Moliere, Giraudoux and Anouilh, performed by actors obviously serious about their work. Most of the Olney staff was composed of either faculty members or graduates of the Catholic U. drama department. Many went on to make names for themselves in New York and elsewhere. James D. Waring, who taught set design and directing during the school year and functioned in these same capacities at Olney in the summer, was responsible for introducing Irish playwright Hugh Leonard to this country. All of Leonard's plays, including the award-winning *Da*, had their American premieres at Olney.

Many good summer theaters have surfaced in the years that followed but, because it occupies a special place in my own development, Olney remains for me unique. Quite apart from the high quality of its productions, it was (and is) a delightful place to visit. One reaches it by means of a road that winds through the idyllic (complete with grazing horses and cows) Maryland countryside. For reasons I've never quite understood the theater itself has always reminded me of a ship, surrounded not by water but by towering shade trees. Waiting to welcome one in those days on the terrace that adjoins the parking lot were Father Hartke (priestly black over rainbow shirt), the genial Jim (Waring) and his colleagues of the Catholic U. drama department, William Graham and Leo Brady, who also functioned as Olney actors and directors.

Dress was informal, the atmosphere relaxed. After the show there was a reception in the vast front room of the rambling building that served as a combination office for the staff and dormitory for the actors. And it was there, among the crush of bending elbows and deviled eggs that I was first exposed to the Washington press corps, including the *Post*'s distinguished critic, Richard L. Coe, who became a close and valued friend. Of all the theaters I covered during those early tenderfoot days, I loved Olney the best. I still do.

EIGHTEEN

My introduction to Olney occurred in the summer of 1954. Five years passed before fate threw me into a similar collision with Washington's Arena Stage. The impact upon my thinking was, if anything, greater.

Theater is supposed to have originated with the Greeks — as part of the annual festivals to their gods. The first theater probably consisted of a mountainside on which the audience sat to watch ceremonies performed in a clearing below. Eventually, the rough surface of the mountain gave way to rows of seats that enclosed the clearing in the manner of an amphitheater.

This basic pattern of an acting area surrounded on three sides by the audience endured for centuries. The stage at Shakespeare's Globe was little more than a platform around which spectators crowded, cheering or heckling the actors as the spirit moved them.

Not only was the arrangement simple but it made possible a rapport between players and audience not unlike that existing today at prize fights and football games. The evolution of this relationship into the relatively sedate sort of thing we find in modern theaters was due mainly to changes in stage design.

THE PURITANS, WHOSE NAME WAS NOTHING IF NOT APT, closed all London theaters when they came to power in 1642. And the ban lasted until the Restoration of Charles II to the throne from which his father had been driven eighteen years before. But the two playhouses he licensed bore little resemblance to the Globe, for in the interim scenery had come into fashion.

Sparked by public reaction to Italian opera (introduced near the end of the Sixteenth Century), productions became more and more elaborate. Auditoriums had to be enlarged to accommodate a burgeoning audience seated in tightly packed rows in *front* of a stage reposing in a "picture frame." The resulting loss in the intimacy previously existing between players and spectators was aggravated by still another factor.

Theater is a door through which we may enter the magic world of make-believe. Shakespeare, a genius, was able to use this door to deepen our understanding of the real world. In the latter half of the Nineteenth Century, a movement was launched to restrict what could happen inside the door to, in Emile Zola's demanding words, an "exact reproduction" of what could happen outside. Theater must reflect life not only in the big sense but also in its boring details.

To put it another way, theater had to stop being theatrical and become realistic — which meant that the audience could no longer be acknowledged (as with the soliloquy and aside) but must be considered as eavesdropping through the invisible fourth wall of a room. It also meant that, in order to preserve the illusion of reality, a curtain must be lowered between scenes to mask the set changes — which imposed unnecessary interruptions to the action. By the middle of the Twentieth Century these traditional strictures had combined with the mundane, unpoetic approach they fostered to rob the theater of much of the magic that had always been its most appealing characteristic. They were finally lifted by the pressure of economic necessity.

Soaring costs had seriously reduced the number of shows available to the country at large. A new factory was needed to replace Broadway. It was found in a cheaper and less pretentious means of production.

Little theaters began to sprout like mushrooms — in cellars, lofts and defunct movie houses. And, since few boasted conventional stages, theater-in-the-round, pioneered by Margo Jones in Texas, was resorted to. I had attended some of these theaters without being particularly impressed. All struck me as unsuccessful efforts to make the best of bad bargains. None gave the slightest hint that I might be in at the beginning of a revolution. Then I went to see a play at Zelda Fichandler's Arena Stage.

Watching, I was suddenly seized by the conviction that arena staging contained in its very nature the power to restore theatricality to the theater and that this particular theater might serve as inspiration for one I now decided must be developed in Baltimore.

Founded in 1950 by Mrs. Fichandler (then a language student at George Washington University) with the help of one of her instructors, Arena Stage by the time I met her had moved from the downtown movie house where it had weathered its first few seasons to an abandoned brewery in Washington's Foggy

Bottom district. It stayed there only long enough for Zelda to raise money for a brand new plant which was in time to house three separate theaters whose facilities compared favorably to any in the country.

My purpose here is not to catalogue the manifold accomplishments of this remarkable woman — who, together with her husband, Tom, built Arena Stage into one of the great theaters of the world — but to acknowledge the impact of her and that theater upon my own development.

I've mentioned that my previous experience with in-the-round staging had yielded only chagrin at the compromises that economics impose upon art. Producers, I felt, resorted to it only because they could not afford anything better. I did not get this impression at Arena Stage.

There the staging was handled not as a necessary expedient but as a raison d'etre of the production and, indeed, of the playhouse itself. And no wonder! For by enabling members of the audience to communicate more intimately with the actors and one another, it helped to re-establish the vibrant spirit of the Elizabethan theater. It also helped to destroy the stultifying preoccupation with realism that had dominated American productions for more than 50 years.

But what really grabbed me in her Foggy Bottom office that afternoon was the personality of Zelda herself. She possessed an energy so electric she almost sent off sparks. Nothing appeared to daunt her. To my tentative questions about how she had managed to raise money for getting Arena Stage started, she replied that money was never the real problem in such ventures. "We just called up some friends," she said, "and we had it in a couple of weeks."

"It becomes increasingly clear," I wrote in an article that took up most of the front page of the *Sunday Sun*'s feature section of May 31, 1959, "that the real hope for the American theater lies in cities like Baltimore." Then followed my reasons for such a statement (Broadway had had it, for one), ending with an account of my interview with Zelda and my conclusion that what she had accomplished in Washington might also be accomplished 40 miles to the north.

"The most important single requirement for establishing a workable professional theater in Baltimore," I declared, quoting her, "is someone with enough interest to find an appropriate location ('department stores can be suburban but a theater should be in the center of things'), enough energy to raise the money to convert that location into a proper theater and enough skill to manage it, once it is in operation.

"The line," I said, "forms on the right."

IT DIDN'T. Though I never ceased to agitate for a new structure to replace the obviously doomed Ford's and a resident theater comparable to Arena Stage, it seemed more and more evident, as the Fifties gave way to the Sixties, that it would take a miracle to achieve either.

Still, the decade had not been wasted. I began it as a district reporter and ended it as a drama critic. The $50-a-week jump in salary entailed in the shift had originally been resisted by Ed Young, but with his departure for the *Providence Journal*, Dorsey had made no bones about it.

"Starting next week," he told me, "we are stepping you up in $10 increments until we can give you the big money."

The "big money" amounted to a total of $6,656 a year.

Also, I was able to wangle a private office for myself, something neither Kirkley nor *Evening Sun* critic Gilbert Kanour had been able to do in the new *Sun* building. Of course, they didn't have the help of Gina Lollobrigida.

To promote their 1956 film *Trapeze*, United Artists sent life-size photographs of the shapely Italian star to news men all over the country. Standing five feet tall on shapely legs, it had been placed by me in a corner of the *Sun*'s city room when Dorsey strode in one morning in his characteristically foul mood.

"Where'd that come from?" he snarled.

"It was sent by —"

"Get it out of here!"

"What do you want me to do with it?"

"Just get it out of here."

But in the years that followed, he often found time to stop by the office I'd used the photograph as an excuse for obtaining and say with an apologetic grin "I just wanted to say hello to Gina."

So I moved out of the city room with all its good-natured confusion into a relatively calm environment in which I never had to worry about wads of copy paper, launched by members of the Sports Department and representing surrogate baseballs, sailing over my head. Though I missed the vitality and companionship inherent in such activities, I felt the change was necessary. I had begun to sense from responses of readers that I had things to say that might better be said under circumstances more conducive to thought.

In short, while the future of the Baltimore theater remained shrouded in clouds of uncertainty, *my* sun continued to rise — each published article adding to my stature as a promising new voice in the community, each opening night to the public's understanding of my critical function and each year to the list of talented people who provided me with an unending source of inspiration and enlightenment.

Preston Jones
Photo courtesy of the John F. Kennedy Center for the Performing Arts.

The Perception
of Form

NINETEEN

I'm hung up with time."

Some statements, however casually uttered, have a ring. This one, made by the late Preston Jones in the rooftop restaurant of Washington's Kennedy Center between sips of something that looked suspiciously like a Pink Lady, did. "I don't know what you call it," he said, noticing the way I was eying the pink concoction. "Somebody sent it over when I came in and I been drinkin' 'em ever since."

Downstairs his *Texas Trilogy*, scheduled to open the following week on Broadway, was playing to packed houses. A press agent had arranged for him to have dinner that evening with a society reporter at an exclusive Washington club. He had been described in the cover story of a national magazine as the new hope of the American theater. Fame had been thrust upon him. But his edges remained as rough and his countenance as wide-open as the Western plains from which he came.

"I'm always asked," he said, taking another swig of his drink, "if my plays are 'metaphors' for contemporary society. I don't even know what that means. I just write about people."

"The people the 40-year-old ex-highway-worker writes about," I observed in an article appearing in the September 19, 1976 edition of the *Sunday Sun*, "are composites of many he met while living in various small towns in West Texas and his native New Mexico before joining the Dallas Theater Center in 1962. For 11 years he alternated between acting and directing, then became a playwright when, as the newly appointed head of the center's experimental theater, he could find no scripts with regional settings." His trilogy was written within a period of six months.

Bradleyville, name of the fictitious town Jones chose as setting for his three plays, was based on Colorado City, Texas, a community of some 7,000 inhabitants where he lived for several years. And it is indicative of his interest in this community that he succeeds in endowing it with a life more than what we see onstage.

With Tennessee Williams and William Inge, two other regional playwrights to whom he has been compared, life is usually circumscribed by the set — to the extent that we receive no clear impression of the world outside it. But like Thornton Wilder's most celebrated work, *A Texas Trilogy* is as much about a town as it is about its inhabitants. After seeing all three plays, we begin to feel that we, too, live there.

Though each has been written to stand by itself, they draw dramatic significance from one another. Thus, while *The Last Meeting of the Knights of the White Magnolia* may to one encountering the trilogy for the first time seem simply an amusing burlesque of an obsolete Ku Klux Klan-type organization, the same person, after viewing the other two plays, will realize it is considerably more.

This is partly because the 20 years covered by the plays provide one with opportunities to know the same characters at different moments in their lives, partly because of the deepening awareness one receives of the town itself. It is this aspect of the "time" that Jones is "hung up with" that gives the three plays the continuity of a single work.

The best and the one that should in my opinion be seen first is *Lu Ann Hampton Laverty Oberlander*. Not only is it the only one whose action embraces the full 20 years but, in tracing the development of an empty-headed, romantic high-school girl through two unsuccessful marriages into a woman of strength and mature responsibility it, better than either of the others, reveals Jones's serious purpose.

For example, Lu Ann's wastrel brother, who comes across as a drunken buffoon in *The Last Meeting of the Knights of the White Magnolia*, is herein revealed as a pathetic figure. In similar fashion, the comically senile old colonel of *Knights* is shown to be a man of deep sensibilities and indeed near-tragic stature in *The Oldest Living Graduate*.

In short, however lightweight the three plays may seem individually — and both *Knights* and *Graduate* can be legitimately criticized in this respect — taken together, they amount to an eminently respectable work which, in the process of illuminating the various social levels of a small town, makes a heartwarming comment on the nature of man.

For though Jones's characters possess most of the human frailties, being selfish, overbearing and impossibly dense, they are usually well-meaning and never vicious. Moreover, they exhibit, along with a noticeable capacity for love and courage, a zest for life that is charming in the lesser and inspiring in the larger.

Some writers manufacture scapegoats for their personal prejudices. Jones loved every one of his characters, loved them for the way they loved one another and for the way, despite time's ravaging effects, they persevered.

In his excellent book *The Theater of Revolt* Robert Brustein describes outstanding modern playwrights as being in a state of rebellion. Sometimes the rebellion is against God. Sometimes it is against the social order. And sometimes it is against the human condition or the nature of life itself.

To be properly modern, one concludes, is to be against something. Yet there are two sides to every question — even the question of life — and the persistent determination of playwrights to concentrate on only one side has resulted in less than a balanced picture. As a man writing without a chip on his shoulder, Jones without really being conscious of what he was doing tended to restore this balance.

"He is not as poetic as Williams," I said at the end of the above-mentioned article, "as brilliant as Albee or as committed as Miller. But because of his ability to view life from a vantage point other than his own sickness, anger or disapproval, his vision may be clearer. Add to this the fact that he has just begun to write and the alarming speed with which he does it, and he could conceivably outdistance them all."

But I failed to take into account the appalling provinciality of the New York critics — who, apparently annoyed by the glowing reviews Jones had received on his way to Broadway, proceeded to destroy him once he got there. *A Texas Trilogy*, which ran for only 63 performances, was dismissed as a minor effort by a Southern yokel. And these were the same art-lovers whose favorable reception a few months earlier enabled Edward Albee's embarrassingly insignificant *Seascape* to win a Pulitzer Prize. Following the trilogy's closing, Jones returned to Texas where he died a couple of years later. Doctors diagnosed the cause as a bleeding ulcer, but those closest to him maintained it was the New York critics who killed Preston Jones.

TWENTY

The word "time" has different meanings depending upon how it's regarded. To most people it stands for the division of hours, minutes and seconds that make up a day. To a poet it is the endless river whose flow embraces all of life. To others it is the quality implicit in Andrew Marvell's "But at my back I always hear/ Time's winged chariot hurrying near." That winged chariot has been on my tail as long as I can remember and never more insistently than when, as the *Sun's* newly appointed theater critic, I began covering opening nights at Ford's.

The curtain usually went up at a quarter to nine. It came down around eleven. My deadline was twelve-thirty — which meant that, after locating a taxicab to carry me back to the *Sun* and waiting an interminable period for the elevator to hoist me to the fifth floor, I had at most an hour to write what I hoped would be an intelligible review.

As hours go, it was never my finest.

Apprehension over what it might produce haunted me as I sat in my third-row aisle seat trying to concentrate on the show. To make matters worse, I discovered that techniques that had stood me well for writing feature stories did not work when reviewing plays. By the simple addition of a few transitional phrases I had been able to turn notes taken in the course of covering an event into a finished article after getting back to my typewriter. Such a procedure was out of the question when I could not anticipate what my estimate of a show might be until I had seen the whole production. Thus, unless relating to scenery and similar matters, all notes jotted down before the final curtain were useless.

Astute reviewers learn this very soon. So when you see somebody across the aisle scribbling all the way through a performance, you can bet he's either a novice or a nincompoop.

Then there's the lead.

The "lead" — or first sentence — is of primary importance in a newspaper article because it must capture the reader's attention to a degree that he will go on to read the second, and possibly even third, sentence. For this reason, reporters — faced with the task of writing a feature piece in which there is (as is often the case) little substance — resort to trick leads.

I once hit upon the perfect trick lead for a luncheon interview I was about to have with a young Italian movie actress. "I ate spaghetti with Anna Maria Alberghetti." It was not until I arrived at the restaurant that I learned that the lady didn't eat spaghetti, and I was left with "I ate spinach salad with Anna Maria Alberghetti" — which was not quite the same thing.

I mention this because it illustrates the writer's dilemma when the trick lead fails to fit the circumstances. And where criticism is concerned it can be a booby trap.

"If this be art God give us trash!" a trick-lead artist might dash off in the heat of inspiration without any clear idea of where he's going from there. A well-constructed review should proceed from first to last without back-tracking. And since most shows are neither all cream nor all crud, the trick-lead artist may create a false initial impression from which his review never recovers. Rash statements may impress his witless camp-followers with what a clever critic he is, but they will never make him a good one.

The only way to be a good critic is through judicious weighing of a work's assets against its faults — and though this may make for a dull review (nothing is so boring as good criticism), the critic can at least know that he's doing his job.

To be clever or to be honest? That is the question all critics face from the moment they don the mantle. Some, I suspect, never realize they're facing it. Carried away by their pretensions to genius, they may imagine they can't help being clever. Others never realize that the biggest problem in a society where everybody is subjected to brain-washing is coming to grips with what one *really* thinks about anything — and why.

This was the problem that, after I had answered to my own satisfaction the question posed above, I settled down to explore.

AMONG THE CONCLUSIONS I REACHED was that stage productions should be judged according to two criteria — their value as "theater" and their value as "drama." I have discussed the distinction between these two terms in *The Splintered Stage* and shall repeat myself here only to the extent of saying that — whereas good theater enchants us through the use of sets, costumes, music, lighting, staging and other devices appealing mainly to the eye and the ear — good drama grabs us by the throat.

Evaluating the former, I decided, lay in the importance played by the non-human elements in a show. The latter I wrestled with a long time.

For one thing I discovered that, while watching a play, I sometimes found myself weeping. "Weeping" is probably too strong a word. What happened is that, suddenly, my larynx would contract, my breathing would become labored, and my eyes would fill with tears.

The reaction seemed to have no relation to any climactic moment in the story (such as Hamlet's discovery of his father's murder) but rather to the introduction of certain themes. And it was, in hopes of learning why, that I became involved with that second definition — the one Hotspur uses when he describes Time as taking "survey of all the world." In short, it brought me to the "river."

We embark upon it at birth and disembark at death. During the journey we become aware not only of those traveling with us but of those who have preceded us and, by extension, those destined to come afterward. We are, that is to say, made conscious of the *continuity* of human life and that we all share experiences and traits in common.

Many of these traits — ambition, jealousy, envy, hate — arise naturally from our selfish instincts. But from what do love, compassion, concern for the welfare of others arise?

"There's a divinity that shapes our ends," says Hamlet, "Rough-hew them how we will." Whether or not this be true, there is a feeling deep in the heart of man that he is part of some pre-existing design. In art, this design is represented by the phenomenon of "form." And it was my perception of this phenomenon through the introduction of one or more themes — suggesting that the intricately connected human family represented something greater than the sum of its parts — that, as I sat in my third-row aisle seat, brought on the tears.

Since he first learned to reason [I wrote in my book] *man has sought nothing so much as form and meaning in his life, some evidence of order and purpose in the universe. It is this search that has produced both religion and science, both God and the hydrogen bomb. So basic is apparently man's need to find meaning in his existence that to encounter even a minute reflection of it — in an example of human kindness, a drop of water under a microscope, or the structure of a play — is enough to evoke an answering flash from something deep and organic inside. The mere realization that something deep and meaningful has been wrought from chaos, as the universe itself may once have been, fills him with such profound emotion — a mixture of hope, gratitude and a strange sense of fulfillment — that he is moved to tears. For in this microcosm of order he sees, or thinks he sees, an affirmation of that ultimate symbol of meaning — God.*

PERHAPS THE MOST OBVIOUS EXAMPLE of the phenomenon is a symphony orchestra, in which all the instruments combine to create a carefully worked-out pattern of sound. For a more primitive example, stand on a corner and watch a band march by. Is it simply the martial music that sends our spirits soaring? Or is it the aspect of parts coming together to make a splendid whole? For an even more primitive one, observe the effect when a group of chorus girls, after cavorting to no discernible purpose about a stage, fall into line and start kicking their legs in unison. The audience will invariably burst into applause.

It is the perception of form that does it. *Any* kind of form, just so long as it's perceivable. And how much more powerful the perception when the perceiver perceives himself as being a part.

I remember a television show back in the Sixties when one of those groups of singing sisters put on a Christmas spectacular involving all the female members of their constantly burgeoning clan. Of those featured among the mothers, grandmothers, aunts, great aunts and cousins by the dozen, was a male child of four or thereabouts whose function was to stand in the center of the stage and bang a tin drum while his mother, grandmother, aunts, great aunts and cousins by the dozen stood in the background singing "The Little Drummer Boy."

He obviously hadn't the foggiest notion as to why he was there. His mother had told him to stand in one spot and beat his drum and he was doing it. Then somewhere in the middle of the number something happened. Suddenly he got the idea! You could see it in his expression — which changed from blankness to stunned comprehension. He straightened, and his movements took on authority. He was no longer a little boy following instructions. He was part of something! And the realization transfigured him.

He must have felt much the same when, as an infant, he got the idea that faces appearing over the sides of his crib boded existence of something beyond the confines of his room. Picturing himself in relation to this something gave him his first concept of form and, since it was the first abstract concept of his life, it must have made an unforgettable impression. Such must be the reason for our emotional reaction to this same concept when evoked in the theater or concert hall. It carries us back to the crib, those faces and the mystery they represent.

THERE IS NO WAY OF KNOWING whether the voyage each of us takes on the river has any meaning. Possibly Preston Jones — whose shock at his sudden success was so great that when I interviewed him that night in the Kennedy Center's rooftop restaurant I could see the wonder in his eyes — thought it did.

He was a good ol' boy headed for glory. But not, as it turned out, the glory he'd anticipated. Death and the New York critics saw to that.

But in the way for a short while it rose and fell, surged and receded like the sun and the tides, his life had — form. And the thread that ran through it, binding its two halves together, was the subject with which I began this chapter.

"AND TIME PASSING," wrote Thomas Wolfe in *The Hills Beyond*, "like the humming of a bee, time passing like the thrumming in a wood, time passing as cloud shadows pass above the hill flanks of the mountain meadows . . . time passing as men pass who never will come back again . . . and leaving us, Great God, with only this knowing that this earth, this time, this life . . . are stranger than a dream."

TWENTY-ONE

Thus did I arrive at the conclusion that, as certain chords struck on a musical instrument will set other instruments to vibrating, certain themes in a play will induce emotional tremors throughout an audience.

The reason for this, I decided, was that the themes tended to reinforce man's cherished view of himself as a creature fundamentally good. But that was not the whole story.

"The tragic hero with Shakespeare," wrote A. C. Bradley in *Shakespearean Tragedy* (Macmillan, 1905) "need not be 'good,' though generally he is 'good' and therefore at once wins sympathy in his error. But it is necessary that he should have so much of greatness that in his error and fall we may be vividly conscious of the possibilities of human nature."

What, I asked myself, makes a man great, as opposed to merely good? It was, I further decided, a combination of three qualities:

1. Genius,
2. The courage to translate that genius into positive action, and
3. Willingness to accept full responsibility for the results.

An examination of new works by the then-prominent American playwrights convinced me that none of the central characters possessed any of these qualities.

Each period creates its own fads. In the 1950's it was neurosis.

I was in Martick's one afternoon when Morris opened the door behind the bar and yelled up the stairs to his mother "When is Jeanette coming back from her psychiatrist? There's nobody down here to take care of the customers and I've got to go to *my* psychiatrist!"

Ludicrous as this may sound, it was no joke. In the Fifties, people with any claim to sensitivity went to psychiatrists. It was fashionable to be an emotional wreck. On the stage, it took the form of characters incapable of coping with life.

They were *victims* of either society or their childhood conditioning and, as such, could not be held responsible for their misery. Nor, by the same token, could they do anything to alleviate it. All they could do was suffer and, of course, complain — which brings us back to the subject of greatness. It consists — like faith, hope and charity — of three things: genius, responsibleness and courage. And the greatest of these is courage.

Though possessing qualities of intellect, aspiration and sensibility that place him at the top of the animal kingdom [I wrote in my book], man, no less than the other members of that kingdom, is a victim of mortality. Like the mosquito, man dies. Yet, unlike the mosquito, he has the power to comprehend and anticipate the event long before it happens. This power saddles man with a burden from which all other living creatures are exempt. And the irony of it all is that the more highly developed his intellect, aspiration and sensibility, the more poignantly aware of this burden man becomes.

Adding to its weight is, moreover, the generally unsatisfactory nature of life itself. Suffering, both in body and in spirit, seems to be the natural state of human existence. And, in the face of all this suffering and its ultimate terminus in death, the phenomenon of courage in a superior, more sensitive and, consequently, more vulnerable human being is an inspiring and magnificent thing.

But, owing to the popularity of freudian psychology in the Fifties, courage, the most dramatic of all human traits, virtually disappeared from the stage. And what replaced it?

"You always had that detached quality as if you were playing a game without much concern over whether you won or lost," Maggie tells her alcoholic husband in *Cat on a Hot Tin Roof,* "and now that you've lost the game, not lost but just quit playing, you have that rare sort of charm that usually happens in the very old or hopelessly sick people, the charm of the defeated."

For the indomitable strength, which enabled the Shakespearean hero to stand up and slug it out with life, the heroes of the 1950's substituted the charm of the defeated. They were also "sick" according to the special meaning Freudians apply to that term. Indeed, by the final curtain in *Death of a Salesman* and *A Streetcar Named Desire* (the two celebrated "masterpieces" of the period), the central characters were virtually certifiable. The refusal to fit into any conventional pattern that had once excited audiences' admiration became simply morbid when the people were obviously insane.

My repeated sounding of this theme in reviews brought me into conflict with groups priding themselves on being in the fashionable mainstream. I've suggested that this book might be, among other things, a chronicle of my love affair with the Baltimore public. But, as Lysander points out in *A Midsummer Night's Dream*, the "course of true love never did run smooth." And, since the course for me was pursued through the columns of the *Sun*, the next section will consist of examples of how I provoked responses from my faithful, if not always loving, readers.

Photo courtesy of the Baltimore Sun.

True Love

TWENTY-TWO

During the winter and spring of 1960, productions based on two major Tennessee Williams plays opened in the Baltimore-Washington area. One was a screen adaptation, the other a touring version of the original Broadway show. Both gave me adequate excuse to air my views as to what was wrong with the American theater in general and Williams in particular.

—0—

Tennessee Williams's *Suddenly Last Summer* [I wrote of the film in the January 29 edition of the *Sun*] is a remarkable performance.

Throughout the Hippodrome's current attraction, adapted with the help of Gore Vidal from one of Williams's own plays, he is forced to walk a tightrope between the revolting and the ridiculous. That he does it — to the extent of keeping the audience spellbound most of the time — is a tribute to his peculiar artistry.

The denouement, it is true, reduces the whole experience to shambles, so that the audience departs feeling more foolish than moved. But that is the fault of Mr. Williams's personal taste, not his craftsmanship. I doubt that even Shakespeare could have made that ending, symbolic though it attempts to be, anything but ludicrous.

In view of the central theme that runs through most of his work, it is difficult to avoid the conclusion that Mr. Williams is obsessed with the idea that sex is dirty. Having embraced it, a person automatically becomes unclean, polluted by the mere encounter, hopelessly infected with evil.

This has led to a preoccupation with the nature of evil, which has led in turn to the following Williams corollary:

Evil exists in pristine form in the deliberate destruction by a brutal force of something too weak and helpless to defend itself. Such is the nature of life — the continuing destruction of the noble weak by the soulless strong. And the principal instrument for effecting this carnage is sex, evil's most trusted ally — which, a fifth column of filth, is present in even the purest of people.

Technically speaking, a Shakespearean tragedy is a contest in which two powerful forces fight to a climactic conclusion. When the hero is finally overcome, so monumentally great has he seemed to us, it is as if some immense structure were toppling, as if a considerable chunk of the earth itself were crashing down into the sea.

Seeing a typical Williams play, on the other hand, is comparable to going to the Roman Colosseum and watching a hungry lion devour an aged Christian. In one the impact lies in the furor of the conflict, in the other in the death screams of the victim. Much of Williams's dialogue, poetic as it is, is but a prolonged cry of agony on the part of the victim-hero.

Aristotle made sympathy the basis of the tragic communication. One cannot, however, sympathize with something one does not respect, and because of their sickness it is difficult to respect the majority of Williams's characters.

The closest we can get to sympathy in a Williams play is the kind of pity produced by the sight of a dumb animal caught in a trap and slowly tortured to death by forces beyond its ability to comprehend. Even this, though, is overcome by our feelings of revulsion and horror.

Thus we see that Williams, in spite of his great dramatic talent, is not a writer of great drama. He is — like Edgar Allan Poe, Mary Wollstonecraft Shelley and Bram Stoker — a writer of horror stories. *Suddenly, Last Summer* — no less than *The Fall of the House of Usher, Frankenstein* or *Dracula* — is a horror story. Not that this damns it — for, in the horror idiom, it is magnificent.

Indeed, its heady Williams atmosphere (compounded of equal elements of festering sickness, the grisly and the sexually bizarre); its marvelous Williams dialogue, its beautifully sustained mood (as the author uncovers before our entranced eyes the hideous face of evil itself), its excellent characterizations and artistic unity may make it the most uniformly successful work in any medium the playwright has turned out to date.

Joseph L. Mankiewicz's direction is imaginative and in perfect harmony with the material. And the performances by Elizabeth Taylor, Katharine Hepburn, Albert Dekker, Mercedes McCambridge, Garry Raymond — virtually everybody, in fact, but Montgomery Clift — are in the same key.

With the exception of the outrageous ending — an extreme Williams conceit — and Mr. Clift's inept contribution, *Suddenly, Last Summer* meets every requirement of a brilliant piece of work.

Since much of the spectator's enjoyment will depend upon his ignorance until the proper moment of exactly what did happen so "suddenly last summer," it would be unfair of me to give a detailed synopsis. I will say only that Williams has made his usual theme a symbolic expression of one of the fundamental laws of nature.

The law ... simply is to eat or be eaten. And it is this subject — the actual feeding of one organism upon another — that Mr. Williams has chosen to treat with grim literalness here. We have carnivorous plants, carnivorous birds, carnivorous people.

The hero, who appears only as a faceless form in flashback, has met a strange death while on a vacation cruise with his cousin (Miss Taylor). Her account of what happened when she returns so upsets the dead man's jealous mother (Miss Hepburn) that she has her niece confined in a mental institution and hires a surgeon (Mr. Clift) to perform a lobotomy with the intention of cutting the event from her memory.

That, I think, should be enough to give you the idea. The story that follows — powerfully enacted by the Misses Taylor and Hepburn — is superbly Williams. The only departure from the usual formula is that this time, instead of the Christian getting it, it is the trainer who taught the lion its tricks in the first place. Irony.

—0—

THE DAY THE ABOVE ARTICLE APPEARED IN PRINT I received a telegram bearing the name Marie Hechter and a Baltimore address. It read "Would you please rewrite your review of *Suddenly, Last Summer* so the average reader (me) would understand exactly what you mean?" I had by then learned that such communications were motivated not by malice but high spirits. The anonymous letter that arrived a couple of days later was another matter.

> *I have just finished reading your review of* Suddenly, Last Summer. *I found it to be the work of an untalented, tasteless smut.*
>
> *Perhaps you have never had any creative leanings. But, as any sensitive intelligent soul will tell you, this film is a classic.*
>
> *The credits go first to Mr. Williams without whose genius the acting and direction would have failed.*
>
> *As for Mr. Williams's thinking of sex as being dirty, sex can be dirty. Mr. Williams is successful because he writes well of sex.*
>
> *Most certainly Gore Vidal deserves credit, as his screenplay is an improvement over the play. But all he gave it was a rearrangement and more polish. This doesn't justify with crediting him with everything good.*
>
> *So according to you poor Tennessee, who is most responsible for the quality of this film, is an ass. This doesn't leave him with much (just money).*
>
> *I really long for the day when people will appreciate the artistry, not the moral deficiency, of Tennessee Williams.*
>
> *I suppose I have been a little harsh with you. I'm sure you have motivation for disliking this work. Perhaps professional jealousy?*
>
> *Yours devotedly,*
> *A Friend*
>
> *P.S. — Tenn. Williams was writing quality plays long before you failed.*

TRY AS I MIGHT, I COULD NOT TAKE "A FRIEND'S" ATTACK SERIOUSLY — as indicated by my reply, which appeared, together with the letter, in the *Sunday Sun* of February 7.

> *There was nothing in my review that could have given anybody the impression that I think Tennessee Williams is an ass. As a matter of fact, I think it very likely that he is not an ass.*
>
> *He employs, I'm told, two psychoanalysts. So, even if he is an ass, he's working on it.*
>
> *I entirely agree that* Suddenly, Last Summer *is a classic. Indeed, I compared it to such existing classics as* Dracula *and* Frankenstein. *What more could one ask?*
>
> *I also agree that full credit for the success of the picture should go to Mr. Williams, with an appropriately smaller share going to Mr. Vidal. As I recall, I made only one slight reference to Mr. Vidal in the whole review and so far have received no letters of any kind from his fans.*
>
> *I am aware of the theory that sex can be dirty, but — let us not forget — life can be beautiful. Keep smiling. As for the statement that Williams is successful because he writes well of sex, it strikes me as dogmatic but (in view of all that money) logical.*

I'm pleased to note that somebody longs for the day when people will appreciate the artistry, rather than the "moral deficiency," of Tennessee Williams. That'll be the day.

The remark about professional jealousy, incisive though it may be, does not conform with the facts. Me jealous of Tennessee Williams! Just because he's probably the most gifted dramatist in the country and was writing quality plays long before I failed? Why on earth should I be jealous of him?

BECAUSE THEY MAKE ENTERTAINING SUBJECT MATTER such letters are welcomed by journalists needing material for a daily column. Some, however, are not so easily dismissed. Take the one from Gerald M. Camp concerning my review of *Sweet Bird of Youth*. Of this play I had written in the May 13 edition of the *Sun* that it had once again demonstrated Williams's ability to mesmerize an audience — then went on to observe:

Sustaining the hushed attention of a large crowd throughout a long evening is no mean trick. That Mr. Williams has succeeded in doing it so often is a tribute to a talent which perhaps only his morbid preoccupation with depravity prevents from producing a truly great play.

Centered upon the sexually sensational, this preoccupation is apparently illimitable. I never attend a Tennessee Williams opening that I don't leave with the feeling that he has gone as far down the road of perverse violence as it is possible to go. Yet he always manages to go a little farther.

Consider the fate of his last three protagonists:

In Orpheus Descending, *the hero was torn to bits by dogs. In* Suddenly, Last Summer, *he was eaten by hungry boys. Now, in* Sweet Bird of Youth, *he is surgically emasculated a la Abelard by the relatives of a girl whom he has unwittingly infected with venereal disease.*

I can't imagine how anyone could possibly beat that, but I am confident Mr. Williams will. If the series continues along established lines, his next play should send them home as sick at their stomachs as they are in their hearts.

Such is the tenor of the contemporary theater.

MR. CAMP'S LETTER, addressed not to me but to the editor of the *Sun*, follows:

Sir:

In the three years which I have spent in Baltimore I have become an admirer of your paper and the many fine writers which you employ. Not the least among these is your drama critic Mr. R. H. Gardner. It has become painfully obvious, however, that Mr. Gardner has a personal dislike for any dramatic effort presented under the name Tennessee Williams. It is clear that Mr. Gardner is incapable of reviewing a Williams effort objectively. My disgust reached its peak in reading the review of Sweet Bird of Youth.

Apparently Mr. Gardner feels that Mr. Williams does have considerable playwriting talent, and objects chiefly to his subject matter, human depravity in all its forms. He would perhaps have Mr. Williams's great talent for tearing the veneer of civilization from the evils which do exist in the world turned to light comedy or meaningless character plays. Perhaps he feels that sadism which can result in a man being "torn to bits by dogs" for being different from the accepted standard is not a real human issue. Perhaps he feels that the neuroses which infect present society and lead to, among other things, homosexuality, can be shown more effectively than in the pure shock value of cannibalism.

It is interesting to note that human depravity has always been the theme of the world's greatest drama. One wonders if Mr. Gardner, reviewing the opening of Oedipus Rex *by Sophocles, would not pan it for dealing with murder of one's father, sexual relations with one's mother and self-mutilation. His comment would undoubtedly be "I never attend a Sophocles opening that I don't leave with the feeling that he has gone as far down the road of perverse violence as it is possible to go. Yet he always manages to go a little bit farther. I can't conceive how anyone could possibly top the patricide and incest of this play, but I'm confident that, in the proposed sequel dealing with the hero's daughter, Mr. Sophocles will."*

The same, of course, could be said of Shakespeare, who has been known to write about such nasty subjects as fratricide with the murderer marrying the murdered's wife and plotting the death of his son; murder by one's closest friend (et tu?); the mental decay of a senile king dominated by his daughters; or the joint suicide of two young lovers because of the hatred of their parents. It is these themes that we think of when we speak of Shakespeare and, were they not clothed in Elizabethan English, they would be no less shocking than the tales of madness, perversion, neurosis and hatred which have won for Tennessee Williams critical acclaim throughout the country, two Pulitzer Prizes and innumerable Academy Award nominations.

THE DIFFERENCE BETWEEN "A FRIEND'S" LETTER AND MR. CAMP'S is that one was obviously written by an idiot and the other by a well-meaning, intelligent and educated man. I was reluctant to subject him to the same treatment I had given "A Friend," though for the record I felt compelled to point out the fly in his ointment. Oedipus, Brutus and even Claudius ("It stinks to heaven") accepted moral responsibility for their acts, thus winning our respect, if not our admiration. Tennessee Williams heroes, following the fashion of the day, tended to place blame on anything but themselves.

I was pleased when the following, from a member of the Department of Classics at Western Maryland College, appeared in the *Sun*'s letter column on June 3.

Sir:

Mr. Gerald M. Camp's letter on May 30 dealing with Tennessee Williams compares the theme of "human depravity" in Sophocles's Oedipus Rex *with themes of Tennessee Williams. He notes that Sophocles deals with murder of one's father, sexual relations with one's mother, and self-mutilation.*

These points of comparison are not well-taken for several reasons. First, Oedipus did not know or suspect that it was his father he was attacking, nor did he know or suspect that it was his mother whom he was marrying....

As for the self-mutilation, it was the act of a man of honor rather than a depraved one. Both it and the murder are only referred to and are not shown on the stage.

The whole tone of the play... is one of great respect for a good and honorable king, Oedipus. He is a man essentially public-spirited and noble, who has tried to do right and has earned respect. The play does not depict or suggest him in any conscious depravity. Other characters from tragedy may be mentioned who are depraved, but often they are represented as masters of their depraved purposes, rather than ruled by them.

William Ridington

AS AN AUTHORITY ON THE CLASSICS, Mr. Ridington was simply trying to clear up what he regarded as popular misconceptions about Greek drama. Addie Weiser, whose letter to the *Sun*'s editor appeared on June 5, was bent on vindicating me.

Sir:

I bitterly resented the letter (May 30) criticizing Mr. Gardner's review of Tennessee Williams's Sweet Bird of Youth. *If the writer read Marya Mannes's article "Plea for Fairer Ladies" in the New York Times magazine section of May 29 he learned that even New York is fed up with that sort of thing.*

To me, Mr. Gardner is completely reliable and his style of writing is so delightful that I read his reviews even when I'm not interested in the film or play. We depend on him to save us from spending good time and money to see sordidness that we can see for nothing just two blocks from where we live on Park Avenue. On the other hand, Mr. Gardner's reviews have been responsible for our seeing such wonderful films as Smiles of a Summer Night *which we would not have gone to see otherwise.*

The fact that Mr. Gardner has the courage not to be influenced by the pseudos who go along with anything that is chic at the moment is highly commendable.

I DO NOT RECALL WHETHER I EVER WROTE A THANK-YOU NOTE to Ms. Weiser for these kind words. If not, I hope she will accept this one now.

As for Tennessee's and my artist-critic conflict, it reached a resolution of sorts with the front-page obituary I wrote on February 25, 1983 in which I said he had been America's greatest living playwright. In so describing him, I was not retreating from my position that he was not a writer of great plays. For there is a difference between writing great plays and being a great playwright. And because of the poetry with which he imbued all his plays Williams was definitely that. Not even O'Neill, who liked to think of himself as a poet, could touch him.

Take the opening lines in his first Broadway hit: "Yes, I have tricks in my pocket. I have things up my sleeve. But I am the opposite of a stage magician. He gives you illusion that has the appearance of truth. I give you truth in the pleasant disguise of illusion." From the moment Eddie Dowling spoke these words in the 1945 premiere of *The Glass Menagerie*, the American theater was never quite the same. Nor was I.

Indeed, it was the promise represented by this first and, for my money, best of Williams plays that, in view of his tendency to descend with each new work more and more into the gutter, seemed to emphasize the waste of a great talent. The greatness of that talent, however, remained.

Even as a writer of "horror stories," he was no less than superb and, as such, anticipated an era that saw *The American Dream*, *Oh, Dad* and *Sweeney Todd* on the stage, along with such films as *The Exorcist*, *The Omen*, *Carrie* and *Halloween*, compared to whose grisly subjects his now seem tame.

"For that matter" — and I am quoting from the obituary — "there is evidence that, before losing himself in drugs and drink, he was exploring other avenues, other themes." Among them the desire for, if not the possession of, courage.

THE CHARACTER OF THE 97-YEAR-OLD POET (modeled undoubtedly upon Williams's grandfather) in *The Night of the Iguana* is an inspiring one, and the poem he spends much of the play composing — the first and last stanzas of which follow — might well serve for the playwright's epitaph.

How calmly does the orange branch
Observe the sky begin to blanch
Without a cry, without a prayer,
With no betrayal of despair.

O, courage, could you not as well
Select a second place to dwell,
Not only in that golden tree
But in the frightened heart of me?

TWENTY-THREE

Tennessee Williams was not the only writer to whom my reactions aroused hostile observations on the part of readers. The same was true — and for much the same reasons — of William Inge, Arthur Miller and, especially, Edward Albee. One critic for a national publication became so upset by my remarks in the few pages I allotted Albee in *The Splintered Stage* that he condemned the whole book.

But this is the sort of thing journalists — who cut their teeth on the maxim that you can't please everybody — come to expect. More disturbing are those times when something one has written seems to release a veritable groundswell of resentment and antagonism.

Before television, most Hollywood films were made on studios' back lots. With the advent of a medium capable of showing pictures in living rooms, Hollywood knew it must come up with something else. Television screens were tiny. They did not lend themselves to spectacle. What was needed were screens of unprecedented enormity — which could be used to transport viewers all over the world, enabling them to visit places and see things they would never have been able to visit and see otherwise. Film-makers must knock down the walls of studios and push out into all the remote corners and byways of the earth.

Tyrone Power galloping his horse through the Kyber Pass. Ava Gardner taking a shower in Africa. Let Milton Berle try to match that!

In February of 1955 — while still attached to the city desk as part-time reporter, critic and rewrite man — I was assigned to cover the world premiere of a film based on a 1927 Broadway musical. My account appeared in the next morning's paper:

By R. H. Gardner
(Sun Staff Correspondent)

Easton, Md., Feb. 25 — Hollywood, which in the course of its picture-making, has visited many far-flung, out-of-the-way places, finally got around to the Eastern Shore today, and the 6,000-odd members of this little farming community were buzzing as a result.

The visit came in the form of a well-equipped (Ann Miller and that sort of thing) safari of M.G.M. personalities who made the long trek across tidewater and estuary to officiate in one of those strange sociological phenomena, a world premiere.

The film being "preemed" in Easton — chosen because Mrs. William A. Tucker, former wife of the composer, the late Vincent Youmans, lives in nearby Bozman — was *Hit the Deck*.

Tribesmen from all over the area gathered for the ceremonies which began with Miss Miller's arrival by way of auto and the Chesapeake Bay Bridge from Washington at 12:30 P.M. and concluded with her appearance on the stage of the Avalon Theater eight hours later.

The premiere, a sell-out at prices ranging from $2.50 to $50, netted the Music Therapy Fund of Easton almost $2,000. The fund was established to buy song books, records, sheet music and musical instruments for mental patients at the Eastern Shore State Hospital at Cambridge.

Musical sessions have been carried on at the hospital for almost two years by two volunteers, Mrs. George S. Wallace and Mrs. Margaret Dickson, co-chairmen of the benefit.

The work, an "extra" not provided for in the State budget for mental hospitals, has proved of great help in relieving the tension of mental patients.

After her arrival at 12:30, Miss Miller — who, along with Debbie Reynolds and Jane Powell, provides the feminine interest in Mr. Youmans's *Hit the Deck*— received a key to the city from Mayor Calvin G. Lomax.

She then spent an hour entertaining 400 patients at the Eastern Shore State Hospital, after which she participated in a parade witnessed by approximately 1,000 Easton citizens.

Miss Miller's attitude toward her excursion into the wilds of darkest Maryland was summed up during a brief appearance before 500 students at Easton High School.

"Hi! This is my first time at Easton and I'm thrilled to see you," she declared. "I love all of you and wish I could stay and talk for hours."

Unfortunately, Hollywood publicity stunts being what they are, she could only stay about fifteen minutes. The rest of her time on the Eastern Shore was spent making personal appearances, being interviewed by members of the press and otherwise promoting the movie.

I HAVE INCLUDED THIS STORY IN FULL not because I think it is well written but because I want to show that, despite its air of flippancy, it touches all the bases, notably the effort to provide much-needed therapy for mental patients.

Shortly before my trip to Easton I had covered a party arranged by the producer of a network television program who flew a planeload of third-rate performers down to Hyattsville, Maryland, to celebrate the last birthday of a guest on one of his recent TV shows — a child dying of cancer. The little girl — shrunken to a pathetic yellow skeleton — was too far gone to understand why all these nice people were huddling around while photographers took her picture. Trying to get a shot of her alone, I was told by a network PR man that the producer had specified that no photograph of her could be made without him in it.

My report of this ghastly affair was killed by Dorsey for reasons I doubt he understood himself — or, if so, didn't want to think about. The point is it left a bitter taste in my mouth concerning the extremes to which the insidious forces of commercialism were prepared to go to sell products. Such was perhaps the unconscious cause for my irreverent approach to the *Hit the Deck* premiere. I can only say that it was aimed at Hollywood, not at the people of Easton, whom I considered as much the unwary victims of obtaining free advertising as the Hyattsville child. They, however, took a different view.

In a letter addressed to the editor of the *Sun*, Easton Mayor Calvin G. Lomax wrote "The news story in last Saturday's paper on the world premiere in Easton of *Hit the Deck*, written by R. H. Gardner, is regarded by me and many others here as an insult to the town and the Eastern Shore in general. We see no justification for the writer's superior and bellicose attitude which belittles the efforts of an energetic group of volunteers, MGM pictures and Miss Ann Miller. There is enough cynicism and pseudo-sophistication in the world. Let's keep it out of news columns in the Sun."

Mayor Lomax's protest proved to be only the beginning. During the next week letters poured in from irate Easton residents of which the following are typical.

Sir:

The article by Mr. Gardner, which was supposed to tell the story of the premiere of Hit the Deck, at Easton last night, was neither clever nor subtle, but in the opinion of the writer and many to whom I have spoken was pretty insulting to the people of the Eastern Shore.

Who is Mr. Gardner and why his belittling article about the finest part of the State and its people? Why don't you let Jimmy Flood take care of the Shore news?

Arthur J. Grymes, Jr.

Sir:

I would like to call to your attention the news article by R. H. Gardner regarding the world premiere of the movie Hit the Deck in Easton, Md.

We presumed that he was sent here as a critic to report the film good, bad or very bad, but instead of rating the film, he has very definitely rated the Eastern Shore "folk" as tribesmen living, quote: "In the wilds of darkest Maryland."

Perhaps Mr. Gardner is not acquainted with Talbot County's wealthy tribes and I doubt very much that he attended the premiere because there were present big chiefs in full dress and some other very smart people who did and his article has set the Sunpapers back 50 years in their estimation.

He is no more fit to be a reporter —than gosh darn —that's all. I hope!

Mary Johnson

UNDER THE HEAD "WE WERE NOT AMUSED" the *Easton Star-Democrat* observed in a lead editorial:

The premiere in Easton last Friday of Hit the Deck for benefit of the Music Therapy Fund had many elements which combined to make it a truly noteworthy event.

There was, first of all, the reason for the benefit: the need to raise funds with which to purchase song books and musical instruments for use in music therapy work at the Eastern Shore State Hospital at Cambridge....

The local citizens — headed by Mrs. George Scott Wallace and Mrs. Margaret Dickson —who comprised the committee for the benefit worked feverishly in the short time available to them to insure the project's unqualified success. They deserve the highest praise for a complex, almost impossible task well done.

In light of the foregoing, it was with somewhat startled eyes that Talbot Countians read Mr. R. H. Gardner's article reporting the premiere in the Baltimore Sun for Saturday, February 26. Mr. Gardner treated the entire proceedings as one might report a Hollywood-contrived sideshow thrust upon a gullible public. Countians found themselves referred to as "tribesmen" inhabiting the "darkest wilds of Maryland." It is little wonder that tempers were generally aroused.

The most charitable comment one can muster regarding this display of intolerable bad taste is that it may somehow have been intended to be "cosmopolitan" or humorous.

We were not amused.

IN DESCRIBING THE GENERAL REACTION TO MY ARTICLE the *Star-Democrat* did not exaggerate. Jim Flood, the *Sun*'s Eastern Shore correspondent, sent a memo to the city desk claiming that he had worked hard to repair all the damage done by Mencken in the Thirties and that now I, with one stroke, had ruined everything. It was in December of 1931 that a Salisbury mob dragged a black man accused of murdering his white employer from a hospital bed and lynched him. Edmund Duffy, the *Sun*'s renowned cartoonist, set the tone of the paper's reporting of this event with a sketch of a body hanging from a tree under the caption "Maryland, My Maryland." Mencken followed it with a column in which he declared that the Eastern Shore was inhabited exclusively by poor white trash and morons.

Eastern Shoremen retaliated by overturning the *Sun*'s delivery trucks and instituting a movement to secede from Maryland for the purpose of forming a new state with Delaware.

Nothing so dramatic happened this time. Rather than discouraging delivery of papers, residents were so eager to buy copies of my article that Herb Reynolds, director of the *Sun*'s circulation department, asked me to let him know the next time I planned to do a story on the Eastern Shore so he could get an adequate supply to the dealers.

But time heals, if not all at least some, wounds. A few years later, going to Easton to act as godfather in the christening of Pete Kumpa's baby, I was told by his mother-in-law, a native, that she found me not nearly so awful as reports had led her to believe. Finally, my reading of the offending article to a group of Eastern Shore women I had been invited to address in the Seventies was received with high good humor and applause.

So I gather that, unlike Mencken, I've been forgiven. After all, I only called them tribesmen. He called them morons.

TWENTY-FOUR

Mary Johnson's reference to "big chiefs in full-dress" was her way of saying that, rather than "poor whites," the Eastern Shore was inhabited by the socially elite. And it probably was. And is. One of the first calls received by the *Sunpapers*' switchboard following publication of my article came from a socially prominent Roland Park woman who demanded to know if I was a Communist, for, in the era of Senator Joseph McCarthy, anyone voicing an unpopular opinion was suspect.

I was accused on various occasions: once for my coverage of a play in favor of world federalism at Hagerstown, once for my report of a speech by Herbert (*I Led Three Lives*) Philbrick at Baltimore's Loyola College, and often for my reviews of films with socio-political themes.

The Hagerstown incident involved a clash between the State adjutant of the American Legion and such notable World Federalists as novelist Rex Stout and *Saturday Review of Literature* editor Norman Cousins over the question of whether Stout and Cousins had ever been members of subversive organizations.

The Philbrick controversy grew out of a private interview I had with the man just before he mounted the rostrum. During it I had asked if, considering McCarthy's talent for shaking the American people's confidence in their leaders, Philbrick thought it possible the Wisconsin senator might be working for the Communists. He said he thought it unlikely but that McCarthy might be their unwitting dupe.

Since Philbrick's speech amounted to little more than a rehash of his book about how he had infiltrated a Communist cell for the FBI (and therefore had no news value), I led my account of his Baltimore visit with this statement. I made it clear that it had been delivered in private and not from the podium at Loyola. This was ignored by those who, having attended the event, wrote letters to the *Sun* insisting Philbrick had said no such thing. Obviously I was a Communist.

But these were incidents involving only a few excitable readers. I'm concerned here with the reaction of large groups, such as that of the Baltimore Jewish community to my review of the film *Exodus* and that occurring regularly among patrons of the Painters Mill Music Fair.

Painters Mill was our local version of the musical tent — a phenomenon that, by the time it reached the Baltimore suburb of Owings Mills in the summer of 1960, had spread throughout the East. This particular one was operated by three Philadelphia business men — Shelly Gross, Frank Ford and Lee Guber — who maintained similar operations in four other states. Gross had a natural amiability and urbane charm that belied his name. Ford was quick-tempered and less easy to get along with. I never knew much about Guber (who rarely came around) except that he was then married to the future darling of TV reporting, Barbara Walters.

Musical tents presented plush Broadway shows in an atmosphere suggestive of a circus. The atmosphere derived not only from the festive effect of the attractively designed tents but also from the happy-go-lucky attitude of the spectators who crowded in, often in chartered buses, from all over the State. The buses were chartered by clubs, lodges and religious organizations, which purchased blocks of tickets at a discount. The tickets were then sold to members and their friends at prices calculated to provide funds for the organizations' pet charities.

GROUP SALES IS A DEPARTMENT NOW EXISTING in most professional theaters. At Painters Mill, it was headed by a suburban housewife with an inexhaustible talent for the job. Rarely was there a performance not attended by one or more groups whose presence its members made no effort to conceal. Having paid through the nose for a gung-ho night away from the boondocks, they were dead set on enjoying themselves to the limit.

Every joke, however feeble, created the kind of reaction that used to occur on radio shows when somebody held up the sign "Applause!" Every song, however garbled by the tent's all-too-fallible sound system, brought down their part of the house.

At the end came the inevitable standing ovation.

This tribute, reserved for performances of unparalleled distinction in the legitimate theater, occurred nightly at Painters Mill. As such "great" actresses as Lana Turner, Jayne Mansfield and Julie Newmar paraded down the aisle in glittering sequins, the various groups, as if simultaneously stuck with pins, leaped to their feet and began pounding their palms. This sometimes caused confusion.

Difficulty in getting in and out of the Painters Mill parking lots led some patrons to attempt head starts before the general crush began. The appearance of these foresighted souls rising here and there about the auditorium gave the faithful the mistaken idea that the end had come. The result was not one but, as the end did come, *two* standing ovations.

I was for a long time mystified by such behavior, which I had never encountered in any theater I had ever attended before. Then, gradually, I came to realize that the people who subscribed in groups to Painters Mill productions were less like theater patrons than the fans that attended sporting events at Memorial Stadium. It brought back a night when I had stood at the Calvert bar drinking boiler-makers with Ned Burks.

Baltimore had just obtained the baseball franchise relinquished by the St. Louis Browns, thus restoring the Orioles to the big-league status they had lost in 1902. Burks, long dissatisfied with his job of covering city hall, had requested and received the plum assignment of reporting on the team's first season. The experience proved to be a revelation to him.

Having been bred on the ironclad rule that news men must be objective, he was astounded to find his colleagues in the sports department using such terms as "our team" and "our Birds." And the after-the-game commentary upset him even more.

"Do you," he asked, "when reviewing a bad play, say 'Well, we didn't make it tonight, gang, but, with luck, we will tomorrow?'"

The idea set me to laughing, but I remembered it later when I began to receive letters reading "This is to let you know that I completely disagreed with your review of this week's show at Painters Mill. *And so did every member of my group!*" The Prudential Life Insurance Company has made a profitable thing of convincing people that, by purchasing a policy, they buy "a piece of the rock," meaning Gibraltar. The Painters Mill Group Sales Department seemed to have given its customers the idea that, by subscribing to a show, they obtained some kind of vested interest in it.

It was, in short, *their* show. They came not simply to see it but to root for it. And no pip-squeak of a critic was going to tell them it was anything but the best! Rah! Rah! Rah!

Such was the background of the situation that developed in the summer of 1964 when the Painters Mill management signed Zachary Scott in the part of Higgins for a three-week engagement of *My Fair Lady*.

The fabulously successful musical, based on a celebrated play, concerns the efforts of an upper-class Britisher to teach a cockney flower girl how to speak correctly. As a professor of phonetics, Higgins is a master of English pronunciation. As a native of the American Southwest, Mr. Scott wasn't.

My review, printed in the August 6 edition of the *Sun*, began as follows:

If you have a special fondness for the musical My Fair Lady, *you would be wise for the next three weeks to stay away from Painters Mill.*

The charm of the material is still evident, but the combination of handicaps represented by the casting of Zachary Scott in the role of Higgins, the poor adaptation of the work to the arena-stage, and the inadequacies of the tent's sound system is too much even for Shaw, Lerner and Loewe.

Mr. Scott's part in all this reflects less upon him than upon the person who hired him. He is, after all, an actor of much experience, whose laconic style and nasal delivery — as American as the plains of Texas whence he came — are familiar to anyone who has ever seen him perform.

And the unsuitability of these highly individualistic traits to the proper portrayal of a character whose very essence derives from his upper-class English status and mastery of the Oxonian accent should have been apparent from the beginning. It may be true that one doesn't have to be an Englishman to play Higgins, but one must be capable of creating the illusion of being an Englishman. Otherwise the show falls to pieces, as it does in the first scene of the production at Painters Mill.

ALMOST IMMEDIATELY THE LETTERS BEGAN. Dorsey, who seemed less disturbed by them than by what my reaction to them might be, summoned me to his office. "I know you're itching to reply to all these attacks," he said with obvious embarrassment, "but I would appreciate it if you didn't. As you know, we're backing Johnson over Goldwater for president, and we're anticipating a lot of trouble from the lunatic fringe."

"The Painters Mill producers have asked to meet with me on the subject," I said. "Would you object to that?"

"Why don't you just tell them to go to hell?" he said with a grimace of distaste. But I got his okay to see them in my office the latter part of the week.

And so they came — one night after everybody but the most dedicated of *Sun* hangers-on had gone home to their wives. Not Guber, but Gross and Ford. Gross, smiling whimsically, spent most of the time squirming about in the more uncomfortable of my two chairs. It was Ford who carried the ball.

I had no right, he said, to tell people to stay away from Painters Mill. My job was to comment upon the artistic merits of a show — not to tell people whether to attend them. I asked him what the difference was between saying a show was lousy and telling people not to attend it. But he was not to be mollified. He even complained about remarks I had made about the problem of getting out of the Painters Mill parking lots.

As they left, Shelly Gross mentioned how much he had agreed with my rave review of *Fiddler on the Roof*, which had opened a pre-Broadway run in Washington that same week. Meanwhile, the letters continued to pour in. The next day I discovered why.

I learned that every night, while receiving the customary standing ovation, Zachary Scott made a curtain speech in which he told the applauding spectators that, if they really liked his performance, they should write to the *Sun* protesting my review. He had obviously been much upset by it. A friend of mine who had occupied a table next to his that week at a restaurant said Scott had spent the whole evening excoriating me. The same thing happened years later when Jack Cassidy and his wife Shirley Jones brought their two-person show to the Owings Mills theater.

I had on a previous occasion praised Cassidy for his performance in Painters Mill's *Vagabond King* and both him and his wife for their work in the National Company of the Broadway hit *Wait Until Dark*. On this occasion I had walked out after the first act because their show, which came to Baltimore directly from an engagement in Las Vegas, was essentially a nightclub act that should not have been reviewed by a theater critic.

Looking back, I now realize that neither Scott nor Cassidy would have dared to advise patrons to take public issue with a critic's review had they not been encouraged to do so by the management — which gave me a new insight into those letters ending with "And so did every member of my group." That suburban housewife never stopped working.

TWENTY-FIVE

The announcement that the world premiere of the film *Exodus* would take place in Baltimore filled me with dismay. I had no wish to be the first critic in the world to pan it, and from what I'd read about the Leon Uris novel, I felt pretty sure I'd have to.

In the *New York Post* of May 17, 1959, David Boroff had described the book as a Jewish Western. "It has the same morality play certitudes. There is never any confusion about hero and villain, no ambiguities about right and wrong."

Adding to my discomfort were letters from friends, including a Jewish professor and a Presbyterian minister, asking if the film was as biased in its treatment of the Israeli-Arab question as the novel. If so, they didn't want to see it. For several days, while waiting for *Exodus* to open, I spent a lot of time sitting in my office staring out the window. Criticizing the film for its anti-Arab bias could be interpreted as an attack on the Jewish State — which, by extension, could be interpreted as an attack on Jews.

I hadn't minded implications from Right Wingers that I was a Communist— a risk that almost all liberal writers ran in the Fifties. But to be suspected of anti-Semitism was more than I could bear.

If only there were a way to show that my opinion, whatever it might turn out to be, was not based on prejudice. I toyed with the idea of having a Jew review the film for me but discarded it as cowardice. Then one day I received a letter that I thought might get me off the hook. And it did. Unfortunately it impaled me on another one.

The movie opened on schedule to a resplendent audience made up largely of members of the Baltimore Jewish community who had come directly from a black-tie dinner in honor of Otto Preminger and the State of Israel. The enthusiasm with which they greeted everything that happened on the screen did little to lighten the load, as I trudged back to the office in my unpressed suit to tackle the review. Under the heading "*Exodus* Opens at Mayfair," it appeared in the *Sun* of December 21, 1960.

> *The American Council for Judaism, an organization of anti-Zionist Jews, has sent me some material purporting to help me to "distinguish between fact and fiction" in the film* Exodus, *now being shown on a reserved-seat basis at the Mayfair. Because some of the comments may be of interest to those who have read the Leon Uris novel and are trying to decide whether or not to see the film, I am reproducing them below.*
>
>> *It was reported widely that while on location in Israel and Cyprus, Otto Preminger, the producer, was under strong pressure from Arab, British and some Jewish sources to "tone down" the film script of* Exodus *— and well he may have been; for in addition to distorting the history of Jews and Judaism,* Exodus, *the novel, is clearly anti-Arab, anti-British, anti-some-Jews and generally unhistorical.*
>> *"Whatever the reason, the film* Exodus *is much nearer the truth than the Uris novel, though it obviously describes still-recent history from a partisan point of view.*

THE COUNCIL'S LETTER WENT ON IN MUCH THE SAME VEIN for several pages. In substance it amounted to a statement by the political opposition that the film was an improvement over the novel and, as such, merited in my opinion inclusion in my review. I also included a quote by Marie Syrkin from the previous Winter issue of *Midstream*, a pro-Zionist quarterly. Regarding the book, she had said:

"Characters orate at each other in canned speeches that sound like particularly unspirited declarations introducing the main speaker at Zionist meetings... The characters are card-board, the dialogue wooden, and the style verges from undistinguished to plain bathos."

HAVING THUS PROVIDED A JEWISH BASIS for any negative remarks I might make, I proceeded to review the film — which I described as a Zionist tract in the form of a good adventure epic. I had not counted on the extreme antagonism of Zionists to Jews not sharing their political beliefs.

From the tone of the letters that began to pour into the *Sun* the day after the review appeared I might just as well have quoted the head of the American Nazi Party or the Grand Dragon of the Ku Klux Klan. Compared to the fury of the reaction, that of the Eastern Shore to my piece on the *Hit the Deck* premiere was mild. It raged so fiercely that the *Sun*, after printing multiple evidences for a week, devoted almost half a page to it, then added in a subsequent edition that it had given the controversy enough attention and would give it no more.

All the letters said virtually the same thing — of which the following are typical:

Sir:

I was shocked to note that the first review to appear in your periodical of the screen version of Leon Uris's novel Exodus, *instead of confining itself to an objective appraisal of the story and its message, started out with a disproportionately large quotation of material furnished by the anti-Zionist American Council for Judaism . . . The distortions by this small group of the truth about Israel were denounced four years ago already by more than 1,500 representatives of the Jewish communal organizations in this country. To use the misrepresentations of such a body of men as a springboard for the evaluation of "a Zionist tract" is like resorting to the columns of Moscow's* Pravda *in order to obtain an accurate picture of life in the United States of America.*

Yet Mr. Gardner, who pretends that he does not "wish to become involved in any interdenominational controversy concerning Zionism," has stooped to this kind of sophistry and allowed himself to become a vehicle for propagating the self-vilifying ideas of the American Council for Judaism in order to "distinguish between fact and fiction" in the film Exodus. . . .

Samuel Rosenblatt
President of the Baltimore
Board of Rabbis. Dec. 22.

Sir:

It seems only fair that another voice, in addition to that of your reviewer, Mr. R. H. Gardner, should be raised in behalf of the movie Exodus. *There is always danger that a critic's own thoughts may be hidden behind the quotations he cites. Furthermore, there is even greater danger that the real thought expressed in the quotation may be obscured by wordy argument.*

Mr. Gardner cites the arguments and conclusions submitted to him by the American Council for Judaism. It hurts me to see the sacred name of my religion used to underscore certain political opinions like those of the American Council. This council wrote to Mr. Gardner that the movie was a good one; that, in their opinion, it is much nearer the truth than the novel . . . . In other words, even the anti-Zionist American Council insists that the cinema version of Exodus *is basically fair to all parties: Jews, Arabs, Great Britain, mankind. [But] as I read Mr. Gardner's review I had to pick out these conclusions from the mass of words obscuring these ideas behind anti-Zionist argumentation . . . .*

Abraham Shusterman
Rabbi, Har Sinai
Congregation
Baltimore, Dec. 23.

THOUGH TOO LONG AND RAMBLING FOR FULL INCLUSION HERE, Rabbi Shusterman's letter was the only one of the scores received by the *Sun* that reflected any understanding of why I had chosen to refer to the American Council in the first place. For, if such an anti-Zionist organization thought the pro-Zionist approach of the film basically fair, it must be. Most of the letters took the partisan stand of K. H. Fink:

Sir:

... In his review of the film Exodus, Mr. R. H. Gardner refers to the criticism by the American Council for Judaism of Preminger's film and Leon Uris's book. While reproducing the comments of the council, your reviewer neglected to describe the true nature of the American Council for Judaism.

To begin with, their membership is at best not more than 5,000, but in any case they represent an infinitesimal, albeit quite vocal, part of the more than 5 million Jews in the United States...

There is one aspect of the American Council for Judaism which is not too well known —namely, its role as an Arab propaganda tool. The leadership of the council is in fact instrumental in taking the Arab side and in collaborating with the Arabs' anti-Israeli propaganda. The leaders of the American Council for Judaism are perennial participants in national conventions of pro-Arab events. While the council constantly denounces anything pro-Israel or pro-Zionist, it patently engages in partisan activities for Arab interests at one and the same time...

K. H. Fink

IT WAS ONLY NATURAL, considering the denunciations in every letter of the American Council for Judaism, that a spokesman for that organization would reply:

Sir:

In view of the letters to the Editor that have resulted from Mr. Gardner's use of the American Council for Judaism's statement on the movie Exodus, I hope I may be permitted a few words of comment and correction.

Zionism attacks the speaker, not the idea expressed. The strange fact here is that the council expressed its satisfaction at the way the movie handled the material in the book. Yet simply because the council was named in the review, there is criticism of the review....

A typical example of this technique is contained in the letter written by Mr. K. H. Fink in which he understates the council's membership by more than 200 per cent and makes the most ridiculous accusations about council association with Arab propaganda and anti-Israel activity. The council is not anti-Israel or pro-Arab. It is anti-Zionist and most emphatically is not, and never has been, involved in any pro-Arab activity...

The reason for the uproar is that Zionists more and more are realizing that the council's position (Judaism is a religion, not a nationality) is widely and sympathetically understood. Zionism, rooted in the belief that there is a public body called the "Jewish people," cannot accept this understanding...

Robert S. Nyburg,
President
Baltimore Chapter,
American Council for
Judaism, Dec. 29.

I NEVER — RABBI ROSENBLATT TO THE CONTRARY — HAD ANY DESIRE to become involved in a dispute between two groups of Jews. I knew virtually

Janetta and Price Day.
(Photo courtesy of Joseph V. Ridgely.)

Patrick Skene Catling.
(Photo by Stephen Green Armytage.)

A corner of the back room at Martick's in 1950 shortly after the bar began presenting exhibits of local artists. (Jeanette and Morris looking at Rose holding painting. In the middle, Grace Weaver, with whom I was much involved at the time.) *(Photo by Hans Marx.)*

Rose and her mother. (Inset—the "expression.")

She didn't really need the alligator. *(Photo courtesy of Blaze Starr.)*

Ford's Theatre in the sixties. (Inset—Morris A. Mechanic.) *(Photo courtesy of Jacques Kelly.)*

The Stratford, Ontario Theatre—outside and in. *(Photos courtesy of Stratford Festival Publicity Dept.)*

(left) Flanked by Roger Stevens, chairman of the National Council of the Arts, Mrs. Clarisse Mechanic officially opens the theatre named after her late husband. *(Photo courtesy of Jacques Kelly.)*

(left below) Hope Quackenbush. *(Photo courtesy of the Mechanic Theatre.)*
(right below) Zelda Fichandler. *(Photo by Annalisa Kraft)*

Shelley Post as Gwendolyn in Center Stage's 1963 production of *The Importance of Being Earnest. (Photo by Ud Bros.)*

(below) Center Stage Managing Director Peter Culman. *(Photo by Richard Anderson.)*

nothing about the American Council for Judaism when I used its statement for the reason I have cited. My ignorance of it has not diminished. For all I know, it may not still exist. If it does, I wish it well.

As for the mess we all had been party to, it ended with a letter I wrote to the *Sun* editor in which I again pointed out that, by including a favorable comment from the political opposition, I felt I was being fair to the film. Shortly after publication of this letter on December 28, I received one from a Jewish dentist who said that, despite himself, he was moved to admiration by the way I was able to keep creating, then escaping from, impossible situations.

The course of true love had begun to reverse itself.

TWENTY-SIX

Whatever damage my popularity had suffered as a result of the *Exodus* controversy was repaired three years later by an article which became a landmark in my relationship with the Baltimore public. Before its appearance, I had been viewed with the caution accorded any new voice in the community. But after December 1, 1963 — except for a few isolated individuals (usually with personal interests in the theater) and, of course, the customers of the Painters Mill Group Sales Department — I was everybody's sweetheart.

Inasmuch as the article has been reprinted in the *Congressional Record*, the Kennedy memorial collection published in 1964 and as a postscript to *The Splintered Stage*, I shall not reproduce it here. A note on the circumstances surrounding it, however, might prove helpful.

As I've mentioned before, the *Sunpapers* editorial department consisted of three separate staffs — morning, evening and Sunday. Members of the first two were paid extra for work done for the third. But because of some prehistoric agreement between my predecessor and management, I was obliged to contribute a weekly theater piece gratis. I loved my job, all but one aspect — the Sunday column.

Money has never meant as much to me as time. And owing to the way the four or five movie and/or theater openings I reviewed every week occurred, most of mine was taken up with covering my beat.

The *Sunday Sun* went to press around 6 P.M. Friday, but Harold A. Williams, its industrious, infinitely civilized editor, preferred my copy to be in on Wednesday. I rarely made it. The reason was that I never knew what I was going to write about until 11 P.M. Thursday. Then, having seen and commented on everything I was supposed to for that week, I could settle down at my typewriter in the silence of the night and bring my thoughts to bear on the task.

It was my practice to gird myself for this weekly ordeal with a drink at the Eager House in the company of Myron Wolbarsht. Myron was a brilliant young scientist who in time became head of the biophysics department at Duke University but who was then doing post-graduate work at Johns Hopkins. He always drank New York sours, I screwdrivers. While so occupied, we liked to discuss weighty subjects such as the psychological effects of space travel, the radiation factor in wrist watches, and the breasts on the prettiest of the Eager House's waitresses.

Myron held a dim view of astronauts. "Not human" was his diagnosis, as he sloshed the ice around in his New York sour. "They've been transmuted into machines." The threat imposed by my radium-painted dial, he insisted, was nothing to worry about. To prove it, he took me on a jaunt after the bars closed one morning to his Johns Hopkins laboratory to run a geiger-counter test. We were accompanied by a number of drunks picked up along the way. Unfortunately, the test reassured neither of us. "Maybe," he said afterward, "you'd better throw the watch away." As for the waitress, he married her.

One subject we scrupulously avoided that particular night was President Kennedy's assassination, which had taken place the previous Friday. Owing to the media's determination to devote themselves almost exclusively to the story for a week, we were tired of it.

Later, walking the half-dozen blocks to the *Sun* building, I racked my brain for a topic to write on. Nothing suggested itself. I pushed through the glass doors at the front and rode the elevator to the fifth floor. I loved working late at night when only the sounds of the cleaning women and the distant cries of the crowd in the sports department getting reports on games around the country broke the silence. My office was anything but sumptuous, lacking the one item that separated the VIPs from the hoi polloi — a carpet. But it was mine. Something I had created out of my heart. A sanctuary containing everything I needed for what I liked to do most. Ponder.

Much of my pondering in those days related to my book. One of its theses was that, contrary to scholarly opinion, tragedy of the classical sort *could* take place in the modern age. The principal argument of the scholars in their rejection of this idea was that the world had changed since the time of Shakespeare and, certainly, Sophocles. Democracy, with its decentralization of authority and responsibility, had decreased the importance of the individual to the extent that the death of a ruler did not have the same impact on society.

Yet people had wept in the streets of Berlin and Rio de Janeiro at the news of the president's assassination. Not even the death of Franklin Roosevelt near the end of World War II had triggered such worldwide evidences of grief. Was it simply a sentimental reaction to the snuffing out of the life of a man so young and charming? Or was it a demonstration of A. C. Bradley's concept that tragedy lay in the waste of the good — in this instance hope for a better world? I still don't know the answer, but, for whatever reason, the people wept.

Moreover, it seemed to me, as I tried to rise above the distraction of the vacuum cleaner wielded by the woman next door, that Kennedy's life, when placed into juxtaposition with his accused murderer's, exhibited that peculiar suggestion of the inevitable the Greeks called fate. He represented everything the other wasn't. To a born loser, he was the ultimate symbol of success. His tragic flaw was that he presented to the Lee Harvey Oswalds of the world the image of a man too perfect to endure.

Subsequent events have indicated that neither John Fitzgerald nor other members of his family can stand close examination as paragons of perfection. But, as I sat there in the dark hours of November 29, 1963, I was not concerned so much with fact as with myth. The Kennedy assassination had provided the Twentieth Century with its first genuine myth. And though my attitude toward Bobby, Jackie and Teddy may have changed since, my evaluation of the dramatic possibilities of that myth, as expressed in the article I then proceeded to write, has not.

I finished the article around 4 A.M., sent it down the tube to the composing room and walked home. I was awakened at 9:30 Sunday morning by a telephone call from a woman who, like Myron, had attended Annapolis's St. John's College whose graduates, because it employed the Great Books approach, were widely considered (especially by themselves) as superior. She told me with a respect I had never before detected in her voice that she was humbly grateful for the solace I had provided her in regard to Kennedy's death. Such a comment, coming from somebody who, I had reason to believe, had actually read the classical tragedies (possibly even in Greek!), compensated for the interruption to my sleep.

And it was only the beginning. If reaction to my *Exodus* review could be described as a flood, my piece on the slain president in the role of a tragic hero loosed an avalanche. The reactions came from professors, ordinary readers and guys who made bets in bars. I claim no credit for the hyperbole of praise the article aroused. The president's death had left a wound in the nation's soul. Anything — even a band-aid — would have been appreciated.

In developing his craft, a writer passes through much the same stages as a maturing individual. For the first ten years of my career on the *Sun*, I was like a college boy running recklessly about in search of new experience — from the comradeship of my fellows to love affairs never intended to last.

But with the Kennedy article, I "settled down". Instead of carousing with Banker, Burks, Catling and the like, at the end of the working day I withdrew to my office and gave myself over to consolidating relationship with my true love.

I kept under my desk a large carton, three feet long, two feet wide and two feet deep, in which I deposited the letters I received daily. Whenever I had an extra bit of space I printed them, along with an appropriate comment. Whenever I had an extra bit of time I answered them privately. But this happened all too rarely. I have always been a lousy correspondent.

About once a year I cleaned the box out, emptying its contents into the trash can, not because they lacked merit but simply because the box was full.

People who write letters to newspapers fall into two categories — those who do it once or twice in their lives and those who do it all the time. I had both. Among the former was a delightful Sicilian immigrant who invited me out to his Monkton home for an Italian dinner. I went and the meal, prepared by the host himself, was delicious.

Among the latter were a civic-minded woman who wrote a dozen or so times a year (usually in verse) and a lady long past 70 who wanted me to make a fourth in the group that met with her regularly for bridge.

Such letters, combined with the pieces that prompted them, little by little and totally without design, forged a bond of intimacy between me and the

Baltimore people. And it was this bond that made my latter years on the *Sun* — or until the introduction of the New Regime in the Eighties — a joy.

When I departed on that March day in 1984, the carton was half full. I took it home and set it in a store room where it waits for me to go through it. I doubt that I ever will, for it will bring back times that, because they were so happy, I shall recall with pain.

But there is one batch of letters I cannot consign to the wastebasket — because they triggered probably the biggest *immediate* reaction of any series ever printed in the *Sun*. Brace yourself, dear reader, for the coming of Quakenbush.

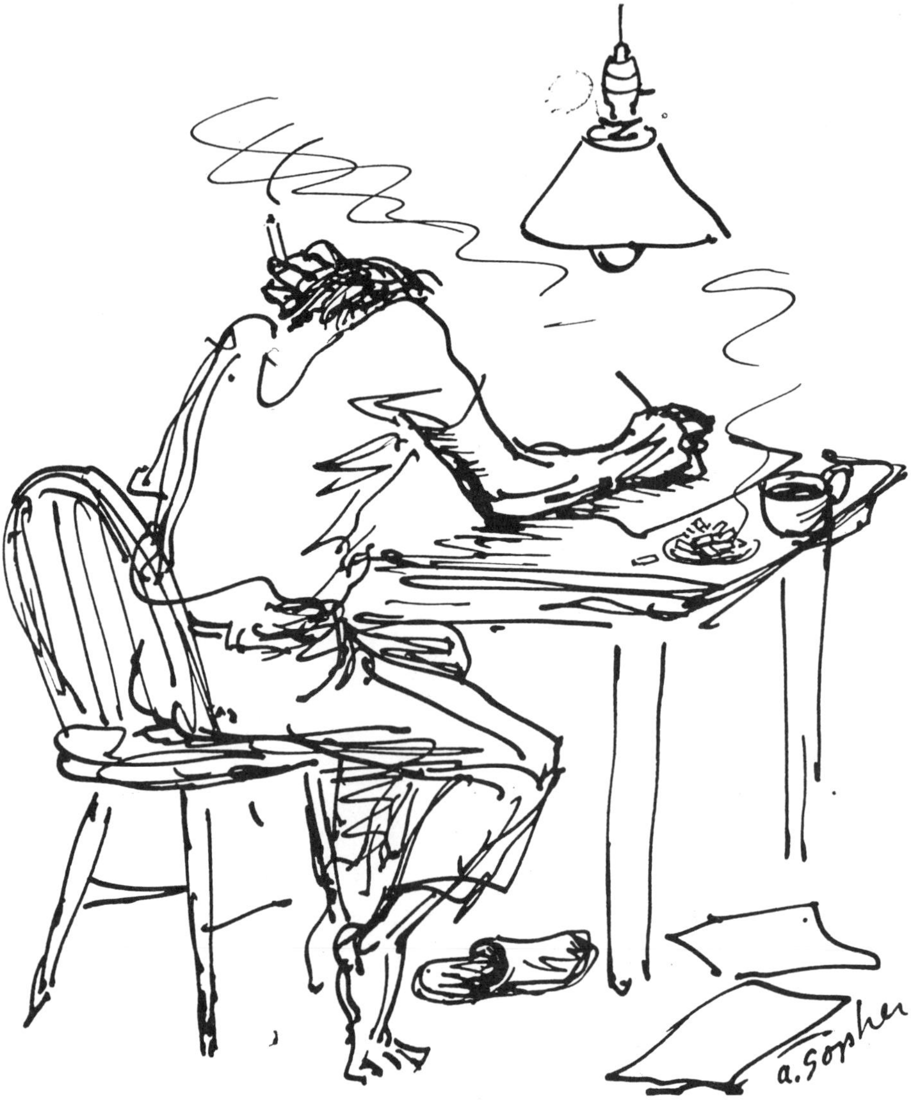
a. Sopher

The Quakenbush Letters

TWENTY-SEVEN

Somewhere around the end of the Fifties the Motion Picture Production Code, which, since the days of the Fatty Arbuckle scandal had determined what could and could not be shown in movie theaters, began to lose authority. Hollywood had originally hoped to combat the competition offered by television with wide-screen spectacle. Now, with the relaxation of censorship, the producers hit upon a cheaper way — the unashamed presentation of — dirt.

In time, film-makers' reliance on "F.F.N." (full frontal nudity), explicit sex and foul language to sell their products reached such nauseous proportions that, by the late Seventies, the trend had begun to turn back upon itself. But in October of 1960, when the following appeared in the Letters-to-the-Editor column of the *Sun*, the possibilities seemed limitless.

Sir:
In these days of sensational and lurid movie advertising complete with illustrations, I find the cinema reporting contained in the Sun *like a breath of fresh air. In my opinion, R. H. Gardner is the greatest. I wouldn't think of attending a show without consulting his column first. This man's gift for separating the worthwhile from the junk is priceless. As far as I am concerned, his views seem to consistently coincide with my own, but in what a hilarious way he can express himself!*

The desire to write a letter like this has been in me each time I have read his material, but after his last two reviews of the current nudist films, I can no longer contain myself. To read the comments of an adult, intelligent mind of candid, casual honesty is really a refreshing way to enjoy a newspaper.

THE LETTER WAS SIGNED A. EMMA ISENNOCK to whom I now tender my sincere and long overdue thanks. One of the reviews to which she referred was printed in the *Sun* of September 30, 1960.

At last the movies have come up with something that may save the industry — nudism!
I'm not one to make predictions, but it's easy to see that the potentialities are vast.
Cinerama, 3-D, VistaVision, bank night — nothing previously resorted to can touch this new development. And as soon as producers familiarize themselves sufficiently with the possibilities to start treating them outside the camps, nudist films may even replace Jack Paar.
*For Members Only, the second such film to play the Century this month, is not quite as nude as the first (*Nature's Paradise*), but what it lacks in authenticity it makes up for in slickness.*
Performances, direction, photography — all are more professional, and the girls are better looking. After that crowd in Nature's Paradise, *I almost gave up nudist films for life.*
The story, which, like Nature's Paradise, *was filmed in England by a British company, concerns a beautiful, thoroughly clothed young lady named Jane (I*

gather from this and Nature's Paradise *that the heroines of all nudist films are called Jane). Her grandfather has just died, leaving her various major industries, an enormous house, a maiden aunt and a nudist camp.*

Actually, he doesn't leave her the camp. He leaves her the ground on which the camp is situated and which he, a confirmed nudist, has leased to the members.

Well, Jane doesn't like the idea of all those undressed uglies (she may have seen Nature's Paradise*) cavorting over her nice land. So she refuses to renew the camp's lease.*

This naturally upsets the nudists who send the camp director, a nice-looking chap who has a real way with women, with or without their clothes on, to plead with her. You'll never guess what happens next.

Carried away by the director's arguments, Jane becomes a nudist herself. And a fine one she makes, too! But that's not the finish. A jealous female nudist almost sabotages Jane's and the director's romance before it gets off the ground so to speak. But the maiden aunt speeds to the rescue, and the film fades out on Jane and the director barefooting it together into the sunset — or, rather, the swimming pool, which is where everybody in nudist films ends up.

There is some skill in the handling of the story. The camera alternates between scenes in the camp and scenes shot elsewhere —such as Jane's office, her home and the director's apartment. As a result, you never know when a scene opens whether the characters are going to have their clothes on or off.

This builds suspense.

The whole thing, I suppose, represents a breakthrough in the commercial movie field, and I anticipate a long string of similar items. We'll have nudist murder films ("The Case of the Unconcealed Motive"), socially significant nudist films ("Nudists Are People") and romantic nudist films ("The Bride Wore Nothing! *").*

Art marches on.

THERE'S AN OLD STORY ABOUT A CECIL B. DEMILLE SPECTACULAR in which a sinful woman (a must in any DeMille movie) lay on a couch and nibbled at a bunch of grapes. The director had a pre-existing notion of how the grapes should look when squashed against the actress's lips. He tried all kinds of fruit — plums, mangoes, persimmons. Nothing seemed right.

Finally an assistant director had a radical idea. "Why not use *grapes*?

The obvious way to compete with television would have been to make a better product but, as indicated by the above story, Hollywood has rarely in such situations chosen the obvious. Still, a small number of superior films did manage to sneak through. One, which opened in Baltimore in October of 1961, was Robert Rosen's *The Hustler*.

Based upon a Walter Tevis novel, *The Hustler* concerned a small-time pool-player named Eddie who makes his living bilking other pool-players unaware that he is a "shark." The story revolves around his efforts to beat Minnesota Fats, the greatest hustler of them all. As played by Paul Newman (Eddie), Jackie Gleason (Fats), George C. Scott (the gambler backing Fats) and Piper Laurie (Eddie's pathetic girlfriend), the film under Mr. Rosen's direction was outstanding, and I said as much in my review. Several days after its appearance on October 28, 1961 I received a letter written in pencil on pages torn from a ten-cent-store tablet. They had been crammed into a small envelope which bore stamps all across the front. None of the stamps had been cancelled. The letter had not been sent through the mail but had been delivered to the *Sun* building by somebody in person.

>Dear Sir:
>Your latest review on *The Hustler* was very accurate and good. I know you will understand what I'm going to say better than me but here it is.
>Since seeing the movie *The Hustler* and being a two-bit pool hustler myself I was able to see what a good relistic movie is supposed to be, and its this.
>Those who are acquainted with the pool world know that its no "Minnesota Fats" or "Fast Eddie" and the other characters to the dercree they were depicted in The Hustler.
>But since the movie was put up with realistic imagination and a lot of art, these people who are not acquainted with the pool world was made richer by thinking that interesting-fascinated people might live somewhere in this world that they had not known about before.
>We all know movies can never show life as it really is. It has to blow it up like 50 times or more and if it is done with realistic imagination plus intertainting the audience can at least say it could be true or if you approve of the world it was depicting you could say I wish it was that way.
>American art such as the movies is moving in such slow pace because the artist never convey what he sees. He only convey what the public see,
>But this movie the artist or director convey what he saw.
>You probably have brought these little points out many times. I just thought I would say it in my own way.
>Some producer said that movies were like sex — none bad but some better than others.
>I don't quit agree with him.
>Thank you

THE LETTER — which bore the return address of a Park Avenue grocery store just around the corner from Martick's — was signed Lorry Quackenbush. Or was it Quakenbush? The question, arising out of the illegibility of my correspondent's handwriting, only added to the general mystery surrounding him in the days that followed. At the moment, unable to discern any suggestion of a "C" between the "A" and "K," I decided to settle for Quakenbush.

But of more interest to me than how he spelled his name was Quakenbush's motivation. Did I not detect a sharp edge of sophistication beneath the softness of his seeming naivete? All that stuff about "realistic imagination" and the probability that I had "brought these little points out many times!" Was he kidding me?

Still, for whatever the reason, he had caught my attention in the way he distinguished between life, as it is, and the illusion of life, as it exists on the stage — one of the more subtle concepts in dramatic philosophy. There is perhaps only one more subtle — the part played by the actor in creating the illusion. This he chose to dispose of in his second letter, which followed immediately after I had responded to the first.

> Dear Sir:
> Thanks for answering my letter. I knew you would understand the real life angle. And thanks for amplifying on it.
> You made it clearer than ever for me.
> I was proud to show your letter to my friends as I happen to like Randolph Scott movies and espiccally the English war desert movies where they throw that plaster on everybody and they come through so palatable so condersiding I hardly knew what a movie critic was before I came out of the hills of N.C. to this Displace Person Camp for southern hillbillys (Yes, there are other kinds) you can see why I was proud.
> Some seems to think that if you like a Randolph Scott movie you couldn't possibly like *Summertime* or *La Strata*.
> Naturally no one take most of the movies serouis, but some seem to be easily anoyed if most of the movies they see are not real good. I have a few stray thoughts on the movies.
> Here they are.
> I think one reason movies stars as a whole do not have as sharp dramatic personality as some of those in the past such as Wallace Berry, Clark Gable and others is that while they was young and their personality was being developed it was forged from life and everyday working people as they had no movies stars *to* draw from as today movies stars unconiously must draw from the movies and T.V. stars so to some decree they will be just an extentsion of past movies stars along with what they bring new to the stage.
> The Phillipines actors has taken on American traits more than others nationality. Thats to be expected.
> I say no one can define what a actor is. We can only reconize it when you see it.
> Just when I think I will be able to come close to express what I think a actor is, it slips away from me.
> So I will stick to comments
> I thought this after seeing Burt Lancaster in *Elmer Gantry*. His hollering and shouting was zeroed into what we thought an evangelist would act like.
> He would let up just when, if he push the ham another inch it would be unbecoming or have a tendency to embarrass the audience as James Dean did by making you fill a little naked in one of his performances.

And since he was portraying a dubious character he had to work on the borderline of becoming vulgar. But he was so crisply in tone that he seemed to make the right gesture, raise or lower his voice just when the audience expected it.

I know all this is simple stuff to you. But since the role was so vivid marked for contrast I was able to see the mechanical unfolding that goes with a good performance. Naturally I have seen some more artful performance such as Peter Finch —*Nun Story* — Arthur Kennedy —*Trial.*

Please remember I am just a hillbilly not a movie critic, and I am not trying to be smart by using left hand english.

Sometime you might comment on the movies and say its not worth $1.25 but I wouldn't miss it for 50c at your neighborhood movie house where it will be shown on a douable bill (I know that would be unethical) but thats where I see all my movies and condersiding all the trouble they went to, to make them I am easily please with the 50c bargain.

No I am not a great movie fan (I wonder why people are so anxious to put that in) you would think so by this rambling on.

This is the reason I was moved to write you. I have a intelligent friend with good taste. He develops this attitude toward you. He said Mike Todd bought you on the *80 Days Around the World* review.

You shouldn't have compared so much of the movie *Exodus* with the book. You should have stuck to the artistic value of the movie.

And then when you gave *The Hustler* a good write up you lost him for good.

The funny part about all this is that he sincere believe what he says. I do not think any of the accustment is true.

I respect his taste and do not understand how he could be so far off. I guess thats always been the $64 qustion when somebody disagrees with our own taste.

Since this was said by a drama critic, the late George Jean Nathan, thought you would like it. He said he dranked so other people would seem interesting.

He also said life was a treadmill to oblivion.

Hope to see a stage show some day as I enjoy your review on them.

Thank you
Lorry Quakenbush

TWENTY-EIGHT

Quakenbush's second letter had arrived in an envelope identical with the first except that all the uncanceled stamps were on the back and had been used to secure the flap the way people use Christmas seals. Whether it was the stamps or the remarks about Randolph Scott I don't know, but for a moment I suddenly felt what I imagined Balboa must have felt when he first sighted the Pacific.

I carried the pile of pages — curled up by double folding and held together with safety pins — down the corridor to Dorsey's office. At that time of day before the sun had gotten anywhere near the yardarm, the managing editor was inclined to be testy. He glared at the smudgy mess I placed on the desk before him. "Cleaning out your wastebasket?" he inquired.

"Mr. Dorsey, I'd like you to take a look at this."

He poked a cautious finger into the pile, as if fearing something might jump out at him. I leaned over and flattened the first letter. "It begins here."

I watched his expression change as he began to read. After a while, he sat back with a grunt. "So?"

"I want to do an in-depth piece on him."

Dorsey stared at me for a moment, then rose to his feet — a trick he often employed to get rid of people. "Why not? He's obviously a fascinating character."

Returning to my typewriter, I began to compose another letter to Quakenbush. I said that he displayed a native wisdom that, combined with his talent for expressing it, had aroused both my admiration and curiosity. Would he please tell me something about himself — his background, his education, his ambitions? I also suggested his spelling might be improved.

I heard nothing for ten days — so long, in fact, that I began to think I had offended him. Then an outsized envelope arrived with seven stamps (canceled this time) on the back and a post-office notation on the front that 12 cents more was due.

In addition to the thick letter, which consisted of a complete 25-cent tablet including the pasteboard covers, the envelope contained two enclosures. One appeared to be an unpublished short story written in Lorry's now-familiar scrawl; the other was an anecdote culled from his past.

> A few winters back when I had just come to Baltimore to look for a job, I found myself with only 50 cents and hungry. So I decided to go to one of those all-night movies they had at that time, instead of paying the 50 cents for a flop.
>
> I went to the movies, but being tired, I took my shoes off and fell asleep.
>
> When I waked up, it was 4 o'closk and the movies was getting ready to close.
>
> My shoes had been stolen, and no one was left in the theater but a moronic doorman. I told him what had happened.

He looked at me and said: "I'm not sure you had any shoes on when you came in here." That did it. I ran out in the street where snow was on the ground.

No stores were open. I took off walking to the bus station, realizing this as the beginning of my Valley Forge.

At the bus station I played cat-and-mouse with the police guard till daybreak. A fellow gave me an old sweater that I tore in half and put on my feet. He told me to go to St. Vincent de Paul on Fallsway and Baltimore streets where I could get some shoes free.

When I arrived numb, they treated me kindly and gave me shoes and threw in an overcoat to boot.

When I bent over to tie my shoes on, I thought about Vivien Leigh in *Gone with the Wind* when she had got back to Tara broke and hungry and reached down to dig a turnip out of the ground.

She said: "God as my witness, if I have to steal, lie or murder, I'll never go hungry again."

My situation did not call for these strong words. But I did say:

"God as my witness, I will never take my shoes off in a movie again."

I COULD NOT HELP NOTICING THAT THE LETTER, which I read next, had been carefully written compared to its predecessors: the penmanship was more legible and, with the exception of a few special problems, the writer exhibited an awareness of the refinements of spelling that was for him quite impressive. I concluded that he had spent a large part of the ten-day interval with a dictionary.

Dear Mr. Gardner:
Your letter with all that flattering sure was nice to the ears. I had the feeling you were talking about somebody else. This is one appraisal where I don't agree with you. (Is it any use to say I am trying to be modest?)

That intellectual friend of mine had this to say about your letter.

Since its your job to criticize movies continuously, when you get a chance to praise something with no artistic taste or judgment at stake, you go overboard. But he always analyzes every hello — to every goodbye.

I have another friend with the taste of a water buffalo who says you were drunk when you wrote that letter.

I think you sensed I needed it and took liberty with your flattering remarks.

I will try to tailor my thoughts to and arround the movies and answer your request by brushing around my life a little.

I saw this in one of those Joseph Levine Italian made pictures. The plot was set in Russia. At the end it actually showed John Derek and his girl riding off into the sunset in a troika.

Zane Grey probably had a guy like Randolph Scott in mind when he was describing the cowboys of the old west. But Scott not being able to act it blends in with the setting and dialog of his movies.

I have tried to buy Frank Sinatra, but i cannot completely buy him. In all his heavy dramatic performances, there is spots in his acting that is not convinceing at all. His over-all performance in musicals is O.K.

I wonder why they are afraid to show bad teeth in those realistic movies. All real cowboys had bad teeth in those days — but not Lancaster and Douglas. Susan Hayward in *I'llCry Tomorrow* had been drinking everything from sterno to sneaky pete but her teeth was still beautiful. If you remember some close ups of some old newsreel shots of Ike before he became president and got some new lower teeth his was black with tobacco tar. Yet the public bought him.

(Not that I am for bad teeth.)

How about Harry Morgan the judge in *Inherit the Wind* and every week playing whatever that is on TV *Gladys and Pete*? He used to be good as the 9th supporting actor.

In all those interviews of actors they all emphasize how they got to make it while they are young. They never seem to have that old fashioned simpleness and courage or dedication to mention for the sake of art. They remind me of Truman talking about the life taking job of the president.

Its old actors and ex-presidents wherever you look.

They should take note from Paul Muni where he would go off and take inventory of himself and try to regenerate that feeling for the real flow of life, or whatever good actors do to improve and grow in stature for his next role — instead of walking through one role to the next to get that money.

One realistic director doesn't let his leading man or woman eat for a day or two before playing a deep love scene. His theory is that hunger for food shows the same expression in the eyes as hunger for love. (He might have something there, since hunger is probably the only real basic feeling there is.)

For the last few pages its been like Psychiatry, tedious theorizing. Now for a few words on my life.

No family, 40 years old, born and raised in small town in N.C., quit school in 6th grade, bummed around the country — caddy, caddy master, odd jobs, the army for four years.

The army was my finest hour because I was part of a cause that was working toward something that was bigger than my own selfish needs and desires.

Only when you are doing something at great personal sacrifice with an unselfish cause for your goal do you rise above your petty self.

(Not that I was a good soldier or did I think like this when I was in the army. Its only when thinking back, I have these thoughts.)

Your pursuit have a noble overtone about it. You are pursuing Artistic Truth, at least as you see it.

Back to my life, out of the army feeling like I would never be fully organized again. (Yes I was shooke up.)

Worked auto parts clerk, pool room, farm, odd jobs. But more personal freedom kept tugging at me — so I took up bootlegging whisky in my small town where I would be my own boss.

I was too much of a success at it.

I kept getting more and more customers and looking out for the law with one eye and the customers with the other and trying to keep up with it all was like fighting a forest fire with an eye dropper.

Spent the fast money on women and gambling.

The whole thing didn't set right with me so I quit.

I should say something about women along here. I was very unlucky in the romance field.

Every woman I ran into said I love you just the way you are and even if you were a ditchdigger I would still love you. What they meant was that if I became the foreman of the crew next week, the supervisor the next month, and then climb Mt. Everrett in my tennis shoes.

Now fisxation has set in in the romance field and my greatest dream of finding a mate is gradually dissolving in mid air.

So I headed north to the big city of Baltimore. Got jobs at the Martin aircraft plant, a bakery, Crown Cork and Seal, attendant at mental hospital. Worked at the hospital 8 months. Felt useful and needed.

Up to this point I had been in Baltimore about 4 years and coming out of those factories feeling like a dish rag after work with no energy left to be a person. And at the hospital some of that atmosphere was beginning to rub off on me.

So I thought I would escape from it all and become a seaman. If I had been tough enough thats where I would have stayed. Shipped for two years.

This brings me up to about 4 years ago.

Now I have heard that most people become a success because they could not sustain themselves on the bottom.

I am not flying under any beatnik flag. I think conformity is a nice word.

However if you have really wanted to and tried to walk in tune with the majority but finding it goes against the grain so much you don't feel like you can survive without becoming something you can't stand. Then you have to walk some other trail. Then maybe you are somekind of a true nonconformity.

But never do I for one moment forget the millions of conformity peoples that take on responsibility — jobs — children — (writers even meeting deadlines) and at times have strong desires to shake it all and become a bum like me but so many things are involved and that feeling of character deep down make them push on.

This trite remark might wrap up this non-conformity and conformity angle — You can't have the cake and eat it too.

Now this bring me up to the present and the last four years.

I am a bushwack pool hustler, dish washer and odd jobs man.

I still feel like I am on the front line but in this front line of life you need a million green points before they will rotate you to the rear for some rest.

But I am fairly contented and reasonably miserable.

I have no illusion of being or want to be a writer. These letters pacify what little urge I have to write.

These letters are the maximum of my talent not the minimum.

What the Letters to the Editor of your paper wants is beautifully constructed sentences more than anything else.

I sent them a good letter on defending Eugene O'Neill *Iceman Cometh* when it was shown on TV and was called trash by some people. I forget what I said but it ran something like this:

It was like a great surgeon cutting deeper and deeper into the body and naming the parts as he went along. The message I got was we all need illusion, and if we saw our self as we relly were, few of us would have the courage to live.

Yes, the dialog and setting was crude but that was his vehicle to make his thoughts come across vivid and clear.

The genius of the craftsmanship of it all was so great you were not offended at all by the crude setting and dialog.

To bring this over clear so a simple man like me could understand it, along with the sweeping and breathtaking dialog made it the best TV show I have ever seen.

(Who knows his message might have been pushing atheism, communism, socialism or why Greek fell.)

As Bertram Russell says, the trouble with this world is that the stupid people are cocksure and the intelligent ones are full of doubts.

I get the feeling I am beginning to sound like a room full of Una Merkles.

So I will try to find an ending along here somewhere.

I brushed over my life a little to try to show you some thread of my philosophy if I have any at all.

I am afraid this twisted remark may fit me — Once you look deep down in him he is rather shallow.

Now all personal previous information was for me to be able to say and know you would unterstand this — I have no desire to meet you, as any contact with success stimulates me and I don't like that feeling.

I have been writing about a year and only when thoughts slips out natural are they worth anything. Any design behind my writing seems to make the whole thing unbecoming.

To give you somekind of jagged background on my little non-designed education, it consists of newspapers, TV, five books — and life.

The Unknown Lincoln.

The Hustler. (It was better than the movie. The only thing I thought I could come close to knowing enough about to write anything on was the pool world. And I used to tinker with the thought of someday winding up in a veterans psycho ward and collaborating with Pete Martin and write a book on it. But Walter Tevis said everything I could have said and a hundred times better than I could have, and I am sure the world can do with one book less.)

Moss Hart Act One.

Mine Enemy Grows Older — Alex King.

And Bridge to Victory.

I am going to pull a Garbo on you and get extremely corny and say again I have no desire to meet you.

Merry Christmas
Lorry Quakenbush

THIS LETTER — WHICH ARRIVED DURING CHRISTMAS WEEK, 1961 — had a depressing effect on me. To begin with, there was the rather pathetic picture it presented of a man whom I had never met but had developed more than a measure of affection for. Secondly, there was the unintentional irony in the implications concerning the great "success" I enjoyed as a writer. In an effort to get my mind off such matters I turned quickly to the envelope's third item, entitled "High Noon at the Bus Station."

This known bad nervy bum had been thrown out of the bus station hundreds of times before.

This night the manager spotted him as he weaved cockily through the door..

The cockily stride inspire the manager to give him the De Luxe bums rush.

The manager grabbed him in the seats of his pants without saying a word and rushed him back through the door into the street.

The humiliated bum falls on his knees reaching in his ragged coat using a Wyatt Earp draw as if he was drawing a gun and with a Humphrey Bogart snarled he says — You have thrown me out for the last time. I am going to blow you to kingdom come.

The manager fear strickin jumped behind a post. About this time the bum has drawn his weapon that turns out to be half filled wine bottle that loses its cap and is dripping wine. He points the bottle toward the half hidden manager and says — bang! — bang?

Lorry Quakenbush

TWENTY-NINE

After reading "High Noon at the Bus Station," I thought I could see what Quakenbush meant when he complained that "any design behind my writing seems to make the whole thing unbecoming." I wondered if I weren't unintentionally contributing to his difficulties by making him feel self-conscious about his creative powers. I decided not to answer this latest and most ambitious of his letters for a while in hopes that a fallow period might in the long run prove beneficial to us both.

My concern, as it turned out, was unnecessary. Two days later I received another bulging envelope bearing eight stamps none of which had been canceled.

I will kick this 4th letter off [it began] with the old saying "Blessed are they who have nothing to say and who cannot be persuaded to say it."

Now since I am not one of the blessed ones, you have flattered me into putting down some more little thoughts, as they were beginning to backwater on me and it has manifest into me writing these letters on the subject.

I am thankful you have given me the opportunity to let these thoughts light against an appreciative understanding mind.

Actors have to see them self very much as other people see them. Thats a pretty good passport into being in tune with people.

Its one of the better traits of an actor because only when you see yourself correctly in your relationship to others do you have that fine sensitive personality we all admire. (I don't mean the type that sensitive to only the things that bother him.)

A good artist in his work sense things that most people have heard or seen before. Before they do or say anything they think is interesting and the more closely he is in tune with what is new and what is not new, the more vivid he comes through. (Yes, thats old stuff but I wanted to say it again.)

Question?

How old are you? How much do you suffer compared to other people as a whole — more, about the same, less, don't have the faintest idea?

You are the only artist I have ever made any contact with, so I was wondering how much a real artist suffer. I am not trying to inject that I am somekind of corny suffering artist — although in my past life the pangs of existing was so sharp I had to walk some unbecoming trail I thought to survive. I am sure that everyone more or less has gone through that.

My definition of a writer is that he says things clear and simple what other people have vaguely thought about. (I still don't think of myself as a writer.)

I think one thing that the people of the mountains of N.C. have over Baltimoreans is that they feel a conscious or unconscious duty to least grope and to show some effort to be in tune with part and parcel with the whole picture.

I am not talking about just education. By just feeling that feeling is better than being educated without that in tune feeling.

Even if they are illiterates and scorn education, for some strange reason that in tune desire seems to be stronger with mountain people than those in Baltimore.

(Probably just my imagination.)

— or could it be the closeness of nature?

On TV Playhouse 90 there was a scene where the star player was very upset and was walking along a river.

The next scene a sea diver was showed coming up out of the water.

I thought the star had commited suicide and they was dragging the river for his body until the diver took his helmut off and said "I keep my hair in place by using Vitalis Hair Tonic."

Then it dawn on me they had gone right into a commercial at a dramatic spot in the story.

I know you must think I see a lot of movies. What it mostly is that I have a pretty good memory and like to kick things arround on all subjects.

(A bad memory and good health is the main ingredients of a contented mind says Dr. Schweitzer.)

When you said write again it was like the first time I walked into a big downtown department store. Not acquainted with the modern ways of the big city and after I purchased my article the saleslady says "Do you wish to charge it?"

I thought do I look that honest or what is it?

Contrast is the truest form of art there is.

I was sitting in Bickford one Sunday morning thinking of the dullness of it all surrounded by the town cream of misfits with the Blue Danube being piped in over the rattling of the dishes and other people conversation when I spotted a lovely woman and a man with three kids having breakfast.

The woman turn to the kids with the projection of a June Allyson and says "Isn't this exciting?"

Breakfast in Bickford exciting! She must have a wonderful imagination or her life was dull. (Bad example but you get the point.) I could spare you this trite saying but I won't — Without bad we wouldn't know what is good.

You ask me my ambition.

It is to become a contented person. I know thats a hellva Vincent Peale type of answer to give.

I have no ambition to my knowledge. I have only joined two things in my life — the human race and the U.S. Army both without my consent.

And as Groucho Marx said I would join no club that would have me as a member.

So you can see I am somekind of unintentionally lone wolf but above all lasy.

Each one of my letters on any subject I hope is the last one, and I will be convinced that I have nothing else to say of any inteerst any more to anybody.

We will be getting some international stars from Japan with the mix breeding resulting from the occupation. It always increase the chances of producing unique people. Tony Quinn, half Irish and half Mexican, Yul Brynner — and many others. (Half Irishman and half American like J.F.K. makes a little frighten combination. He is an eloqunet man and I think he will make a good President if that Irish blood and guts dont get us killed.)

Up to about 50 years ago it was a lot of white and colored mixing.
But for the last three generations the Negro has frown on other Negroes marrying whites. (I guess they are getting even with our past injustice on them by this behavior.) Now I am for all forms of integration (You have to always get that in you know that).

You can keep these letters as long as you want to and do whatever you want to with them. But when you are finish with them please send them back to me.
I want to keep up with what I have covered on the movies as I am writing on other subjects and if I write you again I don't want to bore you with any repeats.
If you have thrown them away I will unterstand and do not give it a second thought.
The questions I asked you was for clinical reason not personal.
(I guess I know what I mean by clinical reason.)

I wonder why they don't use 5 minutes to 12 for a title of a movie. Hitler always ended most of his speeches with that 5 to 12. It meant we have not got much time left.
They have used *12 O'clock High, 3:10 to Yuma*, etc.
Time always makes for suspense.
As someone said the time piece is civilization hand cuff.
Naturally Hitler was terrible. But he was the most dramatic person I have ever seen on the screen.

Now I am allowed one more old saying. Do life draw from the theater or do the theater draw from life?
I think both is interwoven but having a good feel of both but instincly knowing where one stop and the other begin is a mark of a great actor.
Because remember both is in man's mind and knowing what man thinks is the theater and what he thinks is life is the key to a good actor.

Politicians seem to have that instincly feeling such as Roosevelt, Hitler, Wilke, Huey Long and many others.

The movies can well absorb one Joseph Levine but someday they may get one too many and you might be out of a job and if you take up pool hustling I probably will meet you along the trail somewhere. Now for the ending.

Since the big thread of these letters is woven arround the movies I should be allowed to end it by saying — As the sun sinks slowly in the west we will say faerwell to the wonderful natives of Baltimore.

Lorry Quakenbush

I HAD REASON TO RECALL THE SUGGESTION that I might ultimately be reduced to pool hustling when, a few days after receiving the above letter, I became the object of a heated attack in the *Sun*'s letter column because of my unfavorable review of a Broadway bound play called *The Captains and the Kings*.

Theater-hungry Baltimoreans had loved this ill-fated melodrama, which presented on a level not far above that of television soap opera some of the problems faced by the naval officer responsible for the development of this country's first nuclear-powered submarine. Consequently my description of it as "another one of those plays in which everybody shouts at everybody all the time" had aroused a vehement, if short-lived, storm of protest.

One woman, outraged by my cynical and unpatriotic approach to the matter, had gone so far as to compare me to the play's most unattractive character — a man who, in his determination to discredit the courageous and idealistic hero, had shown himself to be not only cynical and unpatriotic, but also vicious, hysterical, perverted and ugly.

It was to this letter that the opening remarks of Quakenbush's fifth were addressed.

Because she thought it was a good play, her main point was that every American should see it because every advancement our country has made was due to the consecration of some man to an idea ahead of his time and for the good of his country.

This is wonderful but for every Billy Mitchell and Hyman Rickover there are thousands of psychos. I guess that was brought out in the play.

Every nut thinks he is ahead of his time and his idea is good for the country. Time is the only thing that tell the good ideas from the bad ones.

To find out about this sifting out process with all this to come through to her brand new and thinking it was good theater then striking a personal blow at you for not liking it, I will have to answer her this way.

She is probably a college graduate, well read, intelligent, unworldly person. And when she is not reading or discussing life she must be wrapped up in cellophane on a mantlepiece.

It moved her so much she wanted you to buy it a 100 per cent.

I was glad you brought out that shouting. (In Raisin in the *Sun* Sidney Poitier got out of bed hollering and nobody stopped till the movie was over.)
Take a nut throwing a fit in a mental hospital, he comes through sharp, alive and loud. But not much what he says is clear or at all palatable.
A good actor being directed by a good director shooting the same scene in the theater conveys the thoughts in the dialog with palatable and clearness and above all he is hooked in with the same mood that the audience is in.
Now to deal with any subject and fulfil the audience appetite you must wrap up the subject, pro and con, by reaching a point where most intelligent have reached, as not to leave loop holes for your audience to cut the subject apart.

Now I don't have the slightest idea how much of this aplyies to *Captains of the Kings,* as I did not see it.

I am looking forward to seeing the movie *Long Day Journey into Night.* I imagine its going to be a lot of hollering but I am sure it will be done artful with O'Neill inspiration behind it.

I kept this letter reasonable short as I am trying to kick this writing habit. Naturally I didn't send it to your letters to the editors as I have given them the gate.

I thought for something to merit being printed you kind of had to tell the truth and it must not be quite common knowledge. I was always under the impression that this was the gauge they used. But I am learning fast.
    So long
    Lorry Quakenbush

THIRTY

By now I had decided how the story on Quakenbush should be handled. I wanted to publish the letters, bad grammar, misspellings and all. And, in that it returned to the subject of *The Hustler,* thus bringing our correspondence full circle, his next seemed a logical place to stop.
 It also provided a surprise twist by revealing that Quakenbush's initial remarks about the film had been made without his actually having seen it.

My first comments on *The Hustler* was based on what I had heard and read from reviews such as yours and as I said before your review was good and accurate from a critic and art viewpoint.

I had to wait and see it at the neighborhood theater.

The movie as a whole was good and as you said the director Robert Rossen should be commented for putting it together. It was remarkable that he was able to put some sustance to such a lose theme as pool hustling (although he had a good book for a guideline).

The characters in the movie was tough roles to play because the actors didn't have other movies to draw from as these characters had never been done before in the movies.

Now I am going to critizied the movie from a pool player angle.

The movie said and emphasies pool was a art — so naturally you couldn't give a few week of lessons to Paul Newman and make him come through as a artist and a great pool player.

His performance was good and only a pool player would have picked out this and the handling of the cue stick flaws.

I am sure the flaws in the cue stick handling was not picked up or expected to be picked up by most people because he only handled the cue stick in the *clear* when he was supposed to be *stalling*. When he was opening up the camera was rather sneaky as it was really the world champion pool player Willie Mosconi shooting.

I am pointing out where I can see where the movie was good and realistic to most people but knowing so much about pool it was hard for them to keep the illusion up to par *for* me.

Jackie Gleason was the only actor in the movie with a real life pool room background and it showed up in the movie.

When the camera showed Gleason shooting pool you felt like he had gotten inside the game and knew what he was doing. Gleason was good.

His main job was to fill out the image of the dialouge spoken about "Mininirsoto Fats" and to bring that image to life by his pool playing and behaiver and as you said his restraint was wonderful.

His suit was the unsung hero of the movie.

The rack man was good. He was able to get his chest, shoulders and face in every rack as he wanted to get in the game so bad. The last thing he pulled out when lifting the rack was his eye glasses.

The scene at Arthurs Pool Room where they broke Newmans fingers was very flat.

The hustler that kept calling him friend was terrible. He looked bored and wanted to get away from it all. He was supposed to have worked "Fast Eddie" up so much that he opened up on him and got his fingers broke.

(In the book this was a good scene. The local hustler would sneer at the 9 ball before sinking it.)

I wish I had seen the movie when it was freshed in your mind.

I hope I don't seem contradictory when I said in my first letter it was a good movie and left the impression I saw it. These criticsm is from the pool playing angle.

A bushwack pool player means one good enough to ambush and beat a average player but not good enough to beat a real good player. I am a bushwack hustler.

In my previous letters I thought I convinced you that by only telling at least 90 per cent of the truth about my life would I come through with any freshness attached to it because surely you have been expose to proffessional material and plenty of sophistication.

But I will try to show you again where pool hustling fits into my existence.

As we know no one can make a living solely hustling pool. I said I did odd jobs — racking balls, washing dishes, etc. And consirdering I live on $22 a week it does play a little part in my existence.

Now this life was a drifting process. But pool hustling has always been interwoved in my life — even when I was shipping, working at the hospital, aircraft plant, etc.

Its a toss up in our society which is the lowest a pool hustler or a horse tout.

Both are two inches below whale manure. In the female society a slut is a pool hustlers counterpart.

Please don't get me mixed up with real good pool players because whatever society thinks of them they are exceptional people.

John McGraw, the late manager of the N.Y. Giants, said it took more raw nerve to be a good pool player than any other sport.

Other sports you can run off the physical tension. Pool is the least supervised. A lot of friction and distraction is attached to it and the buzzards on the roost don't help any.

(This reminds me when I caddied as a kid for those phony bankers and bussniss men, when they were putting I had to stand back from the green so my growling hungry stomach would not bother them as they were playing for 10c a hole. I have shot 9 balls in with Elvis Presley whaling on the radio, pin ball machines going and psychos wandering around the table.)

I am coming to the end of the trail.

I have run out of pool rooms in Baltimore and I don't have the spirit to try some other place. I tried New York a few years back and the biggest of it all overpowered me. I did not know whether to jump in front of the subways or to ride in them.

You ask if I make a living shooting pool.

I make 5 or 6 dollars a week and that help me to exist. Buy it if you want to. Remember you asked the question.

I am glad you didn't ask an important and the oldest mankind question such as why the distribution of our wealth is not more evenly distributed.

Now every social improvement we have made has been through liberal legislation. Soon as most people get a taste of success they are afraid that to much liberal legislation will jeopardise their hard-won position — so they fall back on the old theory that if you make it to easy you will destroy individuality initiative.

My theory is that more people fell at the wayside from the strain of trying.

My theory is that it should be arranged that nobody could go below a certain standard, then after that they would be on their own. You would still have plenty of margin left for all that individuality initiative and the strain to keep up with the Jones.

But since I love individuality freedom I guess its best the way it is now — so we are back where we started.

No I am not a socialist but I do agree with Carl Sandburg when he said Ike is a good noble man but he has never had to wonder where his next meal or suit was coming from since the time he went to West Point. Yet he drags his feet in that social liberalization angle saying you shouldn't make it to easy for people it will spoil them.

I don't know whos right or wrong. All I know is that government is run by people and people are full of flaws. But regardless a politician is still pursuiting a noble pursuit and some do become noble.

(Yes I can become corny about other things than movies.)

Everybody from two bit actors to Fulton Sheen becomes a genious at explaining and making it convincing on how through hard work and determination and a little luck they became the success they are. It takes a lot of luck and the right amount of work and to those who say luck played only a small part in their success I will say to them they was lucky that they didn't need much luck to be a success.

Probably from this letter I sound like one of them last Angry Young Men or a very mixed up man.

Its a little of both. But I feel more mixed up than I do angry.

And if I was too harsh on them pool hustlers in the movie its kind of like you if you was writing about critics. But I am afraid. And forgive me for even remembering this but it explain my attitude toward men in general — in *Suddenly Last Summer* where one of the actors said the history of any man is just one long line of debris.

I say again keep these letters as long as you want to and do with them whatever you want to but when you finish send them back. And now I will say I hope for the last time so long as I am trying hard to kick this writing habit.

Lorry Quakenbush

THUS ENDED — FOR A WHILE — THE QUAKENBUSH LETTERS.

THIRTY-ONE

I spent every spare minute the next week deciphering, editing and typing the letters. It was, to put it mildly, a job!

Then, having reduced the messy pile to a neat one — held together this time with paper clips — I went again to Dorsey's office.

"The story on Quakenbush," I said, handing him the fruits of my labors. "To be printed as is."

He ran his eyes over the first page.

"Absolutely not!"

"But Buck —" I hoped familiarity might breed a more receptive attitude on his part. "This is literature — sort of."

"So is *Huckleberry Finn*, but you'd never get it past the proof room."

I knew what he meant. The proof room had a nasty habit of overlooking the most obvious errors while catching any intentional one a reporter might try to sneak in.

"Understand, I've got nothing against Quakenbush," he said, as I gathered up my papers preparatory to departing. "I like his style. But those letters don't belong in a daily paper."

So I boxed up the manuscript and sent it to my agent, who spent the better part of a year peddling it to magazines. They liked everything about it but the length. After a while, I gave up. Quakenbush and I had tried but we'd failed. Then Banker returned from Europe.

He had replaced Ed Young as city editor when the latter left for a better job on the *Providence Journal*. Then, as another step up the ladder toward managing editor, he had accepted the post as chief of the *Sun*'s Rome bureau. Such assignments lasted a maximum of three years, so in 1962 he came back to resume his responsibilities on the city desk.

Like most returnees from the *Sun*'s foreign bureaus, he was looking for greater opportunities than those offered by straight reporting of local news. We were having a late drink at the Calvert one night when I began talking about Quakenbush. He asked if he could see the letters,

Those were the days when I spent most of my after-midnight hours in the office working on my book. I said if he was really interested I could go back to the paper and get him a copy. Around 3:30, as I sat at my desk writing something about *Hamlet*, the phone rang. "Hal," said Banker in a quiet, purposeful voice, "I want this."

"What are you going to do with it?"

"Put it on the back page."

"But Dorsey has already said no."

"Don't worry about Dorsey. Just get it into a shape where we can print it in four installments."

So I spent another gruelling period of reorganization and, even worse, retyping. But I got through it.

Francis Whittie was night make-up man, a liaison position between those who wrote the paper on the fifth floor and those who put it together on the fourth. His duties included deciding what lines should be cut from stories too long to fit into the spaces provided for them. As such, he occupied a key position in my life, and I lost no time cultivating him.

In this campaign I was surprisingly successful. Though named after the most benevolent of saints, Francis seemed to hate everybody — with one notable exception. Me! It may have been the free tickets I obtained for him to plays appearing at Ford's, but for whatever reason he went out of his way to see that my copy received the best possible treatment. Without his guiding hand my opening-night pieces would doubtless have been butchered as they came to be under a different regime some 20 years later.

From the first, he took a dim view of the Quakenbush letters. Banker and I had had a hard enough time getting them through the copy desk. Now, to hear Francis tell it, their appearance downstairs threatened a new crisis in labor relations.

"Paul," he said after the first letter came down the tube, "you're making a terrible mistake with this Quakenbush thing. The proof readers are ready to walk out."

"Why?" Banker could be infuriating when he wanted to.

"Why? Because the man's *illiterate!*"

"So are the proof-readers," said Banker with a fiendish grin. "They should feel right at home."

"Well" — Francis, who had encountered him before in this mood, threw up his hands — "you're going to regret it."

Everybody on the fifth floor with the exception of Dorsey — whose reversal of his original position puzzled me — agreed. "Banker has flipped his lid" was the consensus.

I wrote Quakenbush telling him what was in the wind and asking permission to publish the letters. I warned him what that permission might entail. He would emerge from the shadows into the public spotlight. Was he willing to run this risk?

He was — with certain conditions. I must never attempt to discover his true identity. I must never even try to meet him personally.

Meanwhile, I contracted with the nationally-known Baltimore artist Aaron Sopher, who had illustrated some of my stories in the past, to do sketches around the theme of Quakenbush. He came up with three — two in poolroom settings and an imaginary portrait of the writer himself bent over a table with his shoes off composing the letters.

Of this sketch, Quakenbush later observed that "it did indeed uncanny captured the way I kinder see myself. The overall atmosphere was in line with my life and the exact kind of image I would want the readers to have of me."

The first of the four installments appeared on the back page of the *Sunday Sun* of November 11, 1962 in a three-column layout under the general heading, "The Quakenbush Letters," and a subheading, "The Real Life Angle." The general head remained the same for all the installments; the subhead changed from "The True Nonconformity" on Monday; to "That In Tune Feeling," on Tuesday, and "The Hustler" on Wednesday.

By 8 A.M. Monday, approximately 24 hours after the first installment had appeared in print, the letters began to arrive. No story or series of stories had created such an overnight sensation. And the reaction snowballed with the passing of each day and the publication of each new letter. My phone, both at home and at the office, never ceased ringing. People stopped me on the street.

A friend of mine, walking along North Charles one afternoon, overheard two intelligent-looking men involved in an intellectual discussion. "Well, that's the same thing Quakenbush says," one observed as she passed. Suddenly, my correspondent had become a household word.

Yet antagonism to him and what he represented continued to grow among my colleagues. The editor of the page on which the *Sun* expresses editorial opinion has always been identified on the masthead as "The Editor." As such, Price Day, a *Sun* Pulitzer Prize-winner, controlled publication of letters sent in by *Sun* readers. He let it be known, as the Quakenbush mail piled up, that he would publish no letters about a man whose existence he had reason to doubt. The implication was clear: I had perpetrated a fraud by writing the letters myself.

Banker was furious. He had gone out on a shaky limb and, now that he had made the journey not only safely but triumphantly, he wanted the acknowledgement due him. Fortunately, Price was not the only recipient of letters. I had a stack myself, which Banker threatened to publish on the back page until Dorsey pointed out that doing so would probably create a long-range breach between the editorial and news departments. A few I managed to get into my Sunday column.

Dear Mr. Gardner:

When reading a really good book I am torn between wanting to see how it all comes out and not wanting to finish because I am enjoying it so much.

This was my reaction to the Quakenbush letters. Let's hope that he cannot "kick the writing habit" for I should certainly like a volume of his work.

Being as suspicious as a prospective car-buyer, I wonder who Lorry really is —but you don't have to know the ingredients to enjoy the cake; so why press?

If he were published I'd have to put him on the shelf with Ambrose Bierce, Mencken, Bemelmans and Pogo. Please give us more!

Sincerely,
Virginia Harding

Dear Mr. Gardner:

The Quakenbush letters are fascinating stuff. If the author is "for real," I hope he is being paid for his contributions. If the Quakenbush letters aren't a spoof (the name Quakenbush is almost too inspired to be real) you and the Sun are to be congratulated upon giving the author encouragement.

Mrs. Herman Stotz

Dear Mr. Gardner:

The Quakenbush letters are marvelous. What a character! What a soul! Thanks for publishing them.

W. C. Troutman

Dear Mr. Gardner:

Hurray for Lorry Quakenbush! When is his book coming out? I want to send it to all my friends.

Mrs. Vida Rouse

Dear Mr. Gardner:

Congratulations on having unearthed Quakenbush. My wife and I are both enthusiastic and proud of this remarkable job.

Arnold Wilkes

Dear Mr. Gardner:

Our sixth grade is studying the newspaper in school. Monday morning we read your interesting article "The Quakenbush Letters." We are curious to know whether Lorry Quakenbush is a real or fictional person. We would appreciate hearing from you giving us this information.

Sincerely,
Mr. J. Conigliaro's Class
Medford Heights Elementary School

"YES, MR. J. CONIGLIARO'S CLASS [I replied in my column of November 18, 1962], there *is* a Lorry Quakenbush. That may not be his real name, but by any other name he would be no less real.

"For one year, his letters — not all of which have been printed — have brightened my day as the awareness of him (bending over a dishpan here, a pool cue there) has brightened my life.

"He has, in fact, exerted a strong influence upon many of us here at the *Sun*, where the ordinary run of news — crime, politics, civic reform — suddenly seems rather colorless without Quakenbush on the back page.

"For myself, I can only repeat the sentiments conveyed to him after receiving his first letter. I hope he will write to me again."

THIRTY-TWO

The last of the four installments appeared on Wednesday. When I entered the city room a few minutes before noon Thursday, Banker, standing up in an aggressive attitude at the city desk, let out a yell.

"Gardner!

"The search for Quakenbush—" There was a note of hysteria in his voice — "is *on!*"

I learned that the minority theory held by Price and others — including a few Johns Hopkins professors — that I had written the letters myself had crystallized into an action on the part of our competitor, the *News-American*, to prove that Quakenbush did not exist. Reporters had been dispatched to all Baltimore pool rooms to ask veteran customers if they knew such a man. The *Sun*, feeling it had better locate my correspondent before the competition did, had telephoned the Army, Selective Service, the North Carolina draft boards and other government agencies, none of which had anybody on record named Lorry Quakenbush.

"But, Paul," I protested, "Quakenbush has always said his name was a phony."

"Well —" He threw a stack of notes down on the desk, as the phones began to buzz — "whatever's the story we'll know soon. I've got a reporter watching that grocery store where he gets his mail. They say he comes around 6."

The reporter, John H. Kostmayer, called in at 5:47. Quakenbush had appeared on schedule but refused to be interviewed. At sight of the reporter, he had scooted into a stockroom in the rear of the establishment and bolted the door.

"He won't come out," said Kostmayer.

"Gardner," said Banker, "get over there."

Fifteen minutes later I was pleading with a crack in the stockroom door. "Lorry, let me in."

"Mistah Gahdner," said a voice I had never heard before but which, owing to my Southern background, seemed all-too-familiar. "Ah told you ah did not want to meet you —"

"I know that, Lorry. But I told *you* that, if you agreed to having the letters published, things might happen you wouldn't like. Now we have to produce you to prove you really exist."

Ten minutes later I had the necessary proof that he indeed really did. Standing before me amid a pile of crates, packing cases and soft-drink containers was a rangy, rawboned figure from whose hawk-like countenance a pair of gentle eyes stared fearfully. A shabby overcoat hung from his slightly stooped shoulders almost to his ankles. A large, floppy-brimmed hat completed the picture. All he needed was a coon gun and a jug of moonshine to look like the popular concept of a mountaineer.

He had, he said in his soft North Carolina drawl while bolting the door behind me, written another letter but had not dared send it. Why? Because he was afraid the Veterans Administration might be so annoyed by all the publicity that it would revoke the pension he received as a former POW who'd had most of his stomach removed. "They're not going to like the idea of somebody on their dole spending all his time in poolrooms and movie theaters."

"But, Lorry! They can't take away your pension. It's guaranteed."

"Yeah." His voice was bitter. "That's what they told Caryl Chessman." In May of 1960, Chessman had been executed on charges of kidnapping and rape. The fact that he had been held for twelve years in San Quentin's death row indicated a certain indecision on the part of authorities as to his guilt. I wasn't sure what Quakenbush's point was, but I had no wish to argue with it.

All in all, our first encounter among the shelves and bottles of the Park Pantry's storeroom was pleasant enough — which was more than I can say for some of our subsequent meetings. For Quakenbush developed the notion that I was exploiting him. And I probably did temporarily increase the *Sun*'s circulation (thus adding to the stockholders' income) but I personally never made a dime out of our correspondence — though I took care to see that he did.

But his animosity lasted only a short time. We kept up our correspondence and chance meetings in the street. And, on December 20, 1972, I published a short story of his that took up the whole front page and part of another in the *Sun*'s feature section.

I preceded the story with the following explanatory remarks:

Almost exactly ten years ago I published a series of letters from a correspondent calling himself Lorry Quakenbush (or Quackenbush). Since then, Quakenbush — whom many at the time thought I had invented — has appeared in other columns, other papers, with the result that he has become familiar to a large number of Baltimoreans.

During the intervening years, I have continued to hear from him on subjects of both local and national interest. He is a frequenter of movie theaters and pool halls, and what he has found therein has combined with his own incorruptible individuality to create a literary view that might be described as romantic realism. Quakenbush knows, perhaps as well as any man alive, that life is not a bowl of cherries, but it has not embittered him. Indeed, the wonder that life still manages to arouse in him is the secret of his charm.

QUAKENBUSH'S STORY STARTS OFF SHOWING A GUY by the name of Lepage Royster, a sickly broken-in-spirit misplaced Southerner (yes, Royster is basic a sad guy — but there is still a little humor and cheerfulness left in his make-up) in a cheap, dingy, light-housekeeping attic room. In a covering letter, Quakenbush describes Royster as "half urban, half countrified, half intelligent, half moron — somebody like me. I would like to have the story set (played out) in a northern city, say Chicago or New York, as I don't want to be recognize as Royster — which I am somewhat is."

Even more was Quakenbush the half-prima donna, half-terrified lover of womanhood reflected in the letter he — still proclaiming his disdain for the fame he had achieved — handed me in the stockroom of the Park Pantry near the end of that Christmas season, 1962. And it is so that I shall, with affection, always remember him.

> Dear Mr. Gardner:
> All them comments about me having creative powers and was some kind of phenomemom made me feel the way George Cohan did after seeing *Yankee Doolde Dandy* — he said I would like to have known that little nice fellow played by James Cagney.
> Now I did cry a long time to be heard and I believe people liked what I said, also I am going to weather that storm of paying the little price of having that miserable pleasant feeling that comes with any unexpected success, espiccally if it brings a little enjoyment to other people. And to weather the storm I should be able to draw a little from all that philosophty lingo I tried to dispense with in my past letters.
> I have walked by the corner of Carrollton and Baltimore Streets 300 times and the same fellow has been standing there telling a different fellow how he won this fight when in the U.S. Army for the champion of England. I do not know how but I have picked up this conversation 67 times while passing the corner spread over the last few years.
> The fellow is reliving his finest hour over and over. Now I will be standing on some corner twenty years from now telling about the time I made some comments and it made news.

All this is to convey sharply to you that I am not fishing for encouragement, because I truly think I am as much of a writer as Loeta Parson think she is, also when I think of myself as a writer I feel as phonie as Fred Allen said Jack Benny was. He said — Jack is such a phonie that he would eat a meal at Bickford, then stand in front of the Stork Club and pick his teeth.

A small instance I experience by those letters being published.

This very pretty interesting maybe foreign looking lady ask for a Monday morning paper at 8:30 P.M. Monday night at Schill book store on Franklin Street so she could read the "Quakenbush Letters." Schill did not have the Monday morning edition.

I was there waiting for the 8:30 P.M. Tuesday bulldog edition and I had the Monday paper with me, so I could not resist offering it to her as she was going out of the door. She reached into her handbag to get me the seven cents.

Now just a moment its something very sad about watching a woman get money out of her handbag.

The sadness must stem from watching her juggling the eight different packages and you feeling helpless to help her or it reflects that security desire that women seem to have more than men by making that money so hard to get (I know they haven't got any pockets) and I am not trying to sound like Jack Parr or Arthur Godfrey talking about crying at the opening of a new supermarket.

Back to the girl I couldn't resist to ask her why she like them, she said she liked them because they was good but she thought a well educated and culture person had wrote them and was passing off as a hillybilly to make them more impressive.

Then I thought if she thought you were that big of a fraud she didn't have a accurate appraiser of your writing and your paper accurate standing, so I was at a roadblock. So I did the most convincing thing I could do to let her know the truth.

So I said I am Lorry Quakenbush. She seem to buy it without too much hesitation and I said I am not well educated or culture (Yes I am sorry to say it shows.)

She then shook hands with me and said the letters was beautiful and she had a good friend who knows you and would I like to meet you. I said no thanks and tried to make an ordly retreat by tipping my hat like Dean Rusk and running.

She was a lovely human being and sincere (I thought she was lovely before she even spoke) but I believe she would be more mentally beautiful if she didn't look for fraud where even thinking it may be some fraud involve in this particular case would mortgage her from seeing the letters clear as she might have without the over suspicion.

(A lot of time we pride ourselves in having an enquiring mind when it may be an over suspicious mind.)

Now on top of all this she happen to have that mysterious overall mental and physical commodation that soothes and irritates at the same time that vacuum that waiting to be fill within us. This strange feeling only shows up four or five times in a life time.

This feeling is so frustration because behind it is 5,000 years of man groping and suffering and trying to pass on a better barrometer for you so you can have a more accurate gauge to find the right woman for you.

You are the inherited keeper and the final resting place for that feeling and it can not be dismiss to easy or can you over use it.

That 5000 year old voice is saying please be sure, don't go way. don't be, do be a little, please let her know you are caught in the same flood and is sinking.

With all that coming at me in a flash with not a moment's notice, I became so unraviled I could not tell her and ran away into the night.

Your friend,
Lorry Quakenbush

Photo courtesy of Mechanic Theatre

(below) Photo courtesy of Center Stage.

Baltimore Busts Out

THIRTY-THREE

One remembers the Sixties as a decade of radical change — of political assassination, youthful rebellion and alteration in the profiles of large American cities. The last, called urban renewal, began in Baltimore with construction of the first of a series of gleaming skyscrapers that eventually replaced the dowdy, if somewhat more charming, office buildings of a downtown area newly designated as the Charles Center.

At some point in the general upheaval, Rose decided to leave the family nest and venture, however tentatively, into the outside world. She held a number of jobs, ranging from secretary for a U.S. Congressman to executive assistant in various social agencies — which, owing to her natural talents, soon established her as even more of a personality in the community than she had been in the bar.

And since I, in my new role of *Sun* theater critic, was also exploring unknown territory, we walked similar roads.

It seemed an appropriate time to renew my efforts in behalf of the project I'd been pushing by way of Sunday columns, appearances before civic groups and personal contacts since my initial meeting with Zelda Fichandler: the creation of a Baltimore equivalent to Washington's Arena Stage.

By then, Hilltop had just about reached the end of its bumpy road, and Ford's was obviously on its last leg. For live theater, the city would soon be obliged to depend upon Painters Mill and such amateur groups as the Johns Hopkins Playshop, the Vagabonds (advertised as the oldest, continuously producing little theater in America) and the Baltimore Actors Theater.

The Playshop, as befitting its academic associations, specialized in the classics, the Vagabonds in works that had appeared on Broadway, the Baltimore Actors Theater (known as BAT) in musicals.

Composed largely of young female socialites with a drive to express themselves, BAT raised money through parties to which I, as the *Sun*'s theater critic, was usually invited. It was thus that I met Betty Bruce, a Baltimore County housewife with a drive that could not be contained. When I met her she had just returned from Africa, where she had visited an old schoolmate, a nun then serving in a leper colony. The experience left her hooked on Africa. It also left her hooked to some extent on leprosy, which interest she pursued through friendship with a cured leper after returning to the States.

Somewhere around the middle Sixties Betty divorced her second husband, the universally liked Dancy Bruce, moved to Kenya and married Jock Leslie-Melville, a British aristocrat with whom she built an international reputation as an author, lecturer and world-traveler. She and Jock, who died in 1984 of a brain tumor, became two of my closest friends.

Betty introduced me to Marilyn Meyerhoff and Linell Smith, both involved in one way or another with BAT activities. Marilyn was married to Harry Meyerhoff, who later became famous as owner of the 1979 Derby and Preakness winner Spectacular Bid. Both Marilyn and Harry played important parts in the founding and support of the theater this chapter is about.

Linell was the daughter of Odgen Nash. Her husband, a member of an old Virginia family, was named John but because his last name happened to be Smith he preferred to be called by his middle name, Marshall. Marshall was an insurance broker who represented, among other companies, Lloyds of London. I had heard that Lloyds insured a number of strange things for enormous amounts — such as Marlene Dietrich's legs. I felt that my only problem as a reviewer lay in the possibility that my eyes might give out. I decided to have them insured for a million dollars.

"Now you understand," said Marshall in his characteristic drawl, "that Lloyds is not an ordinary insurance company. They put their policies up for bids. A guy walks down the aisle and says 'Who wants Gardner's eyes?' They bid and then the next year they do it again."

Having my eyes dealt with in such a cavalier fashion did not appeal to me. But in the process of our discussions I managed to impress Marshall with what had become for me an obsession. Zelda had stressed the importance of a theater's location. Early one spring morning Marshall telephoned to say he had found one. He took me down to the Baltimore waterfront where the Bay Belle, an excursion boat used for moonlight cruises up and down the Chesapeake, was moored. He thought it might make a great floating theater.

And it might have, except that the ceiling in the ballroom wasn't high enough to accommodate the lights.

Another person who shared my dreams — which, as it turned out, were not exclusive to me — was John Bos. John was an extremely talented young man who, as public-relations director of Painters Mill, had become an intimate friend.

John wanted to exert an influence in the regional theater. And he did. He became business manager of Center Stage during its critical second season and, after that, PR director for Arena Stage in Washington. Though I played some small part in his obtaining both jobs, such help proved to be unnecessary. John was so good he didn't need it.

We used to make late-night tours of the city scouting locations for the theater we hoped would soon materialize. But nobody showed any inclination to take the steps necessary to get the project started.

Then, as sometimes happens, something did.

Edward Golden, an engaging young newcomer who, following his graduation from Harvard, had become drama director of Baltimore's Jewish Community Center, announced his intention of vacating that post at the end of 1962. Inasmuch as he had made a deep impression on a small but affluent segment of the public interested not only in attending the theater but in performing in it as well, his departure was considered as something not devoutly to be wished. The result was the founding of a professional resident theater by those most concerned, with him at the head.

Since this was what I had been lobbying for for years, I jumped in with both editorial feet to support it. So enthusiastic was my support that I was accused of promoting the project for my own shady ends. "In the last few weeks," wrote Gavin Fletcher, of Severna Park, Md. in a letter to the *Sun* dated February 1, 1963, "Mr. Gardner has written three articles about Center Stage, one a favorable review. One must question the impartiality of a reviewer who puffs the plays in which he invests."

The suggestion was idiotic. Of all the people involved, I was in the best position to know that, with the exception of a few Broadway shows, musical tents and the ubiquitous dinner operations, no theatrical ventures were making money. It was for this reason that I had advised the original group of Center Stage backers to incorporate as a non-profit organization, which would have enabled them to receive public money. But it took more than one unsuccessful season, the threat of bankruptcy and the urging of their legal counselor, Donald Rothman, for them to act upon the advice.

Replying to Mr. Fletcher's letter on February 6, I observed that, "were I inclined to be dishonest, there are more certain and lucrative ways open to me than this."

The review to which he referred was written of the theater's first presentation, which took place January 22. It began as follows:

Center Stage opened its doors last night, and I am happy to report it is a charming place tastefully decorated in subdued tones of blue and red and exuding an air of luxury with its glass chandeliers and wall-to-wall carpeting.

Though an unwise choice for a premier performance, Edward Golden's modern-dress version of Arthur Schnitzler's La Ronde *was a generally admirable production which seemed to be enjoyed by a sold-out, first-night audience that included the mayor and president of the City Council.*

THEN FOLLOWED A LIST OF REASONS WHY I considered the play an unwise choice, culminating in a statement to the effect that its shortcomings and those of the production seemed to go hand-in-hand. "When the writing was at its best, the show was at its best, and vice versa."

Ed was upset by the review, which I showed him in my office that same evening before the paper went to press. Having apparently concluded from my enthusiasm that it would continue in the form of unqualified rave notices, he felt betrayed.

We didn't get along too well after that. Aware that my support had played an important part in getting Center Stage launched, he lived in terror of my turning the knife the other way. Indeed, throughout the rest of his Baltimore career he acted as if I were a dagger held over his head.

I became particularly conscious of this one night when a *News-American* columnist with whom I had just shared a spot on an Elaine Stein radio show warned that he would take retaliatory measures against me for any harm done to his friend Ed Golden.

I had no wish to harm his friend and even less the theater his friend had, with the considerable help of the Jewish community and the Baltimore press corps, managed to found. For the next 20 years — through recurring economic crises, fire and successive changes in location and artistic directors — I went out of my way to avoid it.

The history of Center Stage falls roughly into three periods: from its 1963 opening in a converted Preston Street gymnasium through its shift two years later to a remodeled North Avenue cafeteria (destroyed by fire in January of 1974) to its present home in a brand new facility (provided by the city and the inspired financial machinations of its board) in a former Catholic school at 700 North Calvert Street.

During the first period, the theater's artistic end was handled — rather well, I now feel, looking back on it — by Mr. Golden. During the second, it was handled by Douglas Seale, a renowned British director with a pronounced talent for flamboyance, and John Stix — less flamboyant but more sound. Jacques Cartier, the third director to occupy this second period, seemed to offer great initial promise, which as time went on slowly diminished.

All of these directors displayed one deadly flaw — the inability to balance their personal desire to create important new productions against their audiences' inability to appreciate them. Stan Wojewodski, Jr., the man who has guided the artistic life of Center Stage since Mr. Cartier's untimely departure, has on occasion revealed the same problem. But, when he is on target, which is more often than not, he is decidedly on.

It is interesting that, with the possible exception of Mr. Wojewodski, all the resident directors at Center Stage have tended to regard me as an enemy. And this despite my continued efforts to be the opposite. Much of the impact of any review depends upon the words with which the critic begins it. If he chooses to begin on a negative note, no matter how many positive factors he may bring in later, the reader will automatically assume the production is a dud. During the entire time I covered Center Stage — which I did up to my retirement from the *Sun* (and even afterward in my public-radio broadcasts) — I always strove to find something good (or at least noncommittal) to say in my opening remarks.

For I knew something the public didn't — that for the first ten years the theater was literally hanging by its economic eyebrows. With the coming of managing director Peter Culman, the infusion of new blood into the board (including my old pal, now the enormously wealthy, Howard Head) and the obtaining of grants from all over, this situation changed.

But I always recalled a night at West Preston Street when only seven people sat in the audience. With one devastating notice I could, I kept reminding myself, destroy this little theater forever. So I continued to write pieces that I hoped wouldn't.

Not that I ever falsified a review. I never said a show was better than it was. The worst that can be said of me is that I did not always spell out in the slashing manner of some of my colleagues just how bad some of them were. But today, looking at Center Stage, which has grown into one of the most economically sound and respected regional theaters in the country, I feel such a nurturing approach was worth it.

Apart from everything else, Center Stage has occupied a special place in my heart because of a lovely woman who came down from New York to appear in several of its second-season productions and stayed on to brighten the city and my life.

THIRTY-FOUR

Center Stage opened in January of 1963. In February of 1964, Morris Mechanic carried out his long-standing threat and closed Ford's. For more than a year, the Stanton — nee Stanley, Baltimore's remaining relic from the glory days when movie theaters were built along the lines of Oriental palaces — was used for the presentation of legitimate productions. Then, on April 17, 1965, he closed that, too.

Both theaters were demolished — being replaced with, in the case of Ford's, a parking garage and, in that of the Stanton, a parking lot.

On the same weekend the Stanton closed its doors a strike by the Baltimore Newspaper Guild shut down the *Sun* for the first time since its founding in 1837. For eight weeks the paper did not publish. At some point during this disturbing series of events my book came out.

It created something less than a sensation. As for the equally unsensational Baltimore theater season, almost two years passed without the city's having a stage upon which to present touring Broadway shows. We reporters were told that Mr. Mechanic was laying plans for the construction of a new theater on the site of the old *Sun* building at Baltimore and Charles Streets. We were also told that the reason such plans were progressing so slowly was that they included space for a number of retail stores and that he refused to break ground until all this space had been leased.

For whatever reason, the theater was not completed until after his death, when it was announced it would bear his name. His widow, Clarisse, a very able woman whom I number among my dearest friends, took over control of all his properties, including the theater. The grand opening took place on January 16, 1967, with a production of *Hello, Dolly!* starring Betty Grable. Though no Carol Channing, Miss Grable filled the bill well enough, and the new theater was hailed by most of those covering the event (including myself) as a big success.

We were wrong.

To begin with, architect John M. Johansen had tried to effect a compromise between the oblong-shaped auditoriums of the past (designed for proscenium stages) and the wide-sweeping amphitheater-type auditoriums (designed for thrust stages) then coming into fashion. His design made provisions for a 15-foot-deep forestage to be added whenever circumstances permitted. Because all touring Broadway shows were designed for the traditional arrangement, circumstances didn't. The forestage was never used.

Despite repeated efforts in my Sunday column to explain the situation, Mechanic patrons continued to be puzzled (and outraged) by their inability to see properly from the extreme left and right sections of the auditorium. Hearing, too, was difficult — and their irritation was given additional impetus by the shoddy nature of some of the productions. The better shows still went to Washington. But for a few notable exceptions, Baltimore had to subsist on bus and truck companies featuring has been stars.

Before its opening, the theater had been leased by Joseph and James Nederlander, brothers who operated similar outlets in Detroit and New York.

Their optimism about the miracle they were going to work for us here in the backwaters was unshakable. Joe told me in a telephone conversation from his Detroit office shortly before his and James's arrival here that demand for Mechanic subscriptions would under their direction become so great that the only way a person could acquire one would be to inherit it from a deceased relative.

The first thing they did was to launch a massive subscription drive based on the rationale that the new playhouse would inaugurate a new era in the Baltimore theater. The drive proved successful, though apparently not as successful as the Nederlanders would have had the Baltimore public believe. According to their press releases, it netted 20,000 subscribers. But I was later told by Tom Fox—who had left his job as assistant to National Theater manager Scott Kirkpatrick in Washington to take over management of the Mechanic—that the total never exceeded 14,000.

Still, compared to the 3,000 or so that had preceded it, 14,000 wasn't bad. Unfortunately, the number shrank in subsequent years to that represented by the old hard-core subscribers at Ford's. So the Nederlanders gathered up their unfulfilled expectations and departed.

During roughly this same period nine new theaters opened in Washington.

Three — the Arena, Kreeger and Old Vat — were part of the complex built and directed by Tom and Zelda Fichandler.

Three more — the 2,318-seat Opera House, the 1,142-seat Eisenhower and the 512-seat Terrace — were contained in the lavish John F. Kennedy Center for the Performing Arts, which began operations in September of 1971.

The Kennedy Center theaters — all of traditional "tennis court" shape — presented for the most part shows on their way to or from New York. The Arena Group — of anything but traditional design — specialized in either new or experimental productions.

A brand new theater, erected on the Catholic University campus and named after Father Hartke, offered revivals of memorable plays.

The two remaining playhouses—the Folger Shakespeare Library Theater and the restored Ford's, reconstructed inside the actual shell of the historic theater in which Lincoln was shot — were flexible in their choice of subjects and styles.

I covered all nine, which meant continual driving back and forth between Baltimore and Washington, but it was worth it.

Meanwhile, back at the Mechanic —

In 1973, the theater was taken over by a triumvirate composed of two of Mr. Mechanic's former business associates and Howard R. Owen (his nephew by marriage) whose management ultimately plunged it into a period of darkness. For a while it looked as if this long-held dream of Baltimore theatergoers would deteriorate into a facility for the exhibition of black exploitation films. Then Mayor William Donald Schaefer stepped in, and the long-range result was a city-backed operation with Hope Quackenbush at the head.

A native of Chicago, Mrs. Quackenbush (no relation of Lorry) had during the Sixties lived in Baltimore where she made a favorable impression on Mr. Schaefer and other dignitaries by her work as executive director of the first City

Fair. Afterwards she moved to Minneapolis. She returned when her husband Bruce, described in a *Sun* article as "an executive on the move," was transferred here by his firm, the Commercial Credit Corporation.

Under the mayor's direction Mrs. Quackenbush, together with Sandy Hillman of the Baltimore Promotion Council and other civic leaders, secured the services of Broadway producer Alexander Cohen, who for 33 months handled the Mechanic's bookings in a manner that replaced with glitter the lacklustre aspects of the productions that had preceded them. He also instituted structural changes that improved the interior shape of the playhouse.

Mr. Cohen believed that promotion was the answer to all things. And he was canny enough to realize that his first job in this connection was changing Baltimoreans' traditional image of themselves as inhabitants of a second-rate city.

"Broadway needs Baltimore just as much as Baltimore needs Broadway," he told a large gathering of civic leaders and press representatives on the occasion of his appointment as guiding genius of the "new" Mechanic. Exactly why Broadway needed Baltimore, in view of its indifference for the past 25 years, wasn't clear. But the statement had a nice sound — and in an effort to prove the point he brought down from New York a whole passel of Broadway celebrities for a luncheon to kick off the 1976-77 subscription campaign. According to an announcement in the *Sunday Sun* of April 11, 1976, those attending were Alfred Drake, Celeste Holm, Lynn Redgrave, Jerry Orbach, Jerry Lewis, Eddie Albert — all well-known actors — and producers Joseph Papp and T. Edward Hambleton.

A couple of months later, Mr. Cohen — still interested in selling subscriptions — brought Carol Channing to Baltimore for a press reception aboard the *Nobska*, a boat recently converted into a restaurant. Sitting on the deck, the woman who had sold the world on the idea that diamonds were a girl's best friend told of an encounter she had once had with former First Lady Pat Nixon.

"We got along so well. I felt we were great friends. Then the next week the 'enemies' list' came out, and my name — it was in alphabetical order — was practically at the top."

By such exposure, Mr. Cohen hoped to keep the Mechanic constantly in the minds of the Baltimore people. His aim — as reported in my Sunday account of his first meeting with members of the community and press — was:

"A 40-week season of the *creme de la creme* of the theatrical world: distinguished shows in the class of the *Hamlet*, with Richard Burton, which he produced on Broadway in the Sixties. Foreign hits like *Beyond the Fringe*, which he imported from England.

"Crowds of customers clamoring for tickets at the box office! Restaurants teeming with before-and-after theater patrons! Traffic making downtown after dark look like the Beltway during rush hour!

"Time alone," I concluded, "will tell whether Mr. Cohen is the magician his prophecies seem to imply, but that he is a spellbinder there can be no doubt. And at Thursday's luncheon, the large group of civic leaders assembled to hear of his 33-month contract with the city listened with open mouths. Even Mayor

Schaefer, noted for his faith in the Baltimore-that-is-to-be, looked a little dazed."

As one who had listened to many such projections, I was not. I became dazed, or rather dazzled, only when a couple of years later subscriptions at the Mechanic passed the 20,000 mark. In some way and despite such disappointing productions as his *Hellzapoppin* revival with Jerry Lewis and *The Bed Before Yesterday* with Miss Channing, Mr. Cohen managed to capture the imagination of the Baltimore public — which eventually enabled the Ms's. Quackenbush and Hillman, aided by Theater Guild director Philip Langner in New York, to build the Mechanic into one of the most successful road theaters in the country.

As I write this, it has 23,000 subscribers, as compared to the Kennedy Center's 7,000. In view of this lead, Broadway producers no longer bypass Baltimore for Washington. Indeed, Harold Prince, who once declared he would never again bring a show to Baltimore, decided to open his musical *Rosa* at Center Stage, which boasts 12,500 subscribers of its own.

Add to this the strides made in the experimental field by Philip Arnoult's Theater Project, the blossoming of the black community's Arena Players in a newly constructed theater of their own and the fact that the city has over the years served as host to an increasing number of international festivals and you can see that, since the middle Fifties when I became the *Sun*'s theater critic, Baltimore has experienced considerable growth as a theater town. For this growth I take no special credit.

But I was there!

James D. Waring

Drowning In The Rubicon

THIRTY-FIVE

I am a liberal in everything but art, in which, alas, I am a reactionary. I long to return to a time when it all made sense — when style was judged by its eloquence and the artist felt an obligation to make himself understood."

These words, opening Chapter 2 of *The Splintered Stage*, were prompted by a revolution then occurring in the field of playwriting. Until the late 1950's, dramatists as a rule had endeavored to make their works comprehensible to an audience. Why characters acted the way they did was considered as important as the actions themselves.

Suddenly it all changed. Characters began to say the damndest things to one another, and their actions often seemed to make no sense whatever. It was called the Theater of the Absurd.

Rationale for this radical new development evolved from the notion that, by "dying" in the Nietzschean sense, God had left a universe in which human behavior had no meaning. Because man's whole history seemed to me devoted to the search for an explanation of himself I considered form and meaning the most dramatic of themes. Now I found myself faced with a theater based on meaninglessness.

Philosophical despair had of course been dealt with before, but the Theater of the Absurd gave it a new twist. Whereas Giraudoux, Anouilh, Sartre and Camus had presented "their sense of the irrationality of the human condition in the form of highly lucid and logically constructed reasoning," declared the apostle of the new theater, Martin Esslin, "the Theater of the Absurd strives to express its sense of the senselessness of the human condition and the inadequacy of the rational approach by the open abandonment of rational devices and discursive thought."

Fortunately, the Theater of the Absurd in a pure sense didn't stay with us long. After all, a philosophy based on meaninglessness has nowhere to go. But, by providing excuses for writers bent on substituting their own undisciplined flights of fancy for properly constructed plays, it has perhaps cursed us forever.

For one thing it combined with the winds of rebellion then sweeping American youth as a result of the Vietnam War to produce a generally anarchistic approach to everything. In the theater, the most notable example was the musical *Hair* — which opened Broadway's back door to nudity, dirty feet, foul language and disgusting behavior in general. Boorishness became the way to make it on the New York stage.

The anarchy was expressed not only in the messy structure of plays but in the physical structure of the playhouses in which they were presented. For *Dude*, a creation of the same writer-composer-director team responsible for *Hair*, the interior of New York's Broadway Theater was rearranged. The audience was seated on the stage and the show performed in the balcony and orchestra. Something of the same thing occurred in Hal Prince's production of *Candide*.

The idea was that any show would gain stature by being presented in a manner new to it. The idea reached deplorable proportions when applied to productions of the classics. Dear God, the horrors I've suffered at the hands of directors and designers determined to inflict their own personal wounds on works written by Shakespeare, Moliere, Chekhov and other great dramatists too dead to protest!

Perhaps the worst wound of all was inflicted on the old Freudian doctrine of motivation. This doctrine had spawned not only a whole era of plays by such distinguished dramatists as Arthur Miller, Tennessee Williams, William Inge, Arthur Laurents, Lillian Hellman and Paddy Chayefsky but also an acting technique that, as espoused by Lee Strasberg of the Actors Studio, eventually became an object of ridicule.

The story is well known of the Method actor ordered by a Broadway director to go to one side of the stage and wait there for three beats before delivering his next line.

"What's my motivation?" asked the actor.

"Your motivation," roared the director — I think it was either George S. Kaufman or George Abbott — "is that, if you don't, I'll fire you!"

Still, in that it helped to clarify characters' behavior, motivation was something that should not have been thrown out like the baby with the bath water.

In a series of interviews on the British Broadcasting Company, Harold Pinter stated that playwrights should not invade the inner consciousness of their characters. Why they (the characters) did the things they did was their own business. He also said, when asked by an interviewer, that his plays were about "the weasel under the cocktail cabinet." He later admitted that he had tossed the remark off the top of his head and that it meant "precisely nothing."

Yet Pinter continued to be taken seriously by not only critics but his fellow artists. During a New York press conference in connection with his play *Butley*, Simon Gray, a close friend of Pinter's, responded to a question as to whether his central character was homosexual with "Oh, I shouldn't think so."

"But," somebody asked (probably me) "shouldn't the playwright know such things?"

"Not necessarily," said Mr. Gray with an airy smile. "A playwright need only know what his characters do during the play. He doesn't have to understand why."

This idea of not even the playwright understanding what is going on in his plays has resulted in a number of works — including Sam Shepard's Pulitzer Prize-winning *Buried Child* — that have defied rational interpretation.

Happily, not everyone working during this period took advantage of the situation. In 1967, Tom Stoppard, a Rumanian-born British subject, wrote a play, *Rosencrantz and Guildenstern Are Dead*, that portrayed the two non-entities of Shakespearean drama in a different light. Never knowing what they were doing in *Hamlet* to begin with, they were like man himself, born into a world beyond their comprehension. But — and this is the important point — Shakespeare knew! And the suggestion that God might, after all, not be dead, Stoppard further developed in *Jumpers*.

Because of their intellectual content, the two plays combined with *A Texas Trilogy* and Peter Shaffer's *Equus* and *Amadeus* to add up to the seven most stimulating theatrical offerings of the Sixties and Seventies. There was only one

170

more stimulating: Peter Weiss's inspired blending of Brecht's (epic) theater of ideas and Artaud's (total) theater of the emotions, *Marat/Sade*.

In addition to making the most of a superbly theatrical play, the magnificent production by the Royal Shakespeare Company under the direction of Peter Brook, challenged the position of the playwright with that of the director. Henceforth, all major productions would reflect this challenge.

I left the playwright in the last chapter of *The Splintered Stage* with his nose pressed against the back wall of a blind alley chanting "I am meaningless; I am absurd." Where, I asked, was he to go from there? I assumed he would retrace his steps to the alley's mouth and resume progress along the path he'd been pursuing before turning into it.

What he did instead was to leap straight up into the air and where he came down — whether under the cocktail cabinet with the weasel or on a glorious new road to greater meaning — is still unclear.

THIRTY-SIX

In 1962, an ex-clothing designer named Ellen Stewart opened a combination boutique and theater in Greenwich Village. She called it La Mama Experimental Theater Club, but, as its fame spread throughout the avant garde circles of that day, it became known as Cafe La Mama.

Ms. Stewart, a black emigre from the deep South, loved the theater. She also loved playwrights, whose works she felt should be produced for, if no other reason, an encouragement to their authors. This philosophy led to her producing plays whose dramatic insignificance did nothing to prevent her following them with others equally bad.

Eventually the law of averages set in — with the result that she discovered, in addition to a number of promising new playwrights, Tom O'Horgan who made a big, if short-lived, name for himself as director of *Hair, Dude, Jesus Christ Superstar* (on Broadway) and *Tom Paine* and *Futz* (off). *Tom Paine* concerned the American Revolutionary War pamphleteer, *Futz* a passionate love affair between a farmer and his pig.

I had met O'Horgan in New York and, later, Baltimore, which he visited to promote Leslie Irons's Corner Theater productions of plays originating at La Mama. And I had found him to be a thoroughly likable young man. His work was another matter. Admittedly, the productions were inventive and often brilliantly performed. But they tended to be repetitious, deafening and, owing to the unwashed bodies of the participants, somewhat gamey. So I was relieved when, after a few years, the trend wore itself out.

During the same period that *Hair, Tom Paine, Futz* and other O'Horgan creations were steaming (some might say stinking) up the New York scene, a gifted hack who had got his start grinding out jokes for radio and TV comics, began the series of scripts that was to make him the most successful playwright in history. Since then Neil Simon has grown sufficiently to transcend his gagwriter beginnings, but at the time I didn't like him any more than I did the La Mama crowd. I knew, however, that he was getting rich. And since his plays fell roughly into the category of a kind I myself had once tried to write, I began to get ideas.

In 1950, I'd had a shaky little comedy produced off-Broadway. It was called *IOU Jeremiah* and, though off-Broadway had not at that time become fashionable, it was reviewed by the city's two leading trade papers, *Billboard* and *Variety*. I never saw the *Variety* review (I didn't even get up to New York for the show's opening), but *Billboard* went so far as to suggest that with a few superficial changes it might make me a lot of money. As a $35-a-week insurance salesman, I was much impressed by the suggestion, and the passing of years had not detracted from its appeal when, as drama critic of the *Sun*, I attended the 1965 tryout of *Cactus Flower* in Washington.

If anything *Cactus Flower*, adapted by Abe Burrows's from a contemporary French comedy, was even lighter in weight than the stuff Simon was turning out. But anyone could see the gold glinting between the lines. I left the National Theater muttering to myself.

I had three weeks of vacation coming, so I thought "Why Not?" My next (and, I sincerely hope, last) play *Christabel and the Rubicon* was the result.

Revolting youth had already begun the process of national brain-washing that was to culminate in the axiom that everything young was good and everything old "irrelevant." But, in 1966, it was too soon for me to know this. Thus, in choosing a 17-year-old girl for my central character I was not consciously pandering to fashion.

What drew me to the subject was the way it demonstrated how a determined child could bend a whole group of adults, including her parents, to her will. It also demonstrated the almost mystical power of women. I am not a feminist according to the political definition of the term. I am, however, a "femalist." God, I'm convinced, created Adam as a first draft. It was only with Eve that He hit His stride.

Though Christabel was the heroine of my play, it was Bobby, the boy next door, through his unwitting motivation of everything she does, who is the pivotal character.

Bobby is a schlemiel. He falls over his feet. As a little girl four years his junior, Christabel sat in a tree in her yard and watched his pathetic efforts to roller skate and, with her maternal, marvelously womanly instinct, decided that life had given her him to watch over and protect. He was, as she says in her final passionate outburst, "Mine! And nobody, nobody is going to take him from me!"

The "nobody" Christabel fears may take Bobby from her is the United States Air Force in which he intends to enlist as first step in his long-range plan to become an astronaut. To forestall this plan, Christabel — convinced that the physically inept Bobby cannot possibly survive military service — deliberately seduces and becomes pregnant by him. Pride, however, prevents her telling him of this decision "to cross the Rubicon." Instead she maintains that Frazier, a famous novelist she and Bobby happened to meet in a Manhattan night club two months before, is the father.

Frazier, in his late 40's, was blind drunk the whole time and is therefore astounded to receive a letter reading "Dear Mr. Frazier: You may not remember me, but I spent the night in your apartment one Saturday about two months ago. Now I am pregnant and have to get married. Please come to dinner Sunday."

Christabel's middle-class parents' confusion upon hearing that their bright-eyed little baby has got herself pregnant by a man old enough to be (as her exasperated father says) *his* father increases when the man shows up for Sunday dinner with a woman he says he has been engaged to for years.

WELL, AS IS TRUE OF ALL FAIRY TALES, everything turns out for the best. I had trouble with the second act but, for something dashed off in such a short time, it, too, came off reasonably well.

I sent the finished manuscript to my agent who sold it instantly to a woman whose last Broadway involvement *The Owl and the Pussycat* had been a howling success. Pat Fowler, I discovered, was a charming woman whose enthusiasm for *Christabel* was exceeded only by my amazement at it. She told me at our first meeting in her luxurious Riverside Drive apartment that, of the several hundred scripts she had read that year, only an unproduced work by Nobel Prize-winner Jean-Paul Sartre had impressed her so much.

Her curiosity as to the identity of the playwright (I had used a pseudonym) reached a peak when she could not find the name in any of the New York telephone directories. Stimulated by this seeming mystery, she had (I never understood why) suspected I might be Bill Manhoff, author of *The Owl and the Pussycat*. She obviously intended this as a compliment. Unfortunately I had seen *The Owl and the Pussycat*.

I had appropriated my grandfather's name, H. J. Moorman, for a reason not in the least mysterious. I knew the Broadway critics might dismiss a trifle like Woody Allen's *Play It Again, Sam* with amused condescension, but when one of their number ventured into their gun-sights they took careful aim. Writing in the New York Post of the 1958 season's disaster *Goldilocks*, Richard Watts, Jr. observed:

> *Since drama critics and their wives are notoriously more brilliant than most people, a great deal is expected of them. And, when they are daring enough to challenge an envious world with a show of their own, nothing less that a masterpiece will satisfy the eager anticipation. Because* Goldilocks, *the musical comedy for which Walter and Jean Kerr wrote the book and their share of the lyrics and which Mr. Kerr directed, seemed, to put it conservatively, rather short of that status in its debut at the Lunt-Fontanne Theater Saturday night, it was a disappointment. What made the dissatisfaction all the more upsetting was that the weaknesses of* Goldilocks *appeared to be chiefly in the writing contribution of the Kerrs.*

THE PROBLEM IN MY CASE was further complicated by the fact that in my book, published only a year before, I had criticized the American theater for not producing anything in the way of great drama. I could easily imagine some snit of a reviewer leading off with "So this is what Mr. Gardner considers great drama?"

I did not want my thin little play judged on the basis of who had written it. Nor — and this was most important — did I want to impose an additional burden upon those colleagues of mine in the Baltimore-Washington area who would feel embarrassed at having to review it.

It soon became evident that the main difficulty in getting *Christabel* into production was finding a suitable actress for the title role. The number of ingenues with names big enough to mean anything on Broadway was severely limited. Tuesday Weld possessed an antipathy to performing on the stage. Marlo Thomas had other commitments. Hayley Mills expressed interest, but nothing came of it.

Finally Pat, having held the play under option for six months, gave up and shifted her attention to something called *Leda Had a Little Swan* which — though boasting a star (Michael J. Pollard) and a director (Andre Gregory) — never opened.

For about a year and a half, *Christabel* went the rounds of the New York offices. Alfred de Liagre, Jr., in his day one of the biggest producers on Broadway, was sufficiently impressed to read it twice — once before and once after I had incorporated some of his recommended changes. Others who gave serious thought to producing it were an associate of the venerable Max Gordon, Leslie Odgen (co-producer of Robert Shaw's *Man in the Glass Booth*) and a teacher of playwriting named Albert Zuckerman.

It was the last — for a while the most enthusiastic of the lot — who raised questions in my mind I felt could be answered only by my seeing the play on the stage. So I sent a copy to Olney, along with a request that it should be treated with no more consideration than any other unsolicited manuscript. A week or so later I received a call from Jim Waring, who said he had read it, liked it and wanted to direct it.

Naturally I was delighted and looked forward to discussing the script with him in detail. But his duties as Olney's full-time designer and director kept him occupied until the very end of the then-current (1969) summer season, for whose final production *Christabel* had been scheduled. Our first real communication on the subject took place early one hot August morning aboard the Metroliner on the way to New York to hold auditions.

His opening remark came in the form of a grunt, as he stared gloomily at the script with eyes that obviously needed sleep. "I see that you've used a motion-picture technique."

"That's right," I said, pleased that he'd noticed. "I know it's unorthodox, but if the action is kept fluid it should work."

He nodded without conviction. "You can do things on the screen you can't do on the stage," he observed.

"True."

"Well," he said with another grunt. "We'll see."

In essence, *Christabel* was a mystery story, the question being is she really pregnant, as she keeps insisting to her unbelieving parents and, if so, who is responsible? Her obvious anger at Bobby throughout suggests that it might conceivably have made her do something she otherwise would not have done. But Frazier, whose character as a boy-man complements Christabel's as a woman-child, wins our affection to the degree that we cannot imagine his taking advantage of a 17-year old girl.

So that leaves only Bobby. My use of the "motion-picture technique" represented an attempt to conceal this fact as long as possible by interrupting the chronological order with flashbacks. Such technique, as it turned out, was also the principal reason for the play's getting as much attention as it did from potential producers.

Much of the action consists of narration by either Christabel, Frazier or Bobby about events that have already transpired. As they describe them, we see the events happening.

I divided the stage into four areas — a large upstage area occupied by a permanent set (representing the living room of Christabel's home) and two small downstage areas a few feet in from the right and left wings that, through the use of "wagons" (wheeled platforms) bearing rudimentary sets, would variously represent Christabel's bedroom and the separate apartments of Frazier and Garmatz, his long-term fiancee. The downstage middle area was used for the Manhattan nightclub where Christabel, furious with Bobby, and the bleary-eyed Frazier meet.

In writing the script, I assumed that the changes in setting, like the "cuts" in a movie, would take no longer than what was required by a couple of stagehands to push a small wagon on and then, a few minutes later, pull it off. I had not counted on the ingenuity of the man who had designed the Olney stage.

The front part was on rollers that enabled it to be pulled either right or left into the wings for set changes. The rear part was also on rollers that enabled it to move backward or forward for the same purpose. The problem was that the designer had not foreseen that such changes might have to be made with split-second timing. It took a full quarter of a minute to drag the segments backward, forward, in and out, as circumstances demanded. The heavy stage, moving on its tracks, produced a deep rumble, like a subway train passing beneath.

I didn't anticipate the threat this arrangement posed during rehearsals (which I viewed clandestinely from a seat in the rear of the darkened theater) because the set of the play then being performed at Olney occupied one whole side of the stage, making it impossible to utilize the equipment. Consequently I did not realize that shifts in scene I had intended to be made in a matter of seconds would entail many times that amount during which the stage would remain in darkness.

And the rumble made anything said while this was going on difficult to hear.

Jim had endeavored to bridge these moments — which became increasingly irritating during all the jumping back and forth in the second act — with music, but the effect was jerky at best. The play lacked the substance to support all the trappings. And the pace suffered.

Jim had been right. One cannot do on the stage what one can do on the screen. He had tried — because he had originally liked the play and, perhaps, because he liked me — a feeling our late-night conferences after those disturbing rehearsals may have lessened. But, without intending to, he had clearly proved his point.

I took care to find a convincing excuse for not reviewing *Christabel*. The assignment was given David Kearse, a conscientious and very gentlemanly *Sun* reporter who of course knew nothing of my connection. Passing his desk the morning after the opening, I was handed a sheet of copy. "Do you think this lead is too flip?" he asked.

"*Christabel*," I read "tried crossing the Rubicon and sank in Olney Theater's premiere of a new comedy this week."

It was my first bulletin from the front, and I contemplated it for a moment before replying.

"No," I said. "It seems just right to me."

And that's the way, much to Banker's glee, the review appeared in the next morning's paper.

AMONG OTHER THINGS, *Christabel* revealed exactly who among my colleagues my real friends were. Without in any way compromising himself concerning the play, Dick Coe, of the *Washington Post*, found redeeming social values in it. Lou Cedrone, of the *Evening Sun*, managed to avoid saying how bad it was without at the same time praising it, while Don Walls, of the *Daily Record*, who — because of remarks I had made about some of his work in the past, had every reason to seize this opportunity to retaliate — didn't. All by opening night had somehow learned who the author was.

In a Sunday column, the *News-American*'s R. P. Harriss took poor Dave Kearse to task for his unwitting part in the drama, and Harry Pouder in a rather charming piece in *Baltimore Magazine* expressed affection for me while pointing out that, as a critic, I would probably have panned *Christabel*. He was right.

Such unsolicited gestures of friendship I found especially heartwarming in view of my state of mind. Only two months before, the dawning of my 51st birthday had reminded me that I was no longer growing up; I was growing old. And the likelihood of my accomplishing anything more of consequence during the time left to me decreased with each day.

I was a man standing at the top of a hill with the choice of looking at the downward path that lay ahead or back at the one scaled on the way up. Without my quite realizing it, the Winged Chariot had closed in.

Mayme

Papa

Me

And
Time Passing...

THIRTY-SEVEN

I sit at the window watching rain puddles form in a parking lot. But it is not the puddles I see.

Like the thrumming in a wood.
Mayme, my mother's older sister, lived in a comfortable old house surrounded by very tall trees. I never knew what they were, for I am ignorant about trees. But they were the kind whose limbs didn't start until 20 or 30 feet up. And the great trunks, standing in towering rows, gave the yard a cathedral quality enhanced by the breezes that murmured through it like the subdued tones of an organ.

On lazy summer mornings during vacations from the Nashville high school I attended the rest of the year, I used to lie in an enormous upstairs room, stretching from one end of the house to the other, and listen to these murmurings, punctuated by the staccato echoes of a woodpecker. The drumming (thrumming?) seemed strangely muted, as if coming from a distance. And the dozing, dream-like nature of my perception of it mingled with the sounds of my mother playing the piano in the living room downstairs and my aunt's rhythmic rocking.

The piano had been the last gift my grandfather (the H. J. Moorman of *Christabel and the Rubicon* fame) had given my mother before his death. And of the few possessions she had managed to salvage from the family financial crisis that had deprived both her and me of the home we were born in — sending us, along with my father, first to Hopkinsville and then to Nashville — she valued it the most. So whenever we visited Aunt Mayme, in whose Mayfield residence it had found sanctuary, the piano was the first thing she headed for.

Toting our luggage, we would climb the steps to the wide front porch, with its peeling paint and swings on squeaky chains at either end. Aunt Mayme, who had been impatiently watching for our arrival, would fling open the door at the first bang of the heavy knocker and welcome us once again to a house filled with antique furniture, family portraits and — love.

Southern women are noted for the effusiveness of their hospitality, and it reaches an apex of sorts when applied to loved ones. My aunt could go on for hours. Eventually, however, the exchange of affection would exhaust itself and my mother would start sidling over to the piano. A moment later, I — upstairs — would hear her sweep into the "waltz."

The name of this piece — which still lingers as a haunting memory — I never knew. I doubt if my mother herself knew. She was a casual, if gifted pianist. She studied under Dr. Hesselberg, Melvin Douglas's father, at Nashville's Belmont College, which she attended before her marriage in May of 1914. He used to say "Miss Moorman, you are playing that goot. But not by the notes. You are playing it by the ear."

She could, it seemed, play anything (including the classics) by ear, and probably the "waltz" was something she had picked up like the style she learned while sitting in with the great jazz pianist Fate Marable at a Riverboat dance in her teens. But whatever it was and from wherever it came, it continues to echo in my head. So, for that matter, does my aunt's rocking.

As befitting a gentlewoman of the old South, Aunt Mayme was pointedly refined — at least in public. But she was short-tempered and addicted (at least, in private) to such utterances as "I'm so goddamn mad I could spit!" She was also fat. Five feet-two, 175 pounds.

In those days, women wore one-piece under garments which successively passed out of, then back into style. They were called "teddies," and one of Aunt Mayme's recurring problems was finding a pair roomy enough to accommodate everything. Not only did they tend to bind the hips, they stuck in the crotch. She developed the habit, when rising from a chair, of reaching in and giving them a tug.

She carried on a running battle with her black cook, an old family retainer who had the palsy. Alice shook under any circumstances but never so much as when confronted with "Miss Maymie" on her high horse about some domestic matter such as why the sheets hadn't been changed.

In the 1950's it became fashionable for Northerners to maintain that Southerners mistreated their servants. Actually black women in the South have always intimidated their white mistresses. And Alice was an old hand at the game. Indeed, so terrorized was Aunt Mayme by the frail and trembling Alice that much of her day was spent composing imaginary responses to Alice's attitudes she never quite dared to deliver.

Sliding oak doors separated the living room from the foyer. My aunt would enter, flinging them back and banging them shut behind her. She rarely did anything quietly. "I'm just going to go in," she would announce to my mother, "and say, 'Alice, you and I have known each other for most of our lives. So we should be able to —'"

During the speech that followed she would flounce over to the big chair by the wicker floor lamp on the south side of the room, plop down, thrust one plump leg under the other, and start rocking. As she rocked — one foot pushing, all the rest riding — the chair would creep across the carpet until it came up against the piano on the north side where my mother was.

Then my aunt would rise, jerk the teddy out of her crotch and, without pausing in her peroration, drag the rocker back to the floor lamp and start all over again.

As cloud shadows pass above the hill-flanks of the mountain meadows... Kentucky has mountains, but Mayfield isn't in them. Yet I knew about cloud shadows. I had seen them move over the grass of our side yard, where I spent much of my childhood playing cowboys and Indians or batting a tennis ball up against the house. I now realize the sound must have driven all within crazy — which was probably why I often caught sight of my grandfather peering out his study window with a twisted smile on his face.

Apart from the yard, the room on the other side of that window was my favorite place in the universe. As a precocious five-year-old, I would get out of bed in the morning and, after eating a breakfast prepared by Alice (who worked for us before she went to Aunt Mayme's) go into my grandfather's study and sit down. He had a tall, high-backed rocking chair with unusually wide arms, one of which had a deep indentation caused by his habit of cracking hickory nuts on it.

He would be in this chair smoking his pipe. The pipe had a curved stem. Once he decided to boil it to improve its flavor. The stem straightened out. Afterwards, whenever he smoked, the lighted tobacco stared him in the eye.

I had a pipe, too. It contained no tobacco, but I "smoked" it anyway. I also had a small rocking chair. My father once told me that he used to be very amused, when passing my grandfather's open door, to see the two of us, sitting there solemnly smoking and rocking without saying a word.

Such silences, however, were rare. My grandfather — or "papa," as we all called him — had opinions about everything, and he never hesitated to share them with me. One of his opinions was that Clarence Darrow was the Antichrist. Dayton, Tennessee was in the same Bible belt as our town, and throughout the sweltering summer of 1925 daily reports of the trial of John Scopes for teaching evolution in the Dayton high school provided a lively subject for papa's and my morning chats. I can't imagine what my reaction would have been had somebody told me that I would someday be working for the newspaper that furnished Scopes's bond and, in the end, paid his fine.

In religious matters, papa was a strict Fundamentalist. He believed in heaven and hell. Especially hell. He had an enormous book devoted to Dante's Inferno, whose Gustave Dore illustrations gave me nightmares. In one of our metaphysical discussions he suggested that the sun might be hell. It was a staggering thought — for at that moment I could see it there in the morning sky, sending its warm beams through a glistening windowpane to light the room where we waited on different thresholds to eternity.

Meanwhile, over the grasses of the side yard cloud shadows passed.

THE INTIMATE RELATIONSHIP THAT DEVELOPED between papa and me before he died at the age of 76 when I was nine is typical of what often happens when an old man and a child live under the same roof. They gravitate toward each other.

The usual explanation for this phenomenon is that the man, being in his dotage, inhabits the same world as the child. I doubt it.

More likely is the possibility that, as a man nears the end, he experiences a need to reach back to the beginning to see if he can discern some form (that word again) in it all.

To put it another way, through close contact with a child an old man may achieve contact with himself as he once was. Men with grandchildren have little live people to help them re-establish this bond. I have only Jerry Todd.

H. L. Mencken said he reread *Huckleberry Finn* every year. The statement confused me until somewhere around my 50th year I understood why. By recalling his feelings when first reading it, the book enabled Mencken to re-enter the world of his childhood. The following appeared in the Sunday *Sun* of March 3, 1974 and, later, in the *Milwaukee Journal*. Reader reaction in both Maryland and Wisconsin was surprisingly big.

Listening with Leo

Among the presents given me by my mother on my eighth Christmas was a book, which started off:

I got into the bushes quick as scat. Biting hard on my breath, sort of. For right there in front of our eyes was a regular old gee-whacker of a dinosaur. Bigger than the town water tower and the Methodist Church steeple put together. I tell you it was risky for us.
My chum got ready with his trusty bow and arrow.
"Do you think you can hit him in the heart?" I said, excited-like, squinting ahead to where the dinosaur was dragging his slimy body out of the pond.
Scoop Ellery's face was rigid.
"Got to," he said, steady-like. "If I miss, he'll turn on us and kill us both."
"It's a lucky thing for Red and Peg, I said, thinking of my other chums, "that they aren't in it."
"They'll miss us," said Scoop, "if we get killed."
My thoughts took a crazy jump.
"Why not aim for a tickly spot in his ribs," I snickered, pointing to the dinosaur, "and let him giggle himself to death?"
"Sh-h-h-h," cautioned Scoop, putting out a hand. "He's listening. The wind is blowing that way. He smells us."
"What of it?" I grinned. "We don't smell bad."

Such was my introduction to the Jerry Todd series of boys' adventure stories. Not make-believe adventures like the dinosaur game played by Jerry and Scoop here, but real experiences involving cops, robbers, ghosts and similarly stimulating subject matter. For having been made "genuine Juvenile Jupiter Detectives" by an old con-artist who sold them membership in a fake detective agency, Jerry, Scoop, Red and Peg spent all their time solving mysteries in their home town of Tutter, Ill., mystery capital of the world.

One would have to have been a small-town boy himself in those dim, pre-television days to understand the fascination these books held for me and others like me all over the country. It is true that the Bob Dexter and Hardy Boys books also concerned boy detectives, but neither was written with the warmth, color and, above all, humor that made the Jerry Todds and Poppy Otts (a companion series for which Jerry also acted as first-person narrator) unique.

To say I loved them would be putting it mildly, but my involvement at first was with the characters only. In my childish ignorance, I had accepted the fiction that Jerry himself was the author. The name, Leo Edwards, on the cover was a meaningless abstraction until a postscript to *Jerry Todd and the Purring Egg*, written not by Edwards but by a real boy like myself, changed everything.

To start with (wrote Eddie Blimke) *I heard this story of the "purring" egg before it was put into a book. That is, I was one of a gang of kids to whom the author read the story aloud. My dad has a summer home at Lake Ripley, near Cambridge, Wisconsin, and that is where Edward Edson Lee spends his summers. Mr. Lee is an author. He writes books for boys. This is one of his books, only it has the name of Leo Edwards on the cover. Some authors, you know, have a pen name, as they call it, and Leo Edwards is Mr. Lee's pen name.*

Well, as you can imagine, we hang around Mr. Lee's cottage quite a lot when we're at the lake. He's jolly and always ready for fun. He likes kids. Whenever he finishes a new book he sends word to us, up and down the lake shore, and that night we crowd around him on his front porch while he reads the book to us. Only it isn't a book then, it's what he calls a manuscript.

Eddie's story concerned an initiation dreamed up by the author and himself in honor of a young summer visitor named Herb Isham. The initiation took place at Hi-Lee Cottage, where the Lees lived, and frankly I found it rather silly. It was the way Eddie wound up his account that impressed me.

I tell you what — if ever you are near Lake Ripley in the summer time drop in and see me for a few minutes. Or, if you prefer, stop in at Hi-Lee Cottage and see Mr. and Mrs. Lee and their boy "Beanie." There's a secret about "Beanie" and Jerry Todd, but I can't put you wise here. I'll whisper the secret to you if you come to see me. A lot of boys come to Lake Ripley to see Mr. Lee. And they all get a warm welcome. I want you to know that.

In J. D. Salinger's *Catcher in the Rye,* Holden Caulfield says that, after reading a book he particularly likes, he has a desire to call up the author. I didn't merely want to telephone. I wanted to catch the next train to Cambridge. In short, Eddie made me conscious of the author as a real person, who lived in a specific locality and whom I might someday meet. The result was that all the affection I felt for the books became focused on him.

My awareness of Leo Edwards, as a living reality as opposed to a name on a dust jacket, was intensified through reading "Our Chatter Box," a sort of open-forum inaugurated with *Poppy Ott and the Tittering Totem*, in which the author published and commented on letters sent in by readers. Among the items included were poems, and if a boy was lucky enough to have his poem published, he received an autographed copy of the book in which it appeared. The following — from Charles Hockett, of Worthington, Ohio — appeared in the first chatter-box and set the tone, not to mention the quality, of most that came after.

OUR GANG
My name is Jerry Todd.
I live in Illinois.
I have a lot of fun
For I play with the boys.
Scoop Ellery and Red Meyers
Are two of my good friends.
Peg Shaw is the other one.
Why? Well, it all depends.

When I read this composition, which went on in much the same vein for nine stanzas, and realized I could earn a book with Edwards's signature in it simply by writing something like it, I got busy with paper and pencil. The poem I finally came up with was every bit as bad as Charles Hockett's, so I didn't see how I could miss. But a quick scanning of the chatter-box in the next Poppy Ott book showed me I had underestimated my competition. For though it contained no less than seven poems — all terrible — mine was not among them.

Disappointment because my literary efforts had not been fully appreciated did not prevent my taking advantage of an offer made by Edwards in one of the chatter-boxes to send his photograph to any who requested it. My parents had named me Rufus Hallette after my father and paternal grandfather and, until I changed to "Hal" at the age of 13, insisted on calling me "Rufe." Consequently, the letter I received in reply to my request began.

My dear Rufe:
I am sending you a picture of myself which I hope you will like and am looking forward to receiving one of you in return.
Hope you will pass Hi-Lee Cottage sometime and stop in and see me. Boys are always welcome and there is always a bunch hanging around. And a good bunch, too, believe me.
Lots of luck and best wishes.
Your pal,
Leo Edwards

Encouraged by all this attention, I decided to try my hand at another poem, which I sent along, together with a snapshot, the next day. But again the Muse let me down. The chatter-box in *Poppy Ott Hits the Trail* had 11 poems, sent in by boys from New York to Texas, but mine was not there. However, under the heading "Pictures," a few pages farther on, I found:

Gee-miny crickets gosh! I've got enough pictures here to fill a picture gallery. Pictures of small boys, big boys, long-legged boys, and all kinds of boys. I doubt if I can mention them all in this "Chatter-Box," but I'll do the best I can.
First on the list is a picture of a boy in overalls. This is Rufe Gardner, Mayfield, Ky., with a little black cap on the side of his head and a grin that spreads from ear to ear. Some guy! He's twelve years old, he says. Accompanying Rufe's swell letter is a poem, but it didn't seem quite as good to me as many I have. Here's hopin' I meet you some time, Rufe.

After that, I stopped writing to Leo Edwards. It wasn't just his crummy attitude about my poetry but the fact that, having reached the pinnacle of being mentioned in a chatter-box, I felt there was no percentage in it. I did not, however, stop reading — or, rather, rereading, for at about this point the quality of the books began to deteriorate. The characters lost their charm, and the stories became downright boring. It was as if they had been written by somebody else.

Or was it simply that I was growing up? Girls — who figured only slightly in the books and then more as good "guys" than as females — were beginning to command my attention. So when, in my early teens, we moved... to Nashville, the books, together with other belongings we had no room for, were left behind in my Aunt Mayme's attic. And in the flurry of adolescent preoccupations that followed, I forgot about them.

Aunt Mayme died in 1966 and the following summer her daughter, my cousin Ann, wrote from Louisville saying she was selling the house and would I please meet her in Mayfield to go through the things in the attic? And there, like a booby trap left for me by my child-self, were the books, with all their memories, waiting. Naturally, I could not resist reading them again, and they aroused in me more than nostalgia.

I had not, I saw, been wrong about Edwards. Unlike the incredible Edward Stratemeyer, who under a number of pseudonyms wrote most of the popular children's series of his day, he had not ground out potboilers with cardboard settings and characters. His Tutter — fictional name for Utica, the tiny Illinois town where he grew up — was three-dimensional, rich in atmosphere and geographical detail. And, combined with his ingenious plots and salty, grass-root characters, it provided a beguiling picture of small-town America during the early part of the century.

Congratulating myself on the discernment I had displayed as a child, I quickly finished all the books recovered from the attic and began haunting the second-hand stores, hoping to pick up the others. No luck. Nor did the public library offer any help. Not only was Edwards not listed in the card-catalogue but no mention of him was made in any of the reference books I consulted on American authors, either living or dead. What was the explanation for this oversight? Surely Jerry and Poppy deserved as much immortality as Stratemeyer's Bobbsey Twins or Bunny Brown and Sister Sue! My indignation thus aroused, I decided to put him on record by writing an article about him myself.

My first move was a letter to G. W. Crump, editor of the *Cambridge News*. Edwards I assumed to be dead, but what about "Beanie?" Did Mr. Crump know of his whereabouts? Weeks passed. Then, arriving at my office one day, I was told I had received a telephone call from a Eugene Lee, of Beloit, who turned out to be "Beanie" himself. An executive with the Beloit Corporation, he still, he said, spent part of every year at Hi-Lee Cottage, and Mr. Crump had forwarded my letter to him.

I learned that "Leo," as he calls his father, had died in 1944 at the age of 60. The date surprised me, because the deterioration in quality to which I have alluded began a good ten years before that, leading me to believe that the books after *Poppy Ott Hits the Trail* had been written by someone else. And the most logical explanation was that Edwards had died.

"No," said Eugene Lee, "he wrote them, but he was in bad shape. Everything sort of fell apart at the end."

Shocked that a man whose attitude, as revealed in his writings, was so unequivocally upbeat should "fall apart at the end," I begged for further information; but Mr. Lee, speaking from the office where he supervises the design of instruments for the operation of paper mills, said he hadn't time to discuss the matter then and referred me to a St. Louis book collector specializing in Edwards lore. For it appeared I was not the only one who cherished the memory of his father.

"There's a big fan club," I was told. "They have a newspaper and everything."

The idea of a Jerry-Poppy fan club composed of middle-aged men intrigued me. And, after receiving Mr. Lee's assurance he would write at his earliest convenience, I hung up and sent off a letter to the St. Louis collector, requesting details. They arrived in the next week's mail.

"I could talk about Leo Edwards for hours," wrote Willis J. Potthoff, a 60-year-old engineer with Emerson Electric, and it was obvious from the material he enclosed that he shared this propensity with others. The envelope contained several issues of the *Tutter Bugle*, identified as the "Voice of the Leo Edwards Juvenile Jupiter Detective Association," the fan club referred to by Mr. Lee.

I have since learned that the *Bugle*, started in 1967 by Robert L. Johnson, of Bisbee, Ariz., only lasted a few years, but at one time its subscribers, reflecting the membership of the club, totaled 100. The first anniversary issue carried the announcement of a projected convention of Edwards fans to be held in his home town during the coming year (1969). Actually, the meeting took place not at Utica but at Hi-Lee Cottage, and, according to a story in the August-September issue of the Methodist publication *Together*, it was well attended by a group that included lawyers, teachers, merchants, engineers and bankers, all of whom came to recall what it was like to be a boy "in the days before Hitler, television and affluence came along to change the world of boys as it used to be."

Mr. Potthoff seemed impressed by the fact that I had been mentioned in one of the chatter-boxes and enclosed a Xeroxed copy of a "mention" concerning himself. A few days later Eugene Lee's letter arrived.

I always find this type of letter difficult to write. I do not know exactly where to start, exactly what to say and more important when I've said enough. So I'll make it brief.

Leo died in 1944 at our home in Rockford, Ill. He was just 60 years old, a broken, sick and bitter man. As far as Betty and I were concerned, his books died with him and that was that. But it wasn't. As the years have passed by it has all gained a head of steam. Book collectors, a magazine published bi-monthly, the rights sold to a Hollywood group, etc.

Many people come to Hi-Lee Cottage at Lake Ripley. Some come to see where the books were written. Others come to see me, son of the author. These are the ones I have qualms about. They have formed a picture of Leo by reading his books, and they are looking for something they do not find; for while I look much like Leo, I'm not much like him in other ways.

Being the son of a popular author of boys' books has its drawbacks, I gathered during a visit of my own to the Lee cottage last summer. "This is where they'd land," said my host, leading me down the steep path from the house to the lake. "He'd read the book to them in two installments, half one night and half the next. At the end of the first half he'd treat them to hotdogs, cooked around a fire in the back yard. The next night there'd be ice cream." Somehow the picture was different from that evoked by Eddie Blimke.

As a child, "Beanie," who typed most of his father's manuscripts, had to share him with all the other boys in the area. Now, a man of pronounced individuality and highly respected in his field, he still has to do it and in a way often at variance with his nature and, at times, a downright nuisance.

For fans, whether they be callow kids or seasoned graybeards, all seem to have one thing in common — the feeling that love gives them proprietary rights. One visitor to the cottage arrived, unheralded, at 3 A.M. with two carloads of friends and relatives. Another, also uninvited, strode in as the Lees were sitting down to dinner and proceeded to join them at the table. Autographed books have disappeared from the shelves such as the two in which Leo acknowledged (the "secret" hinted at so broadly by Eddie) that "Beanie" was the real-life model for Jerry Todd.

Despite such invasions of his privacy and violations of his hospitality, Eugene Lee feels a strong sense of responsibility to the hundreds of people who write seeking information about Leo and help in finding his books, out of print since Grosset & Dunlap scrapped the plates during World War II. Only recently he responded to the requests of a 13-year-old Shreveport boy and a Virginia housewife (who wanted a Poppy Ott to surprise her husband with on Christmas) with free gifts of books, of which he has a good, if rapidly shrinking supply.

A far from sentimental man, he still finds it hard to discuss the final years of his father's life, when diminishing sales and the dissolution of his 30-year marriage left him a virtual recluse. Every time I broached the subject, as we sat looking at the lake he told me Leo loved, he shied away from it. I did, however, get certain impressions.

Edwards left Utica in 1897 at the age of 13 to take a menial job in a Beloit factory. Later, when he began to write, he drew upon his childhood recollections to create the character and characters of Tutter. Thus, though all the Jerry Todd-Poppy Ott books were written after World War I, they must have reflected a life of a much earlier period. This didn't matter too much when the tempo of life was so slow one could detect only superficial changes between one decade and the next. But, as that tempo quickened with the approach of World War II, the books must have lost their "relevance" to a generation whose eyes were turned not to the pleasantries of the past but to the horrors of the future.

At any rate, Edwards's popularity began to wane. His sales — which, according to his son, never totaled much more than 2,000,000 — fell off; and his half-hearted attempts to remedy the situation by changing his format and updating his style proved to be disastrous.

Perhaps most disheartening of all, his boys — those loyal legions who every summer crowded his doorstep, warming him with their love, delighting him with their laughter — grew up, married and moved away to adult responsibilities elsewhere. Forgotten (or so it must have seemed), he lived on at Hi-Lee, the memories of happier times insufficient to lift him from the despondency that reached epic proportions with the discovery that he had incurable cancer.

"Sometimes," Eugene Lee told me, "he would lie on a chair in the back yard all afternoon without moving." A dreadful image for one whose childhood was graced by the felicity of his writing.

Eugene and his charming wife Betty were most gracious during my short stay, enduring my persistent questions, stuffing me with delicious fish he (as acknowledged champion of the lake) had caught that same afternoon and permitting me to spend the night in Leo's room — which, like the rest of the cottage, I found both unpretentious and comfortable.

As I lay there, listening to the midnight voices of boys out on the lake shouting above the racket of an outboard motor, I wondered if, during those last terrible years, Leo had not lain in the same spot and listened to the clamor of similar voices (Jerry, Scoop, Red, Peg?) calling to him from the past. For I well knew that all the pilgrims to Hi-Lee came in answer to such voices. They heard them when they reread the books, and they hoped to hear them even better in the house where the books had been written — the piping, proud, pathetic voices that so many years before had been their own.

With this in mind, I felt my way through the darkened hall to the bookcase and selected from the two shelves of vellum-encased volumes Eugene Lee's personal copy of *Jerry Todd and the Talking Frog*, the book that, given me by my mother on my eighth Christmas, had introduced me to a whole new world. And, returning to Leo's room, I opened it to Chapter One:

"I got into the bushes quick as scat..."

—0—

ACCORDING TO EMILY DICKINSON, there is no frigate like a book to take us lands away. The books found in Aunt Mayme's attic took me back to Rufe Gardner land — sunlight sparkling on papa's bedroom window, mother playing the piano, me in the grass thinking "Ain't nothin' I got to do till school starts in September."

Adding up to what?

An old man watching rain falling in a parking lot?

Form?

Kathleen Moorman Gardner

Father and son

Never Forget

THIRTY-EIGHT

Among the items recovered from Aunt Mayme's attic were some of my mother's school books. Like most Mayfield children of her generation, she had attended West Kentucky College, which was located right across the street from the house where she lived with her parents and two sisters.

West Kentucky College was not really a "college." More like a combination elementary and high school. But it was where my mother used the books I found in the attic.

Most children doodle on their textbooks. My mother — a feisty little thing with enormous eyes and a voice as fresh as a mountain spring — apparently never stopped.

The inside covers and title pages of her books were covered with drawings, words and sentences piled on top of one another in such profusion they looked like mosaics. And the margins were filled with passing thoughts and secret communications aimed at friends across the aisle.

On the flyleaf of Philip Van Ness Myers's *Ancient History* she had written "There's a red-headed boy on both sides of me!" In the margins of pages 148 and 149 of Edward Eggleston's *History of the United States and Its People* was "I am going to ask Prof. Gray to let me be excused, and you come out after me and we will play hopscotch."

Professor Gray appears frequently in her scribblings. He first shows up on the inside front cover of H. A. Guerber's *Story of the Great Republic*:

"Before Xmas Prof. Farrow taught us in the year of 1903. But after Xmas Prof. Gray taught us in the year of 1904. I like Prof. Gray the best."

But on page 248 of Eggleston over a picture of James Lawrence, the American naval commander who uttered the immortal words "Don't give up the ship," I read:

"I hate Prof. Gray, don't you?" Under the picture in a different handwriting was "Yes. He is so mean."

My mother had decorated Lawrence's face with heavy, penciled-in spectacles. Other portraits throughout the books sported mustaches and whiskers the subjects never knew they had.

Starting at the top of page 286 and going all around it and the following page was "S. C. said he was going to bring me some candy at dinner. You had better keep on my good side." And on page 93, over a picture depicting "A wedding in New Amsterdam" were the words "I love S. C., don't you?" Yet on page 266 over John Quincy Adams in a full beard, was "I despise S. C."

In spite of this and similar remarks appearing here and there, strong negative attitudes were not typical of my mother's classroom mood — which was for the most part playful.

"Look on page 211," she tells the reader at the beginning of Guerber. Then on page 211: "Oh! I made a great mistake. Look on page 106." On page 106: "Oh! Please excuse me. Look on page 237." On page 237: "Oh! My toe is hurting."

Above Guerber's table of contents we find: "The shoe said to the stocking 'I'll wear a hole in you.' The stocking said to the shoe 'I'll be darned if you do'."

Thumbing on, I read "If this nut's name you cannot find, look on page 39." Page 39 bore my mother's own name, Kathleen Moorman — a little joke on herself. Beneath it was the statement: "Mary Hunt has the measles."

All of which I assimilated with a mixture of amusement, affection and pain. She had died at age 72 only two years before, and the books provided unexpected insights into a phase of her life I had never known. She had obviously been a lively, if unusually innocent, child.

Then on one side of a map of the Persian Empire opposite page 92 in Myers's *Ancient History* I saw:

"Never forget Wed. night Nov. 20, '07, 7:20 o'clock studying for examination. _____ ____ is here downstairs."

I sat up. Who, I wondered, was _____ ____ and what had led my mother to identify him in such a sneaky fashion? What, moreover, was he doing downstairs in her home? My curiosity was further whetted by an entry on the other side of the Persian Empire in reference to something that had occurred a month earlier.

"Never forget Thurs. morn. History period Oct. 17, '07. The Hon. Kathleen Moorman. And also tonight, Tues. Oct. 22, '07.

"At home studying and thinking of _____ ____." Beneath was written in an emphatic hand "A *Men!*"

I began to flip pages. Myers, I gathered, had served as text for one of my mother's more boring courses. The book was crammed with evidences of the day dreams she had resorted to as a much-needed escape. Or was that really what she, who had just turned 16, needed?

Page 128: "Never forget. Kathleen M. Mon. night, Oct. 21, '07. At home studying." On another part of the page: "Who do you love? _____ ____ and ____ _____. The first the best."

I considered the possibility that Professor Gray had been the object of my mother's affections. But how about that six-letter first name? Then in one of the other books I discovered that Gray's first name had been Thomas, though my mother never referred to him as such. It was either Prof. Gray or, when feeling impish, "old Tom Gray."

Page 136: "Never forget the review of this Tuesday night, Oct. 22, '07. K. M. at home has the blues. Why? Because _____ ____ is going to leave 7:30 o'clock. _____ ____ is upstairs now."

What the devil was _____ ____, who when last heard from was downstairs, doing upstairs? Had he moved in?

Page 155: "Never forget Thurs. night, Oct. 24, '07. Fifteen minutes 'till 9. I expect _____ ____ will leave tomorrow. Two weeks ago tonight. Do I remember? __ and I got mad and about what? Because (s)he went somewhere and did something I did not want h(er)im to do."

Suddenly a new character, _ _, had entered the scene. And what a character he-she must have been! I plunged on.

196

"Two weeks ago tonight. Thurs. Oct. 24, '07. _ _ and I got mad because s(he) was in a play at the M. Church and I did not want h(im)er to be in it with M. S."

My mother, I began to realize, had been a much more complicated person than I had ever suspected:

"Never forget. Sat. morn, Oct. 26, '07. Studying history.

"_ _ not here. Oh, Mur! _ _ _ _ _ _ _ _ _ _ is not in Mayfield!"

After "Oh Mur," I was relieved to find on page 167 the statement that "_ _ _ _ _ _ _ _ _ _ came home Sun. Oct. 27, '07. And I'm so happy."

But the happiness was short-lived!

Page 214: "I am mad at somebody who with _ _ _ _ _ _ _ _ _ _ did me dirty Thurs. night, Nov. 7, '07. They went to town without letting me know."

Finally. Page 303: "Never forget Mon. night, Dec. 9, '07. Mama is at Mrs. Cook's anniversary. Papa has gone to bed. Joe [a boarder who later married my Aunt Mayme] is in Wickliff. Hal [my other aunt] and Will [her husband to be] are in Hal's room. And _ _ and me all alone in Mama's room."

Whichever _ _'s sex and whatever he-she might have been to my mother I was never able to ascertain. Nor could I find any reference to either him-her or _ _ _ _ _ _ _ _ _ _, as such, in any of the other books. I was glad, for by then I was beginning to feel I had pried enough into the privacy of a delightful little girl I was not to meet until emerging from her womb 11 years later.

I EMERGED WITH A BANG. The doctor who delivered me drank. The birth was an agonizingly slow one — and, after hours of sweating it out under the strain of a monumental hangover, he decided upon desperate measures.

He gave my mother a shot of something that brought me out like a blast from a cannon. In the process, it split her uterus down the middle and dislocated her bladder. Years later, a Baltimore surgeon, nourished on Freud, took me into his office after talking to my mother and asked with a dancing light in his eye if she had tried to make me (the baby) feel guilty for her cervical cancer. The question was typical of the ignorance and incompetence displayed by the medical profession toward both my mother and me from the time of my birth, in July of 1918, to the time of her death in May of 1964.

I shall not interrupt this narrative to cite examples. But, looking back, I am amazed that any of us — and I refer to the whole human race — managed to survive.

WHAT ONE CAN BE DEPENDED UPON TO REMEMBER from one's early infancy is debatable. I have a distinct impression of two women laughing while bouncing me up and down on a bed when I was too young even to crawl. One certainly was my mother, the other probably my Aunt Hal, who lived in a house just behind ours with my Uncle Will. They had a son, Harry Moorman Stanfield (named after papa), seven years my senior.

Aunt Hal, whose name was Hallie as distinguished from that of my father (which was Hallette), played an important part in my life — coming close on one occasion to saving it. I have always been a stickler for the genuine as opposed to the imitation. So when my mother, having exhausted her milk supply, tried to switch her nursing baby to the bottle, I refused to go along. It had to be the real thing or nothing.

I was virtually starving when Aunt Hal came into the house one day, crying out, as she always did, "I smell a baby!" Taking one look at me, she said "Let me have him."

She placed me in her lap with my head between her knees so I couldn't wiggle. She then began ladling spoonfuls of milk onto my mouth from a glass in her hand.

Any infant, so provoked, will lick his lips. I did and found the taste not disagreeable. From then on, whenever my stomach told me it was time to eat, I screamed for "Gad-a-milk-a-poon."

AWARENESS OF MY MOTHER AS A SPECIAL ENTITY whose responses to my needs could usually be relied upon must have come around this time. I hated being put to bed — for either a nap in the afternoon or the longer exile from the household at night. Lying there, I would send out urgent appeals to those I felt might come to my aid — my grandfather, my mother and my father, more or less in that order.

My grandfather had a habit of calling me papa's little pig. I, in return, called him Pa-pig. My mother I called Money. "Money!" I would cry from the darkness of the room adjoining the lighted one where I knew they all were. "C'mawn 'n' get me! Pa-pig, mawn! Daddy, mawn!" These nightly ordeals placed enormous strain on my mother and grandfather, whose natural impulse was to rush in and grab me up in their arms. As to the effect upon my father I was never sure.

A peculiar mixture of graciousness and reserve, he lingered on the borders of my life, lending support to any project I might have but sharing with me no part of himself. He was a master at seeming to give everything while actually giving little. When in the chips, there was nothing he would not do for his wife and son except reveal to them what was transpiring in his soul.

I was a sickly child. I had a sensitivity to milk during a time when nobody had heard of allergies. At least not in Mayfield where the treatment for all ills was Dr. Stevens's Red Sour Medicine.

Milk gave me a congestion of the lungs then diagnosed as bronchitis. And this, together with high fever and a general feeling of misery, kept me in bed for long stretches of my childhood. After I recovered from one of these spells my mother, on the advice of good Dr. Stevens, would start plying me with milk to "build me up" — as a result of which I would soon be back in bed again. Every night when he came home from work, my father brought me a present.

He managed Gardner Furniture Company, a business started by his uncle years before. He'd gone into it after my mother insisted he stop traveling around the country selling kitchen cabinets and stay home with her. He was a gifted salesman — almost a genius. He never held a job where he didn't lead the sales force. His uncle had become hopelessly enamored of Aimee Semple McPherson, to whose work he devoted the rest of his life and fortune. My father, with his characteristic willingness to oblige, agreed to run the store without receiving any vested interest in it. Later, the uncle sold out to a chain, and when he died Aimee Semple got everything.

One of my father's newly acquired duties was attending the annual furniture mart in Chicago, to which store-managers from all over the country came to acquaint themselves with the latest in furniture design. Neither my mother nor I quite understood what the term "going to market" meant when the time approached every year. I think she suspected it was just an excuse to whoop it up on the expense account. But she indulged my father in his pretension that it was an important part of his job.

The memory of his first market stands out in my mind. I could not have been more than four. My mother and I took him to the depot. It was around 5 P.M. on a dreary winter's day. We waited on the platform, shivering. As always, my father tried to brighten the situation with banter. It didn't work.

The train arrived, and my father, carrying his suitcase, got on. "See you in a week," he called from the steps with a cheery wave of the hand. The train disappeared around the bend. Much later in life after attending innumerable such departures, it occurred to me that trains when leaving stations never disappear at vanishing points along straight tracks but always around a bend.

And what lies around the bend? The Unknown.

As my mother and I drove home, it began to snow, the flakes whirling away from our headlights like water dividing before the prow of a boat. She sensed my mood. "Don't be unhappy, darling," she said with an unsuccessful attempt to match my father's cheerfulness. "He'll be back before you know it."

But he wouldn't. A whole week would pass before he entered the house again, a smile on his lips and a present in his hand. For me.

BY NATURE A CAREFREE, HAPPILY DISPOSED LITTLE PERSON, Kathleen Moorman, upon becoming a mother, underwent a severe change. Her baby was constantly and inexplicably sick. Several of her close friends had given birth the same year as she, and their babies were as robust and brimming with health as babies should be. Why was hers different? Was it something she had done? Or failed to do?

The question plagued her, along with the fear that I was on a collision course with death. I've mentioned her enormous eyes. Time and again I awakened from a feverish sleep to find these two marvelous orbs fixed upon me.

Anxiety over my health became the prevailing theme of our life together in the old house at Seventh and College Streets where we both had been born. It dominated every hour of the day — especially those involving eating. Dr. Stevens, whom my mother consulted on an average of five times a week, had told her that I must at all costs be made to eat. So she sat beside me at mealtime. "Take a bite of meat," she would say. "Now a bite of potatoes." As I neared the end of each helping, there was always a dish prodding my elbow urging more.

As I grew older, this practice of monitoring my meals became so intolerable that I took to building walls in the form of glasses and ketchup bottles around my plate so she couldn't see it — which at first puzzled, then hurt her.

But eating was only one aspect of the problem. Another was not eating — between meals which conceivably could cut down my appetite for meat and potatoes when the next meal came around. Sweets were a particular threat.

My mother was nothing if not social, and around Christmas she and her many friends spent a lot of time wrapping and exchanging gifts. She would spread an array of beautiful paper, fancy ribbons and Santa Claus stickers over the counterpane and I would toddle in and watch while she put it all together.

For I had learned that Christmas meant, among other things, candy.

She gave and, in turn, received great quantities of Christmas candy. From what she received she allowed me to choose one piece after every meal. Of all the boxes I could choose from I liked Whitman's Sampler the best — for it included on the inside of the boxtop a table of contents. Among the items listed was something described as "Cordial — Be Careful." I soon decided that these cordial-be-carefuls were my favorite.

No child worthy of the name will settle for one piece of candy when opportunities exist for obtaining more. I never failed to take advantage of such opportunities — which sometimes involved pilfering small sums from my mother's purse in order to sneak out and buy some. The accepted punishment for children in those days was lashing their legs with a switch. All the switchings I received (and they were not inconsiderable) resulted from my consuming between-meal things — candy, soda pop, cherries from the tree in our side yard — my mother, in her obsessive concern for my health, considered bad.

The relationship between a sick child and his nurse engenders an intimacy unlike any other. Compared to it, that between husband and wife is rudimentary. Much as I resented my mother's constant attention, I grew to depend upon it. For I knew that, however I might wish her not there, there she would always be.

Sitting at my bedside, while my legs jumped and my head throbbed, she read all the Jerry Todd books out loud to me, as well as others by S. S. Van Dine, Mary Roberts Rinehart and Agatha Christie. We shared both pain and pleasure.

All of which I remembered with shame 35 years later when I became the nurse and she the child.

DURING MOST OF MY CHILDHOOD I LIVED THE LIFE OF A LITTLE PRINCE surrounded by adoring subjects — parents, grandparents, uncles, aunts. Every Christmas my father spent a small fortune upon gifts to put under the 15-foot tree occupying one corner of our high-ceilinged living room and fireworks that, launched from the front yard on Christmas night, drew crowds of awed onlookers from all over town.

He seemed to take special pleasure in indulging my childish fancies. My cousin Moorman, to whom I looked up as only a younger child to an older can, had two electric trains — an Ives and a Lionel. "When the time comes for your father to buy you one," he told me, "be sure it's a Lionel. The Ives is no good."

This information, which I accepted as gospel truth, was duly passed on to my father. "A Lionel," I repeated over and over. "Don't ever get me an Ives!"

Though I didn't know it, my father had already bought an Ives, which investigation had convinced him was the superior product. But he knew how important to me the thing was, so when he presented the train to me the following Christmas he said it was a Lionel.

I had not yet learned to read, but I had the uneasy feeling that something was not right. "Are you sure," I asked anxiously, "that this is a Lionel?"

"Oh, absolutely. See?" He spelled out the letters on the carton with his finger. "I-V-E-S, Lionel."

Well, the train proved to be quite satisfactory. Still, years later, when I came upon the discarded carton in the basement of our South Seventh Street home and realized how my father had fooled me, I was furious.

But any dad can give his boy an electric train. Mine sought the extraordinary. Once, returning from a trip to Chicago, he brought me a toy car the size of a Volkswagen. All it lacked was an engine. It was so heavy my thin legs could not work the pedals that propelled it. So it sat, immobile in the back yard, exciting envy in all the neighborhood children.

Such over-indulgence spoiled me rotten without preparing me for the shocks that were to come. For suddenly he, from whom all blessings flowed, became unglued.

He had never gotten over his uncle's selling Gardner Furniture Company to an outside corporation. He felt the rug had been pulled from under, leaving him in the position of a hired hand. And, as the economic pressures of that depressing period in American history increased, an old vice reappeared. Gambling.

It was perhaps only logical that a man who regularly paid $150 to a Louisville tailor for custom-made suits when most Mayfield business men got theirs for $25 at J. C. Penney's would have difficulty adjusting to the rigors — not to mention boredom — of the Depression. My father simply refused to do it. And in an effort to keep up the style to which he (and his family) had grown accustomed, he gambled. And he gambled big.

At one point his gambling debts amounted to $75,000, no mean sum in those days, so he made a deal with his brother and two sisters to exchange his inheritance upon his mother's death for a settlement then. He thus sacrificed his birthright. He didn't do mine any good either.

What's worse, he continued to gamble. And, as his losses grew, a new vice appeared. Drinking.

The long-range effect first made itself felt on my mother and me when he came home one night with the news that we would soon have to vacate the house at Seventh and College so he could turn it over to the Building and Loan Association. The association, it seemed, held a mortgage it was eager to foreclose. But that did not bother my mother so much as his plan to raise the money needed for moving by selling the furnishings in the same way he sold stuff in his downtown store.

For a week thereafter, she and I prepared tags to be attached to the chairs we had always sat in and the table we had always eaten from. Then, on the appointed day, the doors were thrown open and the townsfolk trooped in. Women my mother had entertained as guests now came as customers to a sale.

Everything — including not simply her own cherished possessions but what remained of her parents' and grandparents' — was thus disposed of. And though the years that followed brought many humiliating experiences, this became the blow from which she never recovered.

Our move from the old house, with its legions of loving memories, was the first in a series that took us from jobs my father held in Hopkinsville, Nashville, Memphis and Fort Worth. And with every change of employment his reserves — both economic and emotional — shrank.

The pattern was always the same. He would take a new job in a new place, where no one knew of his history of drinking and gambling. And for a while, as he applied himself industriously to meeting the new challenge, it would look as if everything were going to be all right. Then the drudgery of going down every day to a less-than-elegant store where he held a less-than-elegant position began to eat on him. And he'd start gambling.

When his debts to friends and loan-sharks reached unmanageable proportions, he'd begin to drink. I've mentioned my allergy to milk. My father apparently was allergic to alcohol — a mere taste of which would inflame his eyes and loosen his tongue to the degree that he would babble in a manner he never did otherwise.

My mother and I, all too familiar with the symptoms, would brace ourselves for the catastrophe we knew was to come. And it invariably did — whereupon we would gather our few belongings together and prepare to move on to the next city.

For much of my youth I shared my mother's hope that he might eventually come to his senses and rise to the level of responsibility he had maintained for the first 15 years of their married life. But as time passed and the pattern became more and more set, I gave up.

My mother, be it a measure of her loyalty or refusal to face facts I could never decide, did not. And her determination that he should abandon his self-destructive habits and become once more the man she had married forced her to assume roles that, because they were demeaning, undermined her respect for herself.

In 1943, my parents, following a crisis of the sort my father was an expert at creating, came to Baltimore where he obtained a job with a Howard Street furniture store completely the opposite of the fashionable West-End shop he had just left in Nashville. As usual, the first couple of years went well. Then he began to exhibit those familiar signs of impending disaster.

My mother knew that an alley running behind the store led directly to a sleazy bar on Franklin Street. Without my knowledge (I was then working full-time at Martin's) she began stationing herself in the door of a cheap hotel across from this bar with the intention of stopping my father's going into it. For if only she could prevent his taking that first drink, maybe — just maybe — our lives would take a different course.

My father's story reached its climax in Tucson, Arizona, where he had gone in a desperate effort to escape the effects of chronic emphysema and asthma. He didn't make it.

Following his death in the fall of 1948 my mother came back from Tucson to live with me in Baltimore. It was a period when I was endeavoring to make the transition from insurance salesman to newspaper reporter, neither of which job paid anything like a living wage. I was also struggling with the problem of how to marry and support a beautiful blond woman with whom I had fallen head-over-heels in love.

It was in such an atmosphere of struggle and despair that I learned my mother was afflicted with terminal cancer.

SHORTLY AFTER MOVING TO FORT WORTH FROM NASHVILLE in the middle Thirties my parents and I went to see a movie called *Born to Dance*. Among the principal characters was Lucy James, a glamorous Broadway star played by Virginia Bruce. One of the better scenes involved a visit by this star to a naval vessel for publicity purposes. As the launch bearing her gorgeous person neared the vessel where the company was standing at rigid attention, a sailor announced over the ship's public-address system:

"Miss Lucy James's approaching Starb'rd B."

The announcement passed from man to man in the ranks until it became a chant: "Miss Lucy James's approaching Starb'rd B."

For some reason this scene stuck in my father's mind, and he developed the habit, when hugging my mother on arriving home at nights, of beating out a tattoo on her rear end to "Miss Lucy James's approaching Starb'rd B."

From here it was but a short step to calling *her* Miss Lucy and, in time, Lucy — a name which others, including myself, began to use.

Approaching the *Sun*'s city desk one afternoon, I was greeted with a howl of laughter from Al Sehlstedt, with whom I had spent many a happy hour playing pool and working rewrite. A devout Catholic, Al had always been a little awed by what he regarded as my crowded love life.

"Gardner, you're too much!" he roared. "A new girl every minute. Lucy wants you to call her whenever you get a chance. I hope she's as delightful in person as she sounds on the telephone."

It was the final stage of my mother's life, and I didn't feel up to explaining that the Lucy of the lilting voice was a dying lady of 72.

AS A NURSE, I FELL FAR SHORT OF MY MOTHER. Of course, she had help. During most of my childhood illnesses she had the financial support of her husband and the emotional support of one or more of her parents and sisters. She also had servants to relieve her of the responsibility of ordinary housekeeping chores. In short, she had nothing that really demanded her time but me, and to me she gave that time unstintingly.

I had none of these advantages. Consequently, when I learned in the fall of 1961 that a malignancy her physician and I thought had been eliminated years before had spread throughout her frail body, I knew I faced a problem that would involve more than what it cost me in grief.

My job required that I spend much of the day and even more of the evening attending movies and plays, along with interviews, news conferences, luncheons, dinners, receptions and other stupid events relating thereto. Worse still, I had to write stories about them.

Fortunately, I was able to obtain the services of two wonderful black women. Anna May came at 2 P.M. when I went to work. Bonnie came around dinner time and stayed until 2 A.M. when I returned. This arrangement, though costing me every penny I made, provided care and, probably even more important, company for my mother when I was elsewhere. And I made a point of being elsewhere most of the time.

Writing, if it is to be any good, should express not only the thoughts but the feelings of the writer. As one whose job it was to write about oftentimes trivial things, I realized the danger of allowing the depression I felt over my mother's approaching death to creep into the tone of the four or more articles I had to pound out every week. More dangerous was the likelihood that, as she got worse, I might be unable to write at all.

I have described how, as a young man, I built a wall of ketchup bottles around my plate to keep her concern for my eating from invading my digestive process. I now built a wall of distance to keep her suffering from invading my soul.

Thank God for Bonnie and Anna May. During the two and a half years it took for my mother to die, they enabled me to stay away from home as much as possible. Even when I was there, I administered to her needs — giving her medicine, taking her to the bathroom, simple things like that — with a detachment that kept the lock tight on my emotions.

"Son," she said, looking at me out of those big eyes which had undergone operations for cataracts only a few months before, "you always seem so stern."

Indeed, sternness may have been the only way I managed to get through the final days when pain made it impossible for her to rise from bed, thus confining her for the rest of her short life to a chair.

And there she sat — day in, day out — with only her two black angels to give her the comfort her son, preoccupied as he was with his own concerns, denied her. Bonnie said that the Saturday night before her death, while I was out getting drunk somewhere, the two of them had held an improvised religious service.

At my mother's request, Bonnie had read the "In my father's house there are many mansions" passage from the Bible, one of her favorites. Afterwards, they had sung a hymn. And after that, my mother had closed her big eyes and said "It's all right, Bonnie. My papa's coming to get me."

And he did. At 2 P.M. on Monday Bonnie arrived in the place of Anna May, who often had things to do for her school-age daughter. I had not gone over to the part of the room where my mother lay, having mistaken her heavy breathing for sleep. And I did not want to disturb her. But it was Bonnie who, after a quick glance in her direction, seemed disturbed.

"If anything happens today," she asked, "what do you want me to do?"

Something in her tone caused me to go around and look at my mother — who, though still breathing heavily, had her eyes open. Aunt Mayme told me, after being at the bedside of Uncle Joe when he died, that there *is* such a thing as the death rattle. With my little mother it was not a rattle but a song.

She seemed to be in a state of intense concentration, as if endeavoring to put the pieces of a difficult puzzle together.

"Lucy?" I said not so much in alarm as interrogation. "Lucy?"

And she gave that dainty, high-above-the-mountain sigh that will live in memory forever and simply — stopped breathing. Ten more days and it would have been her 50th wedding anniversary.

IN SMUDGY PENCIL ON THE LAST PAGE of Guerber's *Story of the Great Republic* is written:

"My name is Kathleen Moorman. I live in Mayfield. I go to West Kentucky College. My teacher is Prof. Gray. My parents are Mr. and Mrs. H. J. Moorman, Hal and Mayme are my sisters. Essie Douthit and I are pardners. Robert Davis is her sweetheart. I am going to grow up and get married and be very happy.
"I am 12 years old."

Never forget.

The Sun Sets

THIRTY-NINE

In the jargon of show business a class act is one of acknowledged superiority. The *Sun* used to be a class act.

Price Day called it the best unread newspaper in the country. "Unread" because its dignified (as opposed to sensational) style made it to the millions nurtured on television seem stodgy. And because at least twenty per cent of them couldn't read.

According to a 60 Minutes TV segment aired in February of 1988, one out of every five Americans is illiterate. Add to this 50 million or so an equal number whose interests run mainly to sports, making money, sex, gossip, rock music and the latest fads in clothes, cars and food, and you have an idea of the audience the average commercial television program is designed for.

It is, I suspect, the same audience the Pepsi Cola people have in mind when they describe their product as the choice of a "New" generation. The adjective is not exclusive with them. It is the practice to advertise everything on the market today as "new." A *New Yorker* cartoon a couple of years back showed an executive in a conference room holding a carton of breakfast food while exclaiming to others around the table "You want to know what's new about our new product? It's the word 'new' on the box. That's what's new!"

My remarks should not be interpreted as an unqualified condemnation of the television industry. For when it makes a conscious appeal to the intelligent viewer, it does a respectable job. But for every hour of David Brinkley, Donahue and 60 Minutes there are countless others devoted to banal soap operas, idiotic sit-coms, violent crime-dramas and nauseating game-and-give-away shows. Taste depends upon values, and such shows have helped to debase the values of not only the individual viewer but of society as well.

Newspapers responded to the threat of television by trying to be just as bad — with writing laced with the latest slang, increasingly trendy subject matter, larger picture layouts and color. The pictures were interesting for the way they reflected feature-page editors' efforts to shift focus from the written word. Sometimes acres of space would be given a shot lacking any kind of distinction.

As for color, newsprint — the paper upon which most newspapers are printed — does not lend itself easily to it. And though some strides have been made in improving reproduction over the years, the effect to the sensitive eye is still garish. Thus what Catling once affectionately referred to as "those neat little pages of gray type" have at times taken on the appearance of circus posters.

IN THE COMPETITION TO MATCH TELEVISION'S PANDERING to "New" tastes the *Sun* was not a leader. It continued to display the same restraint in make-up and reporting it had since the days of Arunah S. Abell. It also continued to lose circulation.

"Vulgar" is defined in *The American Heritage Dictionary* as "Of or associated with the great masses of people as distinguished from the educated and cultivated classes." Newspapers with the largest circulation have usually been the most vulgar, and at some point somebody in the *Sun*'s upper echelons must have decided the paper should become more vulgar in the hope of persuading at least some of the younger members of those great masses to read it.

Young employees who had proved their worth were placed in key positions — copy readers, assistant city editors and, in one case, TV critic. Among them was a recent graduate of the Columbia School of Journalism who used to drop by my office in the late afternoon to tell me how good she was. And for somebody just out of college, she *was* good.

One afternoon she asked me to read a piece she'd just written about the astronaut Wally Schirra. She said she considered it the best thing she'd ever done and hoped I would share her enthusiasm for it. And I did — until I read the first sentence:

"Wally Schirra is a man who could never commit a dishonest act."

I asked how she could know this.

"What?"

"How can you be sure he's never going to commit a dishonest act? What if tomorrow he's charged with income-tax evasion?"

She gave me a blank look. Then — "You don't," she snapped with a contemptuous toss of the head, "understand the new journalism." She was right. And as I became more familiar with it, I understood it even less.

The "new journalism" was once defined by a wag in the business as the reporter himself sitting on top of a single fact. It encouraged writers to embroider supposedly objective accounts with a lot of subjective doodling. It thus opened journalism's door to devices hitherto reserved for fiction.

But the real problem derived not so much from breaches of the laws of journalism as the breakdown in education — which, I discovered while teaching a course in world drama at Goucher College in 1968, was by no means confined to the elementary schools.

Lecturing on Shaw's *Major Barbara*, I mentioned the influence of the munition-makers on events leading to World War I. As I continued, I noticed the peculiar expression that comes over students' faces when they have lost the trend of a teacher's remarks. I stopped.

"You do know there was another war, don't you?"

They did, but they weren't sure what caused it or who the combatants were. "History," according to a famous statement attributed to Henry Ford, "is bunk." I'm sure my students, who displayed little interest in anything happening to the world before they came into it, would have agreed.

THE COPY DESK ON ANY NEWSPAPER HAS TWO MAJOR FUNCTIONS. It writes heads (headlines) and checks copy for accuracy. It is not supposed to rearrange sentences to suit the taste of the individual copy reader.

For more than 30 years my copy was seldom touched, owing to the respect I received from Martha Schoeps and Charley Flowers, as consecutive editors of the *Sun*'s feature section. Suddenly, everything I turned in seemed by the time it got into print to have been written by somebody else.

Carefully constructed sentences were replaced with sloppy ones. In a review of a Sherlock Holmes movie I twice referred to a "hansom" cab.

Somebody changed it to "handsome." A couple of days after the review appeared I got a letter from a reader I hadn't heard from in years.

"My God, Gardner! A *handsome* cab!"

Then there were the heads that said the exact opposite of what the copy said. I could think of only two explanations for this. Either the editors had not bothered to read the copy or they couldn't read.

Stunned at first, I was moved to make a formal protest when one of my pieces suffered eight changes, all of which were arbitrary, several of which substituted ungrammatical sentences for grammatical ones and none of which improved the quality of the original.

But young militants, coming into an old establishment, are driven by need to make their presence felt. Sniping at my copy continued until one of their number was appointed editor of the black-and-white sections of the *Sunday Sun*.

FROM THE BEGINNING HER ATTITUDE TOWARD ME WAS HOSTILE. I suspected she might have been responsible for some of the changes I had complained about. But, for whatever reason, once in the saddle, she began to apply the whip.

She sent memos to Hal Williams, then assistant managing editor in charge of features, urging that I be replaced in my movie critic role by a *Sunday Sun* copy-reader whose collusion with her was obvious. She assigned her ex-husband, a reporter on the *Morning Sun*, to do a piece on a play she knew I planned to review that week.

She claimed his assignment was only to write a feature story. But, as printed above my review on the front page of the following Sunday's *Spectator* section, it took up twice the space, discussing the play's plot, theme and characters. It was also a very disconnected story — probably, in its new-journalistic wanderings from Nietzsche to the Three-Mile-Island episode to current fashions in playwriting, the most overblown since my description of how the flag went up the pole at Williamsburg.

And it represented a deliberate affront to me, whose province as theater critic it flagrantly invaded.

Having failed in an effort to persuade the new editor to postpone publication of my own story until a later date, I tacked a notice on the *Sun*'s bulletin board in the spirit of Luther's Ninety-Five Theses pointing out the sophomoric aspect of the piece and blaming editors for the frequency with which the paper's space was being thus wasted.

I ended with the statement that, if any such humiliation were visited upon me again, I would fire-bomb all parties involved, starting with Banker and working up.

The reference to Banker was included to emphasize the facetiousness of the threat — for there was nobody in the news department above him. Yet not all who read the notice, among them Banker himself, were sure.

This admittedly foolish gesture resulted in a big brouhaha, somewhere around the middle of which the appointment of the first outside (of the *Sun*) publisher since Charles H. Grasty in 1910 was announced.

I HAD HEARD OF JOHN R. MURPHY, but the only thing I really knew about him was that in 1974, while editor of the *Atlanta Constitution*, he had been kidnapped and held for ransom. As related by him afterwards, the story had all the glitz of a TV crime melodrama and, as such, attracted national attention. Among those attracted was Randolph A. Hearst whose daughter, Patty, had been kidnapped a few weeks earlier. The upshot was that Murphy became editor-publisher of the Hearst chain's *San Francisco Examiner*, from which he came to the *Sun*.

Shortly before his arrival in the summer of 1981 I had lunch with William S. Abell, a member of the *Sun*'s board of directors and founding family. He and I had become friends through his interest in the theater and my comments upon it. So I felt no hesitancy in asking what sort of person the new publisher was.

"Hal, you'll love him" was the answer. "He's going to get rid of a lot of dead wood around here."

Several weeks later I gave Mr. Abell a call. "You're right," I told him. "Dead wood's falling all over the place. He just fired me from my job as movie critic."

There was a heavy silence. Then in a shaky voice from the other end of the line came "I — I don't know what to say, since an important condition of our agreement was that he was to have complete freedom."

ONCE ASKED WHY HE HAD RELINQUISHED HIS POSITION as film critic on *The New Yorker*, Wolcott Gibbs replied that he had come to realize that he had been reviewing for his friends films that had been made for his servants. I had no servants but I knew what Gibbs meant.

Movies have always been a good barometer of the nation's taste. The most popular film of the mid-Sixties was *The Sound of Music*, an overly sentimental, Rodgers-Hammerstein musical about the Trapp family singers of Austria. Among the box office champions of the Seventies were *The Last Tango in Paris*, *The Exorcist*, *Star Wars*, and *The Texas Chain-Saw Massacre*. Explicit sex, nudity, drug addiction, the supernatural, comic-strip heroes and violence of a most unspeakable kind replaced romance and mom's apple pie as favorite themes.

The popularity of such films, combined with the parallel popularity of similar works on television, reflected a growing infantilism on the part of the American public. As a child, I had loved Buck Rogers, Flash Gordon, Tarzan, Superman, as well as the hokey violence of the Saturday-afternoon-movie serials. Now a middle-aged critic, I found myself among colleagues who discussed with absolute seriousness movies of the same subject matter.

The *Sunday Sun* copy-reader who replaced me as film critic wrote a glowing review of *Raiders of the Lost Ark*, based on the Saturday-afternoon serials. His published list of the ten best films of all time included *The Wizard of Oz*.

After years of enduring the strain of space wars, body snatching, perverse sex and other miseries in an environment of spilled cola and scattered popcorn, I was happy to be relieved of the chore. But I couldn't help thinking the change might have been handled with more tact.

As a *Sun* employee of more than 30 years, during which I had built not only a national reputation but a large local following, I deserved more courtesy than that contained in the curt announcement that, following publication of a review Murphy didn't like, my services as film critic were being terminated.

Neither of his immediate predecessors would have been guilty of such crudeness or of the blatant censorship it represented. But there may have been method in it. For in the way the act bypassed Banker in the chain of command many on the *Sun* interpreted it as a move against him. And indeed he was the next to go.

"Did he give you any idea when he expected you to leave?" I asked on hearing the news. "Oh yes." The reply was typically Banker. "He said any time next week would do." For somebody born and raised in the old South the new publisher seemed to have inherited none of its graces.

Thus did management rid itself of its dead wood in an evident plan to reshape the *Sun* in the image of the "New" tastes. Then, having increased circulation (in which effort the collapse of the *News-American* doubtless helped), it sold the whole business to the Times Mirror Corporation for $600 million, 14 million of which went into the pocket of the new publisher.

ACCORDING TO THE GUILD CONTRACT THEN IN EFFECT, *Sun* employees, after a brief probationary period, could be fired only for "gross neglect of duty". My removal as film critic did not constitute firing since I continued in my job as drama critic with no decrease in salary. But management's intentions toward me were not long left in doubt.

Stories involving grievances are a bore, and I do not want these recollections, which on the whole have been a labor of love, to descend to that level. So I shall not list the countless times my articles were held up, cut and otherwise mangled in an obvious effort to force my resignation.

And that was only part of it.

Because they have to work all hours of the day and night, critics on the *Sun* have never been required to appear in the office at any specific times. Suddenly I was given times not only to be at my desk but to report in by telephone. Observance of these "deadlines", I was told, was mandatory.

It got worse with the man who replaced Hal Williams on the latter's retirement and who seemed to regard hounding me as his primary mission in life. Until then, I had tried to hang on — for, as Rosie had observed, my job was my life. But when this person declared that he was looking for any technicality as a pretext for firing me, I knew the time had come.

Much as I hated to admit it, the *Sun* I had always known and loved had set.

Goodspeed and me at entrance to TCU. *(From 1941 yearbook.)*

Goodspeed and me at the Belvedere. *(Photo by Robert Goldman.)*

Digging
In My Garden

FORTY

Sometime during the spring of 1982, as the pressure on me to resign mounted, Hope Quackenbush telephoned to ask my opinion of a show she was considering bringing to the Mechanic. I gave her what she wanted but added that, by the time the show reached Baltimore, I might no longer be on the *Sun*. She immediately conveyed the information to Philip Langner, director of the Theater Guild and the Mechanic's New York booking agent, who went straight up the wall.

The result was a flood of mail from the entire theatrical establishment politely but firmly asking the *Sun*'s new management to take steps to prevent my leaving. In printing excerpts from these letters I am not endeavoring to toot my horn. It has simply occurred to me that there might be a question in the reader's mind as to whether the efforts to phase me out could have arisen from the possibility I was no longer any good.

ALEXANDER COHEN WROTE THAT I WAS one of the reasons Broadway producers brought their shows to Baltimore. "We know that we can have the advantage of reading an intelligent critique of our work which will most likely parallel our New York critics' point of view. Gardner is readable, astute, constructive, perceptive and, above all, helpful. If the city loses him, the Mechanic and other theaters will suffer."

Hope Quackenbush:
Mr. Gardner enjoys a large and devoted readership; his reviews and features are widely read and discussed. His opinions on the theater (and on films as well) have always been noted by our subscribers who have come to depend upon him for insight, information and consumer guidance. We know that his readers are loyal and their substantial numbers should not be underestimated. For, in addition to the wit and intelligence that have made people everywhere admire his reviews, he has proven to be a major force in the creation and sustaining of theater.

Peter Culman:
I have been associated with Center Stage for over 15 years. During that time, I know of few people in the community who have done as much to promote good theater as Hal has. While I may quibble with him for a point or two, he is nonetheless fair, thorough and, most importantly, knows what goes into making the art of theater. For he understands a part of theater that few critics do, namely, the terms of a theater production and how well a given production achieves these terms.

HAPPY AS THESE LETTERS MADE ME, my cup did not run over until I saw the one Roger L. Stevens, chairman of the John F. Kennedy Center for the Performing Arts and probably the most distinguished theatrical producer in America, wrote to the chairman of the *Sun*'s Board of Directors on April 19, 1982:

Having been involved in close to 200 productions in my life and having read many thousands of opening night reviews, I can only say that with this experience in the theater I regard Hal Gardner as one of the most lively and competent critics in the field. What is most important: he does not try to express his personal feelings to show how smart he is, which is more than can be said of most critics today. His style most resembles Brooks Atkinson, who in my opinion was the greatest critic of the century, and I think Washington/Baltimore would be the poorer for losing a man of his skill and talents.

My apologies for appearing to try to tell the management of a newspaper what to do, but my respect for Hal Gardner is so great that I would be remiss if I did not register my opinion.

MY REMOVAL AS MOVIE CRITIC HAD BROUGHT IN A STORM of protesting letters, none of which had been printed. But the announcement of my retirement on Sunday, March 11, 1984 — 33 years to the day from when I had started on the paper — loosed a second storm that could not be ignored.

One reason was the importance of some of the people the letters came from, such as the following from Mr. Langner. Though sent to the *Sun*, he had addressed it to me personally.

I have been in the theater 37 years now and I want to say I have never known a finer critic than you . . . What I mean is that you know what you're talking about in the theater. If you say the direction is bad it is the direction and not the acting. If you say the scenery overwhelms the actors it does. That is the difference between those rare people and the people whose credo is "I may not know about the theater but I know what I like."

I shall miss you a great deal. You have done wonders in helping the city of Baltimore acquire its new reputation as a theater of importance in the United States.

IN THE THEN-STILL-PUBLISHING *News-American*, R. P. Harriss, described me as "the best theater critic the *Morning Sun* has had within memory, and one of the best in America.

His newspaper criticism was neither harsh nor bland, but invariably fair. Even in the case of an obvious disaster, he was courteous. . . . So it is to be hoped that his rich store of experience, his shrewdly penetrating critical insights, his integrity and his grace with words —and all that went into his work as a newspaper critic —will continue to be available.

ERNESTINE WALKER, PROFESSOR OF HISTORY at Morgan State College, on March 18, 1984, wrote:

Last Sunday when I read your column announcing your retirement I was shocked. So much had I come to expect and enjoy your perceptive, excellent reviews that I must have considered you timeless. I have always considered you much better than the New York critics. Your humanity, good taste, common sense and lack of snobbery put you ahead of them everytime. Even before Harbor Place and

Baltimore's 'Renaissance' I often told local people who were critical of our town 'Any city having Walters Art Gallery and R. H. Gardner has greater potential than you realize.'

Please accept my sincere thanks for your sterling contributions as a masterful critic who has offered so much. All good wishes for many fruitful years of retirement.

SUCH LETTERS FROM PEOPLE WHO, LIKE PROFESSOR WALKER, I'd had no prior contact with, made me feel that the tens of thousand of words written over the years, had not been wasted.

Not that all came from professors, producers and similar notables. By far the most came from regular readers — such as William H. Engleman, Louise T. Goldman, Sylvia Schoen, Dorothy Siegal and J. T. King, all of whose letters were printed in the Sun's Letter column. The following, from Mr. King, is typical:

In his swan song R. H. Gardner said that his 33 years as the Sun's drama critic paid him a 'continuing return in joy.' He also brought joy to his readers and this is a sad parting time for those of us who learned to rely on his judgment and to profit from his good taste in deciding how to spend an evening. He gave us the pleasure of attending first-rate productions and guided us gently away from the turkeys, all with great style. For this I am grateful. As an ancient Roman once said, 'to like and dislike the same things, that is indeed true friendship.'

MUCH AS I WANTED TO, I COULD NOT ANSWER ALL THE LETTERS personally. It was not only a matter of time but of emotions. What could I have said to either Professor Walker or Mr. King that would have conveyed any part of the feelings I was experiencing as a result of their tributes? So I addressed the following to the Letters to the Editor column of the *Morning Sun*:

Editor:

It is the custom in large organizations whenever a member of one's family dies, gets married or has a baby to post a notice on the bulletin board thanking people for their expressions of sympathy, congratulations or joy.

With your permission, I would like to use this column as a "bulletin board" to thank the many people who have made a special effort to express praise for me along with their regrets over my retirement.

They include professionals in the fields of both journalism and the theater (my long-time colleague R. P. Harriss, who devoted a whole column to the subject, Peter Culman, Clarisse Mechanic, Philip Langner, Zelda Fichandler, Leo Sullivan, Don Walls, Norman Zaiger, Robert Rappaport), old friends I haven't seen for years (Virginia Tracy, Joseph Bandiera, Sara Levi), old friends I've never seen but know intimately through the eloquence of their letters (Alice Farmer, Rae Miller Heneson) and countless others whose good wishes for my future have touched me deeply.

During my 33 years of employment, the Sun *nominated me for several prizes and awards. I won none of them. But I did, I now realize, win something greater*

— *respect from my colleagues, admiration from my readers and a measure of affection from both.*

In short, the most valuable prizes any writer can aspire to, tokens of which I shall treasure always — if not in plaques on the wall, in my heart.

FORTY-ONE

A couple of months before I left the *Sun*, Charley Flowers went without my knowledge into the office of the man who had replaced Hal Williams as assistant managing editor in charge of features and registered a protest about the way I was being treated. Charley was a native of Knoxville, Tennessee. Tennessee is next door to Kentucky, where I was born, and Knoxville is next door to Nashville, where I went to high school. From the time Charley came on the *Sun* in the early Sixties, we developed a kindred feeling for each other. He was that most charming of creatures — a natural Southerner. To my question (prompted by Rose's concern about a dinner she was planning) as to whether he liked chili, his answer was:

"Yea boy."

He also had a natural sense of justice. He could not abide the way I was being kicked around. Unfortunately, his concern for me rebounded to his own disadvantage — with the result that my problems suddenly became his.

His copy was either held up or not printed. When he asked why it was not used, he was told it wasn't any good. At this point, Charley had been chief of the *Sun*'s London Bureau (1966-69), editor of Perspective, the paper's prestigious political-analysis section (1969-73) and editor of its daily feature section (1973-80).

He had filed dispatches from all over Europe. Now he was told by a man who, according to some accounts had never even been a reporter, that his work wasn't any good.

Having always considered the source, I had not let such pressures get me down. Charley was of a different disposition. He resigned and immediately got a better job on the *Washington Times.* He was the dearest of friends, and his death in February of 1990 left a hole in my life that can never be filled.

His resignation was followed by that of Jack Dawson (not the TV sportscaster but a colleague and fellow sufferer of Charley's and mine on the *Sun*). All three of us felt we had been victimized, but I doubt any of us would have wanted to remain in view of the *Sun*'s new journalism, new style and new look suggestive of not only the *News-American* but all Hearst papers everywhere. So it was probably just as well we left. To put it another way, rather than victims, were we not simply casualties of the process of change?

I don't know or, for that matter, care. I am more interested in why, after being so eager to get rid of me, management did not appoint anyone to take my place. For though J. Wynn Rousuck, an able and conscientious reporter on the Sunday staff continued to cover theater openings, as of March 11, 1988 — four years after my retirement — the *Sun* still had no officially designated drama critic.

LIKE THE WOMAN WHO WROTE IN ABOUT QUAKENBUSH, I too am loath to finish books I love. The prospect of bidding farewell to characters I've formed a special affection for is too wrenching. I feel the same about this book. So forgive me if I indulge in one final round of reminiscences before cutting out.

Reggie Bromiley was a Canadian scientist who came to Baltimore at the end of World War II to conduct experiments on laboratory animals at the Johns Hopkins University. Though his educational background more than qualified him for a commission in the British army at the beginning of the war, he had insisted on being inducted as a private. Where emotional conflict is usually enough reason for severing most marital ties, Reggie had divorced his wife for political differences.

He was, to put it simply, anything but an ordinary man. And he had friends of the same order.

Among them was a couple raising a chimpanzee as if it were a human child. The object was to determine if, by wearing rompers, eating at the table and assuming other human characteristics, the chimpanzee could learn to talk. And, when not running up and down the draperies or swinging from the chandelier, he did. He learned to say the word "cup."

Reggie introduced Goodspeed and me to this nuclear family when mother, father and ape came through Baltimore on their way from Florida to New York. Later, driving through midtown Manhattan, they got caught in a traffic jam. A mounted policeman galloped up and began yelling at them. The chimpanzee stuck his head out the window and said "cup." The policeman thought he said "cop," and put it down as a hostile remark.

Reggie — who, as an ex-infantryman and former POW, had had a much more exciting life than either Goodspeed or me — shared with us a penchant for polemics. He always won in such arguments because of a secret weapon — the Zuni Indians. The Zunis, as described by Reggie, defied all laws of human behavior. Whenever John or I brought up a point we considered irrefutable, Reggie would purse his lips, shake his head and say "Well, the Zuni Indians —"

The most annoying thing about the Zuni Indians from John's and my point of view was their refusal to excel. In foot races, they preferred to lose.

One night, leaving Goodspeed's where we usually held these intellectual free-for-alls, I asked Reggie what, if not the desire to excel, he thought man's basic motivation was. "Man's basic motivation," he declared after taking his usual time to weigh the matter, "is to find his place in life."

But how can he find his place if he doesn't know what it is or how to get there?

FOR MUCH OF OUR LIVES, WE POKE ALONG BACK ROADS, often losing our way because we have no clear idea of where we're going. The road is narrow, the traffic heavy. After a while we give up, eyes glazed, mind dulled, as we resign ourselves to simply crawling along.

Then, unexpectedly, we arrive at a highway—down whose uninterrupted length we leap, accelerator pressed to the floor! And it is in the exhilaration we feel while plunging, hair flying, spirits soaring, down this lovely road that we come as close as we ever can to happiness.

I've experienced it three times — each of which has represented a breakthrough from one stage of my life to the next.

LIKE MY MOTHER, I GREW UP IN THE OLD HOUSE across the street from West Kentucky College, whose dignified Victorian structures were replaced in the early 1920's by the neo-classical architecture of Mayfield High School. But the broad expanse of lawn that fronted the new edifice was still called the "campus", and it was into its flourishing life that I — a small boy watching from a porch swing — was drawn.

Every morning at 8, the janitor would come out and ring an enormous bell mounted on a tall concrete pyramid at the side of the main building. During the next 30 minutes, all school-age children throughout the town summoned by the clanging, would straggle past my swing up the wide sidewalk that ran to the school's central door. Then, somewhere around the middle of the afternoon, they'd all straggle back again.

I used to wonder what they did behind that imposing facade of bricks and windows but, being too young even for kindergarten, I assumed such information would be forever denied me. In the late afternoon after they'd gone home, I and other small residents of the neighborhood would converge upon the campus and play Wolf over the River.

I loved Wolf over the River, but the only thing I remember about it now is that one afternoon I skinned my knee and got grass stains on a new pair of pants, after which my mother put her foot down.

Another game we played was Draw a Magic Circle and Sign It with a Punch. "It" would lean against a tree, covering his eyes with his bent arm. Somebody would draw the circle on his back and add the punch. "It" would then have to guess who had punched him. If he got it right, the game was over. Otherwise, the children would run shrieking away and hide in the bushes — from which "It" would have to root them out before they had the chance to run shrieking back to the tree.

My Draw-a-Magic-Circle and Wolf-over-the-River phases gave way in time to another. I doubt that many children in this day of electronic war games have ever heard of rubber guns, but they were very big in my side yard during the 1920's.

A "rubber gun" consisted of a crude wooden replica (usually hacked out by the child himself) of a Colt .44, over whose long barrel was stretched a one-inch-wide segment cut from a discarded inner tube. The segment (or "rubber") was held at the stock by a reinforced clothes pin which, when pressed, would send it zinging through the air into the seat of a playmate's pants. Even then, violence was the name of all games. Especially for pre-pubescent boys — for, at 10, I had not yet discovered girls.

IN THE SUMMER OF 1931, MY FATHER BEGAN the first in the series of disastrous moves that was to take us during the next seventeen years back and forth between Mayfield and Hopkinsville, Memphis and Nashville, Fort Worth and Baltimore. His last move was in a baggage car from Tucson to Mayfield where he found a permanent home along with papa and mama in the Moorman family plot.

I hated all but the first of these moves. The reason I didn't hate that one was because my mother's old schoolmate, Essie Douthet, had married and moved to Hopkinsville before us. Essie had a daughter, Mollie, several months older than I — which is a negligible age difference when you are 60 but can be vast when you are not quite 13.

Mollie ran with a crowd that had already weathered puberty. As my only contact in Hopkinsville, she introduced me to a world somewhat advanced over the one I had known in Mayfield.

A prominent inhabitant of this world was Tom Fairleigh, youngest member of a colorful Hopkinsville family. His parents made their own home-brew, which sometimes exploded, spewing fermented yeast and hops all over the dining-room ceiling. According to legend, June, elder of Tom's two teen-age sisters, had a habit of dancing naked before an open window in an upstairs bedroom. Ann, the younger, played soprano saxophone in the high-school band in which I played snare drum.

I was never fortunate enough to catch June's act, but I have a special reason for remembering Ann.

Aware that we were on the way to becoming "grown-ups," we kids went to parties almost every weekend. Our problem was that — being too young for sex and too old for drop the handkerchief — we never knew what was supposed to happen once we got there. For the most part we sat stiffly in chairs around the walls talking. We were so engaged at Tom's one night when Ann stormed in from a party of her own.

"What are you doing?" she yelled. "Why aren't you dancing?"

Dancing!

In another minute she had grabbed me up, and we were prancing around the floor to the music of a phonograph. "You have a natural talent for this sort of thing," she said. "Step, bend. Step, bend. Step, step, step, bend. Keep it up, and you'll be in the movies."

Ann taught me how to dance. She also taught me how to kiss — not childish puckerings but the sloppy, open-mouthed kind I've never gotten over. The Fairleighs had a tennis court, and almost every afternoon during the hot summer of 1932 I would bicycle out to their suburban home and play tennis. Then I would go into the cool house and Ann would give me a kissing lesson.

Five years later, after becoming a New York actress, Ann sailed through Fort Worth in a touring production of Clare Boothe's *Kiss the Boys Goodbye* (a natural for her). I went backstage, hoping for a refresher course, but she had acute laryngitis and could hardly even speak.

But I shall always remember her for transporting me in one swirling embrace from the world of grubby children playing with rubber guns in a side yard to that of lovely girls swaying on polished ballroom floors beneath rotating crystal balls.

Such was my first "breakthrough", which lasted hardly a year — for the difficulties plaguing my father soon sent us back to Mayfield where social life for people in my age group was limited.

AS ALWAYS, AUNT MAYME OPENED HER HOME AND HEART TO US. Of all the wonderful people I've known, none has been warmer or more giving than this bouncy little woman with her profane tongue and creeping teddies. Money was virtually non-existent in 1933. Yet she never made us feel unwelcomed, though she had to maintain a household which — in addition to my mother, father and me — included herself, Uncle Joe, my cousin Ann and two family retainers.

Alice, without whose nervous ministrations everything would have ground to a stop, usually got her pay on time. Sam, the furnace man, was a different matter. "Sam," my aunt would say when his teetering hulk (he drank a little) loomed in the door around 7 every Saturday night, "you'll have to wait. I don't have any money now." After several weeks of this, Sam (he'd had a couple) told her "Miss Maymie, you know even *I* have to eat."

My father had taken a job as salesman with the Mayfield furniture store that had been his principal competitor in the old days. He worked there, receiving a net income of something less than $75 a month until January of 1934 when he got a slightly better job with a furniture store in Nashville. We lived in the James Robertson, an old apartment-hotel directly across the street from the forbidding stone edifice (we inmates called it the Bastille) of Hume-Fogg High School from which I graduated in June of 1936.

The year marked the one-hundredth anniversary of the founding of the State of Texas. My Aunt Hal, who lived in Mineral Wells, used this as an argument to get us to do something she'd been after us to do for years. Visit her. There was a big centennial celebration being presented in Dallas in the form of a world's fair. She would pay our expenses down and back if we would come.

We went, but because my father — again in trouble — joined us toward the end of the summer we didn't go back for five years. He had an eerie ability to find jobs, and this time it was with one of the most respected furniture stores in the Southwest — Ellison's of Fort Worth. Meanwhile my mother and I stayed in Mineral Wells, dependent upon the hospitality of my Aunt Hal as we had upon that of my Aunt Mayme in Mayfield. It was a situation intolerable to me. So I jumped at the chance, following my father's arrival in Fort Worth, to take a job on an Ellison delivery truck.

I do not wish to suggest that truck-drivers as a group are inferior to other members of the human race, only that the ones I had to put up with were — especially a big, red-necked Irishman named Ollie. Thus when Aunt Hal at the beginning of the next school year insisted that I resume my education I did not protest. She put me through college for which I am still grateful. Yet I might not have appreciated the experience half as much had it not been for that year on the truck. One of the problems in motivating children to go to school has always been their tendency to regard it as a chore rather than a privilege. They should have to work with Ollie.

From the moment I stepped onto the TCU campus that golden September day in 1937 I realized for the first time since the day I had stepped onto the Mayfield campus at age six that knowledge, not muscle, was the answer.

And this discovery, combined with other things, put me on the "highway." I rode it for two glorious years. Then war clouds began to gather over Europe and me.

THE OTHER THINGS HAD TO DO PARTLY WITH MY SUCCESS as a student (straight "A's" my freshman year), partly with the friendship I formed with Goodspeed and Pat Steel. Pat was a natural-born comedian; he could not help being a stand-up comic even when he was sitting down. He had a remarkable way with words and a wit so quick it was almost frightening.

Returning from the opening of the American Shakespeare Festival at Stratford, Connecticut. in the summer of 1955, I stopped by New York where Pat was working as an executive in a large advertising agency.

"How was Jack Palance's performance in *Julius Caesar?*" he asked over a drink in the Plaza's Palm Court.

"Okay." I shrugged. "My problem with him is always how he looks. Like a death's head."

"Yeah." Pat hardly paused for breath. "He played Yorick in *Hamlet*." As anyone familiar with the Shakespeare play knows, the part of Yorick consists of nothing but a skull. Hamlet describes the once-living Yorick to his friend Horatio as being a man of "infinite jest." So was Steel.

A strolling player, he roamed the TCU campus, cornering anybody he thought might make a good audience for his repertory of one-liners. It was as such that he approached me one day during our freshman year. His imitation of Groucho Marx evoked an appreciative reaction, as did his equally effective impression of the dance techniques of Fred Astaire. We became instant friends.

A week later, Goodspeed and I were waiting for a bus opposite the school's entrance when Pat appeared and engaged us in spirited doubletalk. I was amused. Goodspeed wasn't. As the other sauntered off, chortling softly to himself, John observed with more than his usual venom, "I hate that little bastard."

He had, it seemed, worked as Pat's assistant putting out the yearbook of the Fort Worth high school from which both had graduated. According to John, he (Goodspeed) had done all the work and Pat had got all the credit. Whether or not this was true I never knew (or cared), but the fun we derived (and still do) from our three-cornered friendship soon set all bitterness to rest.

This friendship before our graduation in 1941 resulted in scripts of two varsity shows and a weekly radio program which Goodspeed and I wrote and in which Steel starred.

In addition to everything else, John and Pat performed a valuable service for me of which neither was ever aware. I had been, as I've mentioned, a sickly child — which fact my mother in her over-protectiveness never let me forget. "I know you'd like to be out there with them," she used to say when she saw me staring wistfully through the window at children frolicking in the snow. "But it would make you sick. You have to remember you're not as strong as they are."

Not as strong as they are. The feeling of physical inferiority haunted my childhood and — despite repeated efforts to compensate with swimming, tennis and weight-lifting — much of my adolescence as well. Football constituted the ultimate threat. TCU had no fraternities. The social elite was represented by its championship football team whose members inspired a combination of envy and awe. At least in everybody but Goodspeed and Steel.

They laughed at the athletes, and their disdain helped me to reorganize my opinion of myself and the values that opinion reflected.

Hopkinsville carried me across the threshold of adolescence, TCU to the threshold of maturity, the *Sun* to the "place" we all seek and some even find.

YOU KNOW YOU'VE FOUND IT WHEN OTHERS BEGIN to accept you on your terms. I knew I'd found mine that memorable afternoon I walked into the city room, handed Cauly my story about the flower show and he put it on the back page. Nothing that happened over the next 30 years ever succeeded in shaking the sense of belonging I felt at that moment.

After my mother died I discovered an interesting fact. While people live you think of them as they are — or, at least, were when you last saw them. And if they were old and infirm, that's the way you think of them.

But death releases them into the crucible of memory, and you are free to choose from whatever stage of their lives you wish to recall. In similar fashion I, having retired from the *Sun*, am free to blot out the years I prefer to forget and concentrate on those I love. And they are, as I've mentioned, the early ones before all our careers took off in different directions. Before Janetta left the local staff to become an editorial-writer, I to become a theater critic, Sehlstedt to become a space-specialist and Baker, Burks, Miller, Catling and Kumpa to become chiefs of foreign bureaus. When we were all, so to speak, stewing in the same pot.

Those years when, having spent the afternoon away from our desks covering events of the day, interviewing notables and obtaining other printable material, we would surge into the city room to exchange quips and choice bits of information relating to our recent experiences, while writing the next edition. Then sally forth to recap the whole process over beer at the Calvert or pool at the Press Club.

Those years, with jazz sweetening the night at Martick's, Cauly sinking the 8-ball in the side pocket and Jones banging out Mozart in the next room.

Those years when we were still young enough to dream, when all horizons seemed to beckon and each new day was filled with promise.

Those years—

SO STEP UP TO THE BAR — John, Patrick, Pete, Janetta, Dave, Albert, Charley, Nathan, Ned — and let's lift a last one to those years we shared so many years ago.

Addenda

My last days on the *Sun* were so painful that for a long time after leaving I was immobilized by the wounds. Then my writer's instinct asserted itself, and I began work on this book.

I finished it in the summer of 1987 and settled down to wondering what to do with it. I had no illusions about the eagerness of publishers to beat a path to my door. So, hoping for suggestions, I sent the manuscript to a few friends — Nathan Miller, William Mueller, Josephine Jacobsen, Harold Williams, James Bready, Edgar Berman. I had selected them because, in addition to being friends, all were published authors. And I knew that, if you want an opinion untainted by sentiment, ask another writer.

To my surprise all professed to like *Those Years* — even to offering advice on how to market it.

Nathan introduced me (via telephone) to the agent who had been instrumental in getting seven of his books published. Hal Williams recommended it to Jack Goellner, whose Johns Hopkins University Press had just brought out his own book on the *Sun*. Goellner showed strong initial interest, only to inform me after reading the manuscript that the Hopkins press had a rule against autobiographies — and, though I had not originally considered it in that light, an autobiography is what *Those Years* really amounts to.

In the most flattering rejection I'd ever received Goellner wrote: "I remain confident that your agent will place the book under a good imprint, and I wish you all success in that. I hope to see it one day soon in a local book store, and if the owner has the good sense to set up an autographing party, I'll get in line, newly published book in hand, and ask you to sign my copy."

Meanwhile, Edgar Berman was sending copies to *his* agent and publisher. Both praised it but ended up concluding that it was too "regional" in appeal. As time passed and the thing traveled back and forth between my mailbox and those of various publishers, the objection became a consensus.

In short, everybody loved my book, but nobody wanted anything to do with it. I took the problem to Goellner. "Why not," he suggested, "bring it out yourself?"

I had been conditioned to believe that any author reduced to publishing his own stuff was unworthy of respect. "Not true!" declared Goellner. It was perfectly respectable as long as the author did not turn his book over to a "vanity press," thereby losing control of it. And it did seem to me, now that I thought about it, that such a procedure was no different from a composer conducting his own symphony or a playwright producing his own play.

So I decided to "bring out" *Those Years* myself.

I located a very nice publishing firm whose director, Ann Hughes, was not only respectful but friendly. Hal Williams agreed to copy-edit the manuscript without fee, and my old friend from the early *Sun* days, cartoonist Jim Hartzell, spent an entire afternoon advising me as to picture layouts and similar details.

Then, in the fall of 1988, as Ann and I were bracing ourselves to go to press, the unexpected happened. Margaretta Finn, a delightful young woman I had met while she was working as assistant to a local publisher, called up to say that she thought *Those Years* too good to be brought out by its author. She asked permission to show it around herself. It was a request I was only too happy to grant, and in less than a month the book was accepted by the Galileo Press.

I HAVE INCLUDED THESE ANECDOTES TO SHOW HOW FREQUENTLY people seemed to have gone out of their way to help me. Margaretta might be considered an unusual case, but really no more than Hal Williams and Edgar Berman.

As one commissioned to write the official biography of the *Sun*, Hal's willingness to lend support to a work not entirely uncritical of that organization puzzled almost as much as it pleased me. Edgar was even more puzzling. I had met him back in the Forties, when he was courting his future wife, Phoebe. Phoebe, whom I knew through a mutual friend, Betty Stone, had read a play of mine. She showed it to Edgar who showed it to two friends of his — actors Eddie Albert and his wife Margo. What Eddie and Margo thought of the play I never learned, though Margo sent me an imprint of her heavily rouged lips, which I found nice if not particularly illuminating. Maybe she thought it was too regional.

But why did Edgar — well on his way to becoming nationally prominent in both scientific and political fields — bother to help a nonentity he knew only through his girlfriend?

Nor was that all.

Somewhere in the book I describe a meeting with Richard Tucker in the Park Plaza restaurant to discuss my hope of getting a job on the *Sun*. Edgar, who was Tucker's physician, arranged the meeting. This concern for my welfare continued through the years. Two days before his death from cardiac arrest on the way downtown from his Greenspring Valley home, he came to the hospital, where I was being treated for a bloodclot in the leg, to give me an autographed copy of his recently published *In Africa with Schweitzer*. He liked to depict himself in his books and syndicated columns as a hard-bitten cynic, but those who knew him knew better. He was profoundly sensitive and, like Hal Williams and Margaretta, a true friend.

I FOUND THE GALILEO PRESS AND ITS NON-FICTION EDITOR, Loyola College Professor Andrew Ciofalo and his assistant Susan Walsh, much to my liking. The only thing I didn't like was that, owing to previous commitments, they could not bring out my book until the middle of 1990 — six years after my retirement and three after I had finished writing it.

Three years in this day of push-button change is a long time. Should I, I wondered, go over the manuscript with an eye to updating it? I was particularly concerned about the second installment of Russell Baker's autobiography, which came out in the summer of 1989 and covered some of the same territory.

Despite such bothersome matters, I decided to leave my book as I had written it. Every work creates its own form and style. I did not want to complicate the form of *Those Years* with a lot of added material. Nor did I wish to muddy the style, which I had endeavored to keep lively — tripping, as it were, over the surface rather than bogging down in the depths.

Unfortunately this, I discovered as I took another look at the manuscript, has led to my leaving loose ends. What, for example, ever happened to Goodspeed, whom I left dangling somewhere between the burlesque show and "Mr. Peep's Diary?" As his many fans know, he resigned from the *Sun* in the middle Sixties to work for various publications throughout the area. His longest stint was as a book reviewer on Channel 67's Critics' Place.

I, too, had a fling in the Seventies and Eighties at TV and public radio reviewing. It was fun but not nearly so much as writing for a daily newspaper where, God and management willing, you can open up and let your spirits soar.

Unwillingness to have my story stray off in diverse directions also resulted in my inadvertently omitting mention of scores of people who became part of my daily life on the *Sun* and the source of lasting friendships afterwards. They range from assistant managing editors (John Plunkett, James Keat), editorial writers (Edgar Jones, Gwinn Owens, Mike Bowler, Jerry Kelly, Dudley Digges, Brad Jacobs), librarians (Clem Vitek, Fred Rasmussen, Dorothy Schmidt, Dee Lyon), reporters (Frank Somerville, Weldon Wallace, Jesse Glasgow, Jim Elliot, David Ettlin) to Financial editor John Ward, veteran copy-boy Glen Egerton and Barney, the elevator man.

I should also mention Bill Stump, a loyal friend who left the *Sun* shortly after my arrival to take over various editorial assignments on Baltimore Magazine and The News American.

To all such people, named and unnamed, who have extended an open hand and heart to me over the years, I now extend my gratitude for many happy memories.

IT IS CUSTOMARY IN THE THEATER to bring the actors back at the end of a performance to take bows and be applauded by the audience. I would like to end this account with "curtain calls" by some of the beloved friends and esteemed colleagues whose lives touched mine with felicity before passing on. The months and years represent times of death.

Charles V. Flowers, Jr., February 1990; Robert Preston Harriss, October, 1989; Jay Spry, March, 1989; Clarence J. Caulfield, December 1986; Janetta Somerset Ridgely, March, 1986; Edward C. Burks, December, 1983; Edwin P. Young, December, 1982; Martha Schoeps, July, 1981; David Lee Maulsby, November, 1975; Charles H. Dorsey, Jr., October, 1973.

May we all meet in heaven — or, if that's inconvenient, the other place will do.

FINALLY, I WISH TO THANK SHELLEY POST, without whose steadfast devotion over more than a quarter of a century this book, along with its author, simply would not be.

687 6656

B
G   Gardner, Rufus Hallette
                Those years.   1990 $15
             (Autobiographical)

                              1/91

WESTMINSTER
90-9717
91 D

                              Theater
                           3. Sun

                        0913123293